Biochemistry of Brain
and Behavior

Biochemistry of Brain and Behavior

Proceedings of a Symposium held at The University of
Wisconsin-Parkside, Kenosha, Wisconsin May 25-26, 1970

Edited by Robert E. Bowman and Surinder P. Datta
The University of Wisconsin

℗ PLENUM PRESS • NEW YORK – LONDON • 1970

Library of Congress Catalog Card Number 76-133840

SBN 306-30507-0

© 1970 Plenum Press, New York
A Division of Plenum Publishing Corporation
227 West 17th Street, New York, N.Y. 10011

United Kingdom edition published by Plenum Press, London
A Division of Plenum Publishing Corporation, Ltd.
Donington House, 30 Norfolk Street, London W.C. 2, England

Library of Congress Catalog Card Number 76-133840

TO

UW–PARKSIDE, KENOSHA, WISCONSIN

A

New Campus of

THE UNIVERSITY OF WISCONSIN

ACKNOWLEDGEMENTS

The editors of these Proceedings express their gratitude to the following persons who have contributed graciously and generously of their time and effort to make this Symposium and Proceedings a success. Thanks are due to the participants of the Symposium who supplied manuscripts in time to insure rapid publication of the Proceedings. Thanks are also due to Raul DeLuna and Barbara Beremen of the Wisconsin Regional Primate Research Center, who assisted in assembling the subject index. Our special gratitude is extended to Miss Jennifer A. Bruce, Associate Director of the Word Processing and Faculty Support Center of the University of Wisconsin—Parkside; and her staff, Grace Zdanowicz, Linda Wischmann, Barbara Grewenow and Christine Meyer, MT/ST Operators at the Center, who spent many days, evenings and weekends of work to prepare the manuscripts in final form. We are also grateful to the following firms who provided gifts to help support the Symposium: Abbot Laboratories, Chicago, Illinois; Ciba Pharmaceuticals, Summit, New Jersey; Eli Lilly and Co., Indianapolis, Indiana; Lakeside Laboratories, Milwaukee, Wisconsin; Lederle Laboratories, Pearl River, New York; Roche Laboratories, Nutley, New Jersey; Sandoz Pharmaceuticals, Hanover, New Jersey; Schering Corporation, Bloomfield, New Jersey; Smith, Kline and French Laboratories, Philadelphia, Pennsylvania and Squibb Institute for Medical Research, New Brunswick, New Jersey.

CONTENTS

INTRODUCTION

BIOCHEMISTRY OF NERVOUS SYSTEM

BIOCHEMISTRY OF MENTAL DISORDERS

BIOCHEMISTRY OF MEMORY

CONTRIBUTORS TO

THE UNIVERSITY OF WISCONSIN—PARKSIDE
SYMPOSIUM "BIOCHEMISTRY OF BRAIN & MEMORY"
MAY 25-26, 1970, KENOSHA, WISCONSIN

BERNARD W. AGRANOFF

Chief, Section on Biochemistry
Mental Health Research Institute
University of Michigan
Ann Arbor, Michigan

ROBERT E. BOWMAN

Head, Psychochemistry Unit
and
Professor of Psychology
University of Wisconsin Psychology Department
Madison, Wisconsin

HERMAN C. B. DENBER

Director of Psychiatric Research
Manhattan State Hospital
Wards Island, New York
and
Clinical Professor of Psychiatry
New York Medical College
New York, New York

EDWARD GLASSMAN

Director, The Neurobiology Curriculum
and
Professor of Biochemistry and Genetics
University of North Carolina
Chapel Hill, North Carolina

HAROLD E. HIMWICH

Director, Thudichum Psychiatric Research Laboratory
Galesburg State Research Hospital
Galesburg, Illinois

HYAM J. HOFFMAN

Senior Principal Research Scientist
C. S. I. R. O.
Division of Animal Genetics
P. O. Box 90, Epping 2121
Sydney, Australia

HOLGER HYDÉN

Director, Institute of Neurobiology
Faculty of Medicine
University of Göteborg
Göteborg, Sweden

MURRAY E. JARVIK

Professor of Psychiatry & Pharmacology
Department of Psychiatry & Pharmacology
Albert Einstein College of Medicine
Bronx, New York

JULIAN N. KANFER

Director of Biochemical Research
Eunice B. Shriver Kennedy Center for Mental Retardation Research
Waverley, Massachusetts

ARNOLD J. MANDELL

Professor and Chairman
Department of Psychiatry
University of California at San Diego
La Jolla, California

BRUCE S. MCEWEN

Assistant Professor
Rockefeller University
New York, New York

ERIC M. SHOOTER

Professor of Genetics & Biochemistry
Stanford University School of Medicine
Stanford, California

HARRY A. WAISMAN

Professor of Pediatrics
Joseph P. Kennedy, Jr. Memorial Laboratories
University of Wisconsin Medical Center
Madison, Wisconsin

RICHARD J. WURTMAN

Professor of Endocrinology & Metabolism
Massachusetts Institute of Technology
Cambridge, Massachusetts

INTRODUCTION AND SUMMARY

SYMPOSIUM: BIOCHEMISTRY OF BRAIN AND MEMORY

An Introduction and Summary

Robert E. Bowman

Head, Psychochemistry Unit
University of Wisconsin Psychology
Department

Madison, Wisconsin

In recent years, the concept of a scientific interdiscipline of neurobiology has emerged to define the activities of many scientific disciplines which all converge on the problems of the organization and functioning of nervous tissue. An advent of considerable promise in neurobiology has been the burgeoning of interest and research on the biochemical properties of brain, and this research has already added considerably to our understanding of mechanisms whereby the brain produces behavior. The scientific excitement, the relevance of this research to many current human problems, and the rapid growth of knowledge in the behavioral aspects of neurobiology has already spawned a number of symposia and conferences and seems likely to lead to many more.

The present symposium grew out of questions asked by seminar students at the University of Wisconsin, Parkside, about the biochemistry of brain and memory. The questions led Dr. Surinder Datta first to the scientific journals and then to an organization of this symposium as a means of assembling a report to the academic community at large on some recent progress and the status of knowledge relevant to these student questions. The participants were selected in three main topic

areas, one dealing with the biochemistry of neurons
and neuronal growth factors, the second relating
to the biochemistry of mental disorders and mental
retardation, and the last concerned with the biochemistry of memory. In assembling the Proceedings
of this Symposium, we have altered the order of
the papers from that in which they were presented.

There is so much current and important work
being done to understand biochemical factors
related to behavior that there were many possible
participants for this symposium. The limitations
of time, resources, and sometimes availability of
speakers dictated the present restricted sampling.
Nevertheless, the papers presented here represent
areas of recent interesting progress, as well as
work of potential relevance to human welfare.

These Proceedings begin with papers which
discuss biochemical properties of neuronal systems.
An understanding of the biochemical processes by
which neural tissue develops could well prove basic
to a variety of problems, and a beginning has been
made in this respect with the discovery of nerve
growth factors (NGF). In particular, one such NGF
for neurons of peripheral ganglia has been extensively studied, as described by Hoffman. In
addition, considerable excellent work on chemical-
biological characterizations of this NGF, in the
form of the 7S NGF complex and its subunits, is
discussed by Varon and Shooter. It seems plausible
that during neuronal growth, there would be substances produced which would stimulate and direct
that growth. However, considering the source of
7S NGF in salivary glands, it is not clear whether
the 7S NGF complex normally plays any biological
role in the regulation of neuronal growth. Nevertheless, 7S NGF (or antibodies to it) provides a
potential tool for altering the development of
peripheral ganglia, which has not yet been fully
exploited by neurobiologists. Furthermore, the
study of NGF by Hoffman has led him to the development of simple and elegant techniques for culturing
neurons directly over protein bands separated on
acrylamide gel by electrophoresis. This may well
provide the necessary tool by which extracts of

brain tissue can be screened for nerve growth
factors actually elaborated during brain growth,
or by which proteins from any source may be
screened for NGF activity on neurons of the CNS.
The discovery of NGF for brain neurons could open
up tremendous possibilities in neurobiological
research, including the stimulation of neurons in
culture or even in brain. The effect of such
stimulation on behavioral capacities can only be
speculated. The discovery of NGF for brain might
also lead ultimately to the possibility of stimulating neuronal growth in brain for therapeutic
reasons. Finally, it is even possible that such
nerve growth factors might normally operate in
adult brain to stimulate whatever modification in
neurons underlies the storage of memories. Although these possibilities are now only dreams
and guesses, the remarkable progress already made
in the study of NGF indicate that this area of
study has important consequences for neurobiology.

     The second neurochemical problem considered
in these Proceedings focuses on an aspect of myelin
chemistry. Myelin constitutes a wide spread
structural feature of the nervous system, about
which much still remains to be learned. The
importance of myelin biologically to the functioning brain is underscored by the tragic consequences
of mental retardation or death in humans suffering
genetic defects in metabolic pathways for myelin
development, and is also shown by the behavioral
deficits of inbred strains of mice which exhibit
dysfunctions in brain myelin. Such inbred strains
of myelin deficient mice in fact provide a useful
biochemical model for studying the metabolic features of myelin. Studies of this type are described by Kanfer in this Symposium, and illustrate
some of the complexities in elucidating metabolic
processes in brain. The eventual knowledge of
myelin chemistry which studies of these inbred mice
will yield, will provide the techniques and basic
knowledge for understanding a number of neurobiological problems, including those of lipid defects
in human brain.

     One of the major contributions of neurochemis-

try to the understanding of brain and behavior has
been the expansion of knowledge regarding chemical
transmission at the synapse. The identification
of a number of likely neurotransmitter substances
(briefly discussed by Mandell in the next paper in
these Proceedings) has served as a keystone for
research directed toward understanding several
phenomena related to behavior and drug effects.
Histochemically, it has been possible through the
fluorescence of several of the amine transmitters
(norepinephrine, dopamine and serotonin) when
reacted with formaldehyde to trace the course of
neurons containing these substances, and other
work has related these aminergic neurons to various
behavioral functions such as motor function
(dopamine), slow wave sleep (serotonin), paradoxical sleep (norepinephrine), response of the organism to reward (norepinephrine), response to painful
stimuli (serotonin) and the regulation of food and
water intake (norepinephrine and acetylocholine).
Furthermore, the energizing and tranquillizing
effects of numerous drugs are now understood in
terms of alterations in the metabolism or storage
of the above transmitters.

    From among all the rich fields of research
directed towards synaptic transmitter systems,
the present Symposium concentrated on two neurochemical approaches. The paper by Wurtman focuses
on problems in the measurement of norepinephrine
turnover in brain, and the relationship of this
turnover to various endocrine and behavioral
factors. Wurtman makes clear by example that much
careful work needs to go into our neurochemical
measurements in order to yield an accurate account
of the metabolism of transmitter substances, and
thereby to elucidate the relationships between
transmitter substances and behavioral variables.

    On the thesis that the brain regulates behav-
ior, and must in turn be regulated by inputs,
Mandell has looked to the transmitter systems as
potentially the systems at the most critical
juncture for this regulation. He has approached
the regulation of transmitter substances through
the regulation of biosynthesis, and has thus in-

vestigated the activity of the enzymes of biosynthesis for norepinephrine, for acetylocholine,
and for serotonin. His paper presents evidence
for alterations in the activity of these biosynthetic enzymes induced by various drugs.

As Mandell indicated, we have now reached a
point in the investigation of neurochemical factors
in behavior at which we have sufficient knowledge
and techniques to ask questions about regulation
in brain. (However, as other papers in these
Proceedings attest, the era of neurochemical
identification and mapping, or of study of the
metabolic pathways and kinetics, is not over; as
an additional example, it seems probable that a
number of neurotransmitter substances remain to
be identified.) Mandell's investigations of
enzyme induction in brain transmitter systems dis-
close a mechanism for the modifiability of synaptic
function. The modifiability of synapses, in one
way or another, has long been held to account for
the "neuronal plasticity" necessary to explain
learning and memory. The data of Mandell are
thus of considerable interest.

McEwen and colleagues have also directed their
work toward possible processes of enzyme induction
in brain, but along the endocrinological route by
studying the effects of steroid hormones. These
hormones are known to induce protein synthesis in
various target organs, are known to be regulated
themselves via the brain, and finally are known
to affect mating and parental behavior, as well
as behavior during stress and fear. In addition,
androgenic hormones presented to the infant brain
are known to organize the development of subsequent
brain mechanisms for the regulation of gonadotropic
and gonadal hormones. A similar role has been
postulated for corticosteroid hormones in organizing regulatory mechanisms of brain directed toward
subsequent control of corticosteroid secretions.
There are thus several reasons for expecting
metabolic effects of steroids on brain. The main
data presented by McEwen and coworkers indicate
highly specific, low saturation mechanisms in cell
nuclei for the uptake of estradiol in regions of

the hypothalamus and amygdala and of corticosterone
in the hippocampus. These data suggest regions
where metabolic sequelae such as protein induction
may occur during endocrinological regulation of
brain, and have implications for understanding
various behavioral-neurochemical relationships.
For example, these data make it plausible that
endocrine factors could play a role in alterations
of RNA metabolism of limbic structures of brain that
occur during learning (see the papers of Glassman &
Wilson and of Bowman & Kottler in these Proceedings).

The balance of these Proceedings deal with
relationships between biochemistry of brain and
behavior. It is perhaps natural in this respect
that there has been extensive work on those
behaviors which represent very profound health or
functional consequences to the human organism,
namely the behavioral disorders (psychoses) and
mental retardation.

The search for neurological bases for the
psychoses has strongly turned in recent years to a
search specifically for neurochemical bases. This
turn has been fostered no doubt by the development
of the concept of the neuron as a biochemical
machine, or as a miniature gland secreting transmitter substance at the synapse. In addition, much
impetus was given by the dramatic discovery of
LSD and the discovery and rediscovery of other
psychotomimetic compounds. This latter work suggested the possibility that metabolic aberrancies
in the human might produce endogenous compounds
with psychotogenic properties, thereby accounting
for mental disorders. Despite all these portents,
as well as the confidence and hope that organic
(and hence biochemical) defects do underlie the
psychoses, the history of this research has been
distressingly negative. The paper of Denber in
this Symposium discusses the most prominent and
promising theories and data relevant to the biological bases for psychoses. These researches
have employed a variety of strategies. Correlative
studies have compared the chemical profile of
urine for normals and from psychotics, turning up

such differences as the "pink spot" and the "mauve
factor." Subsequent studies, however, have not
substantiated that these factors are uniquely
related to the psychoses. Other correlative
approaches have examined protein profiles in blood
plasma in a similar fashion. Another approach
has compared tissue samples from normals and
schizophrenics for their capacity to produce some
response in a test organism. This was the strategy
employed by Frohman's group in isolating from
schizophrenic serum an alpha-2-globulin fraction
with the ability to affect lactate/pyruvate ratios
in chicken erythrocytes. The relevance of this work
for understanding psychoses is still undecided.
Similarly, Heath and coworkers injected schizophrenic serum or extracts into monkeys and man and
concluded from these data that there existed a
protein factor, taraxein, which produced psychotic-
like reaction in these subjects. This factor
remains to be adequately documented.

Denber, himself, and coworkers have taken a
drug model, namely mescaline-induced psychosis,
as a model for psychosis, and have utilized this
model in animals to study neurochemistry related
to psychosis. This last approach, that of the
model for psychosis, is potentially a most useful
one for research, because it opens the way to
research on animals. Despite various attempts, no
appropriate behavioral model yet exists for animal
psychoses, and the approach of utilizing drug
models of psychotomimetic behavior in lieu of
behavioral models is an intriguing one. In this
respect, it seems plausible that many suitable
drug models may eventually emerge, each reflecting
one or more of many different bits of brain chemistry that can go awry to produce behavioral
symptomatologies classed as psychotomimetic. At
any rate, Denber's approach of studying the pharmacology and neurochemistry of the mescaline model
is certainly defensible. At the least, it will
tell us much about mescaline-brain-behavioral
relationships, which certainly will offer us clues
of more or less relevance to schizophrenia. On
the same basis, other drug models might profitably
be studied. For example, the psychosis in humans

following amphetamine abuse suggests the usefulness
of systematic neurochemical studies in animals
subjected to chronic amphetamine administration.

The recent approach of Himwich's group to the
neurochemical study of schizophrenia is next
described by Himwich. This approach examines the
urine of schizophrenics and normals for abnormal
metabolites which might occur following blockade of
monoamine oxidase, a catabolic enzyme of aminergic
neurons of brain. This approach has led to the
detection of tryptamine derivatives with psychotomimetic properties in the urine of schizophrenics,
but not of normals, the occurrence of which coin-
cided with the exacerbation of behavioral symptoms
in the schizophrenics. Whether these compounds
accounted for the behavioral symptoms during
periods in which they were not detectable in the
urine is an unanswered question. However, these
data clearly establish a difference in metabolic
activity between the normal and schizophrenic
groups, and these experiments deserve to be extended to more subjects to follow up this promising
lead. It is interesting that this enzyme blockade
model for studying schizophrenia has similarities
to the research model of precursor loading and
enzyme blockade which has proven useful in animal
studies of phenylketonuria and mental retardation.

The study of biochemical disease states which
encompass mental retardation has had its most
success in investigations of inborn errors of amino
acid metabolism, particularly phenylketonuria.
Waisman describes the variety of these metabolic
defects now known, and indicates the usefulness
of biochemical modeling of these diseases in
animals for purposes of study. Waisman's group
has used phenylalanine loading to mimic in animals
the biochemical profiles associated with the lack
of enzyme activity of phenylalanine hydroxylase
in natural phenylketonurics. Recently, they have
obtained evidence that phenylalanine loading
disrupts protein synthesis in the brains of young
rats, but not of older rats. It is known that high
phenylalanine levels in the older human do not
have the same serious consequences for the develop-

ment of mental retardation as in the young human.
These two facts together suggest that the disruption of brain protein synthesis by high phenylala-
mine levels in infants may account for the mental
retardation observed later in these children.
Much work remains to be done to confirm this
possibility. However, it is clear from the review
and research described by Waisman that neurochemistry has the tools that will lead to an understanding of - and therefore perhaps control of - these
inborn errors of metabolism which otherwise can
lead to lifetimes of personal tragedy for the affected persons and their families.

     The final section of these Proceedings deals
with neurochemical processes which occur during
brief behavioral experiences, particularly learning. The reported research has been motivated by
the search for processes which underlie the
encoding of memory, although the identification
of these processes is not yet certain in the
various studies.

     Geller and Jarvik begin with a discussion of
short term and long term memory storage processes,
and describe the induction of retrograde amnesia
by various agents as evidence for these processes.
The use of electroconclusive shock soon after one
trial learning has been extensively used to produce
a retrograde amnesia which has been widely interpreted as indicative of disruption of consolidation
of long term memory. Geller and Jarvik indicate
the behavioral complexities of this problem which
includes evidence for an "incubation" process
following learning, which may be different from the
consolidation process, and for possible endocrine
involvement in post learning processes. In
addition, they discuss research using antibiotics
to inhibit brain protein synthesis immediately
following learning, thereby producing retrograde
amnesia. It is clear from this work that we cannot yet be certain about the period of time over
which the consolidation of memory proceeds, and
that there may be several post learning processes
besides consolidation which act in the brain and
which complicate interpretations of the data both

on retrograde amnesia and on measurement of biochemical changes.

The approach of measuring brain RNA changes
during a simple, short learning task is discussed
by Glassman and Wilson, who present evidence for
altered brain RNA metabolism in mice during 15
minutes of learning of one-way avoidance of
electric shock. This brief experience reliably
increases the uptake of precursor into brain RNA.
Glassman and Wilson have devised a variety of
control experiments and an interesting behavioral
analysis whereby they are able to demonstrate that
the brain RNA changes occur during new learning
phases of their task, whether the mice are first
learning the task, or are subjected to their first
extinction of the task. Their work is particularly
instructive of the elaboration of biochemical and
behavioral knowledge in this field which can be
produced by a careful research program, and by a
clear and detailed theoretical analysis underlying
that program.

Bowman and Kottler present a similar approach
in which they find increased uptake of precursor
into RNA of the hippocampus in rats learning a
maze habit for water reinforcements. The same
kind of RNA change was noted in rats receiving
their initial experience in novel environments, or
consuming water under novel circumstances. Thus,
the role of hippocampal RNA changes during behavioral experiences is not clearly confined to
learning situations. Bowman and Kottler suggest
conceiving of these metabolic effects simply as
chemoencephalographic events, similar in logic
to electroencephalographic events, thereby recognizing that a variety of behavioral or neural
processes might give rise to these events. They
also point out that these chemoencephalographic
processes may not necessarily be accompanied by
electrical signals, and may thus be measuring
neuronal processes not detectable by electrical
measurement.

Next, Hydén and Lange describe protein changes
in brain resulting during an induced change in

handedness in rats. They note increased amounts
of S100 protein in hippocampus, and find that
antiserum to S100 blocks further improvement in
performance when injected into the brains of
learning rats. The S100 protein is the most
studied of several proteins found only in brain,
and the investigation by Hydén and Lange on a
possible role of this brain specific protein in
response to learning a behavioral task illustrates
the possible gain to be had by studying the proteins which are special to brain. Furthermore,
since any RNA changes important to brain-behavioral
functions would need to be expressed through protein manufacture, the data of Hydén and Lange offer
a critical substantiation of the findings of RNA
changes during learning, as well as of the disruptive effects of inhibitors of protein synthesis on
memory. The use of protein antisera to alter brain
function also illustrates an interesting technique
that may eventually allow highly specific experimental intervention in brain.

Finally, Agranoff summarizes work on the use
of antibiotics to inhibit the synthesis of DNA, of
RNA and of protein in the brain of goldfish during
or following learning. These data confirm that
short term and long term memory employ different
metabolic or cellular processes, since the former
is not hindered by antibiotics while the latter is.
Agranoff also discusses, as moderator for the
session on memory, the possible interrelationships
of the work of the previous four papers, and states
the case for a neuronal connectivity theory of
memory.

The variety of tasks which yield measurable
neurochemical changes, and the efficacy of inhibitors of protein synthesis in producing retrograde
amnesia, reveal that the metabolic processes of
nucleic acids and protein in brain are intimately
related in lawful ways to the functioning of
definable behavioral processes. The evidence does
not discourage the theory that the encoding of
memory involves RNA and protein synthesis in
brain, although the data can also generally be
explained by other theories as well. Whatever the

behavioral or neurological reasons for the biochemical effects noted in these studies, the
eventual understanding of those reasons through
continued research seems certain to broaden, and
perhaps even to change drastically, our concepts
of the functioning of the massively complex
neural machinery which stores our experience and
generates our behavior.

BIOCHEMISTRY OF NERVOUS SYSTEM

BIOLOGICAL SIGNIFICANCE AND ACTION OF THE "NERVE GROWTH" FACTOR

H. Hoffman

C.S.I.R.O., Division of Animal Genetics

Sydney, Australia

The discovery of a 'Nerve Growth Factor', NGF, which induces embryonic ganglion cells to differentiate, was made during a study of the development of the embryonic nervous system.

Hamburger and Keefe (1944) and Hamburger and Levi-Montalcini (1949) showed that reducing the size of a peripheral field, e.g., the limb bud in a chick embryo, resulted in fewer and smaller nerve cells, with fewer and smaller axons, in the ganglia and spinal cord segments innervating the limb; grafting extra limb buds into the region in a two day chick, resulting in later fusion to form an over-sized limb, produced the opposite results- there were more and larger nerve cells with more and larger axons.

Levi-Montalcini and Hamburger (1951) analyzed this inductive effect more precisely by replacing the limb bud used in earlier transplantation ex- periments with specific, more homogeneous tissues- but all substitute tissues were ineffective. Meanwhile Bueker (1948) had attempted a similar simplification of the experiment by using a frag- ment of transplantable rat sarcoma 180 in place of the limb bud graft. The tumor was invaded by large numbers of sensory nerve-fibers and the sensory ganglia supplying the area became hyper-

3

plastic. Levi-Montalcini and Hamburger (1951)
further extended these experiments, demonstrating
that the tumor was invaded by sensory and sympathetic axons only, with concomitant hypertrophy
and hyperplasia of the ganglia from which they
came. Motor neurons, failing to innervate, became
atrophic. Even when the tumor was transplanted
onto a part of the chorio-allantois distant from
the embryo, considerable hyperplasia of sensory
and sympathetic ganglia occurred; bundles of
nerve-fibers from these ganglia entered organs
and tissues in an abnormal manner, instanced by
invasion of the mesonephres, and the formation of
neuromas in the lumens of veins (Levi-Montalcini
& Hamburger, 1953). Many other types of tumors
failed to evoke this response. These observations
led the authors to attribute the effect to a
diffusible agent, released from the tumor, and
acting specifically on sensory and sympathetic
neuroblasts. This conclusion was further reinforced by the results of explanting small fragments
of tumor into tissue cultures alongside sensory or
sympathetic ganglia from chick embryos (Levi-
Montalcini, Meyer & Hamburger, 1954). The presence
of tumor fragments greatly augmented the outgrowth
of neurites, which formed a halo around the
ganglion.

ISOLATION OF THE "NERVE GROWTH FACTOR"

Cell-free homogenates from the tumor were
prepared by Cohen, Levi-Montalcini and Hamburger
(1954) and partially purified. These preparations
exerted the same action *in vitro* as did tumor
fragments. Further purification resulted in the
characterization of the active substance as a
protein (Cohen & Levi-Montalcini, 1957). Later
studies (Cohen, 1958, 1959) revealed that rather
greater NGF activity could be obtained with
preparations from snake venom (originally introduced as a phosphodiesterase reagent to break up
the tumor extract) and from the salivary glands of
mouse and rat, especially the male mouse submaxillary gland. The Nerve Growth Factor emerged
from these studies as a heat labile protein, in-

activated by acid, alkali, trypsin, chymotrypsin
and papain, with a molecular weight of 22,000 or
44,000. As the culture method used by most workers reveals little of the behavior of individual
neurites, and shows only an opaque ganglionic
mass surrounded by a halo of neurites, the effect
of this purified NGF on neuroblasts has been
studied primarily in chick embryos and newborn
mice. When injected into chick embryos of 6 to 7
days incubation, the neuroblasts of both sympathetic and sensory ganglia undergo enlargement,
precocious differentiation, and become excessively
basophilic. The growth of neurites is also considerably increased. There is little description
of the changes in the cell population of ganglia
incubated with NGF *in vitro*, but Blood (1969)
found that, in her cultures, the stimulated neuroblasts were smaller than control ones, although
there were far more neuroblasts in the cultures.
Her observations indicated that the neuroblast
numbers increased at the expense of the Schwann
and satellite cells. Although both she and Levi-
Montalcini had observed waves of mitotic activity
in some stages of developing ganglia stimulated
with NGF, it seems at least likely that the increased numbers of neuroblasts found in these
experiments result from an increasingly high level
of differentiation of embryonic ganglion cells,
which might otherwise have formed.

Cohen (1958) found no NGF activity in extracts
of numerous normal mouse tissues-liver, kidney,
brain, pancreas, intestine, stomach and mammary
gland. He also failed to find activity in chick
embryo extract, while in one experiment, muscle
extract showed some NGF activity. On the other
hand Bueker, Schenkein and Bane (1960) found NGF
activity in extracts of kidney, spleen, thymus,
placenta, heart muscle and voluntary muscle, and
in the axial components of seven day chicks.
Levi-Montalcini and Angeletti (1960) found experimentally induced granulomas to be a potent source
of NGF. NGF from a specific source is quite
species-unspecific in action: mouse submaxillary
NGF is effective on neuroblasts of other mammals,
birds, and even in Urodele embryos (Weis, 1969).

The identification of NGF as a single protein
of defined characteristics was challenged by
Schenkein and Bueker (1962, 1964) who found that
Cohen's preparation could be separated on DEAE
cellulose into two fractions, neither of which
was active as NGF when isolated, but the two
fractions, when recombined, yielded an active
preparation. One component had a molecular weight
of 8,600, the other of 3,500. Later Schenkein
(1968) reported isolating a new NGF 10^7 times more
potent than any previously obtained. Its
molecular weight was 12,000 or more.

Varon, Nomura and Shooter (1967a, b) showed
that a protein of M.W. 140,000 could be isolated
from mouse submaxillary gland which at acid and
alkaline pH's dissociated into three dissimilar
molecular species, named alpha, beta and gamma,
one of which (beta) still acted as NGF, but with
lower potency: the dissociation was reversible.
Later work (Greene, Shooter and Varon, 1969)
showed that one component of the NGF 7S complex of
M.W. 140,000 was enzymatic, a specific esteropeptidase when free but not when combined with
the two components of the complex. Soon after
publication of the first paper from this group,
Angeletti, Calissano, Chen and Levi-Montalcini
(1967) also published evidence for the existence
of an NGF complex of M.W. about 130,000, which
dissociated readily. Meanwhile Angeletti (1968)
had described a molecule from snake venom, with a
molecular weight no greater than 5,000, possessing
NGF activity.

ACRYLAMIDE GEL ELECTROPHORESIS AND
THE IDENTIFICATION OF NGF

Our interest in this subject arose from the
many differing accounts of the nature of NGF, and
speculations as to what changes it induced, and
how it acted. We (Hoffman, Naughton, McDougall &
Hamilton, 1967; Hoffman and McDougall, 1968)
distributed a crude extract of mouse submaxillary
gland electrophoretically along a cylinder of
acrylamide gel, then cut a 0.5 mm thick slice out

of the middle longitudinally, and cultured ganglia
from ten day old chicks along the length of the
slice, directly on it, in a layer of medium.
Although acrylamide monomer is toxic, electrophoresis effectively removes monomer, and soaking
for one-half hour in physiological solution,
containing a low concentration of antibiotic
ensures that the surface of the slice is sterile,
and innocuous to cells. After 48 hours we examined the gel slice, and found that individual
ganglion cells had migrated to some extent out of
the ganglia, onto the surface of the gel (Figs. 1,
2) along most of its length. In certain specific
regions (N in Text Fig. 1) many more neuroblasts
moved out, often covering the gel in these regions
(see Figs. 3, 4, 5): these cells were appreciably
larger than seen in other regions, and a high
proportion of them extruded one or more neurites

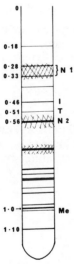

Text Fig. 1. A map of the stained protein bands
seen in an electrophoretic acrylamide gel prepared from male mouse submaxillary gland. On the
right are Rf values, while on the left is indicated
the biological activity detected over the specific
band. N1 and N2 represent regions of NGF activity,
I represents a region of marked inhibition of
neuroblasts.

Fig. 1.   Portion of the surface of a 10 day chick sensory ganglion,
                           incubated in normal fowl plasma on acrylamide gel (48
                           hours). No neuroblasts have migrated out. Unless other-
                           wise stated all figures are photographed fresh with phase
                           contrast optics with 40x water immersion objective (x 500).

Fig. 2.   Similar field to Fig. 1, but of a control ganglion incubated
                           in Eagle's basal medium : numerous neuroblasts are
                           migrating out of the ganglion, over the surface of the gel
                           (x 500).

Figs. 3 & 4.   Two fields from a culture of sensory ganglion in plasma
                           containing $10\,\mu$gm/ml of purified NGF. The photographs
                           typify areas of gel extensively invaded by migrating neuro-
                           blasts, many of which have extruded neurites (x 500).

Fig. 5.   Although this figure illustrates a culture stimulated by
                           thrombin (100 units/ml) rather than NGF, the area has
                           been similarly invaded by comparable neuroblasts, many
                           of which are extruding neurites (x 500).

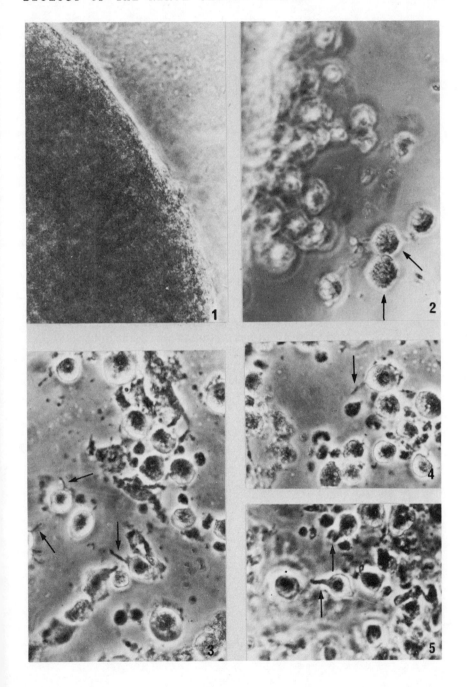

Figs. 6-17.   All these photographs represent the manifold appearances
                     of sprouting neuroblasts, migrating on acrylamide gel sur-
                     faces, when stimulated by NGF. In some instances varico-
                     sities typical of growing neurites *in vivo* are seen (Figs. 6,
                     8, 14 & 17) forked neurites are not rare (Figs. 12 & 15)
                     while in Fig. 9 a bipolar cell is shown (All x 600).

Fig. 18.   An electron microscopic view of numerous neurites,
                     wandering about in a culture of sensory neuroblasts
                     stimulated with 25 units/ml of thrombin. The neurites
                     typically contain little except ribosomes. Glutaraldehyde
                     and osmium tetroxide fixation, Epon imbedding (x 25,000).

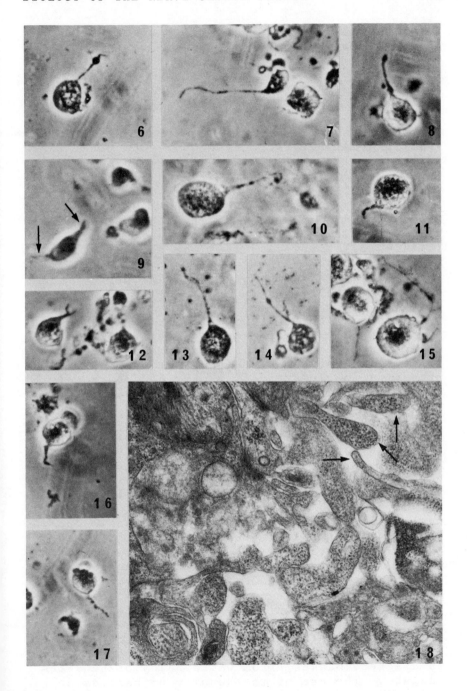

(see Figs. 6 to 17) - up to three neurites per
cell have been observed (a bipolar cell is seen
in Fig. 9). As a result of this examination we
could recognize three bands of stimulatory
activity, which corresponded with the bands visible when the gels were stained (see Text Fig. 1).
This method of examining the effects of specific
protein bands on individual free neuroblasts is
readily available for microscopy. One other band
worthy of mention at this stage was the one seen
in Text Fig. 1, labelled I. In this region no
migration occurred, in other words the activity
of neuroblasts over this band was less than control; in addition, there was evidence of destruction of cells. Careful examination of ganglia
in this region revealed that the surface of the
neuroblasts was to some degree stripped off, and
the cells appeared to have shed some of their
internal organelles.

The ability to examine individual neuroblasts,
in direct contact with specific, electrophoretically homogeneous proteins, enables the observer
to study the effect of these proteins on neurite
extrusion, cellular hypertrophy, and destructive
changes. The migration of cells in cultures of
dorsal root ganglia has been described (Lamont
and Vernon, 1967). Such cultures, as described in
this work, enable the study *in vitro* of aspects
of the action of NGF on neuroblasts closely
related to the phenomena observed *in vivo*. Observations *in vivo* suggest that the principal effects
of administration of NGF are increase in size,
number and rate of differentiation of mature
neurones. In chick embryos a considerable increase
in the number of differentiated cells followed
the administration of NGF. Although there is a
marked increase in mitotic index in ganglia of
embryos treated with NGF (Levi-Montalcini, 1966)
the principal effect appears to be a differentiating one. When young mice were injected with NGF,
only cell size was affected - there was no change
in cell number (Levi-Montalcini and Angeletti,
1960). When ganglia are grown on glass they remain
as discrete masses, from which halos of neurites
radiate. The use of the density of halo as an

assay method is essentially a compromise one, since
no other indices of growth are available from this
type of culture. The free migration of ganglion
cells on acrylamide gel not only makes possible
the observation of behavior of individual cells,
but also demonstrates that NGF stimulates migration as well as differentiation of neuroblasts.
Thus tumor transplants in chick embryos resulted
not only in the hypertrophy of pre-existing
ganglia, but in the appearance *de novo* of hyper-
trophic ganglionic masses in the body of the tumor
transplant (Levi-Montalcini, 1958).

The behavior of explanted, migrating neuroblasts, which we have characterized as responses to
NGF, were always correlated with the presence of
NGF. Thus beta-NGF, or the 7S NGF always produced
these responses, identical to those seen in
association with the three bands we have characterized as NGF in our gels. These three bands were
completely consistent in their occurrence in gels
prepared from submaxillary gland homogenates; they
may represent differently charged molecules, as a
result of buffer adsorption, or may be differing
fragments of a single NGF molecule.

We have observed a characteristic pattern of
response to changing concentration of NGF. With
increasing concentration above a threshold level,
more neuroblasts appear on the gel surface; these
cells become larger and more densely granular,
and a higher proportion extrude neurites as the
concentration of NGF rises. An optimal concentration is reached, above which less response is
observed; as the concentration increases further
the cells wandering over the surface of the gel
clump and begin to disrupt. This effect is consistent for any given NGF preparation, and reminiscent of observations of Schenkein (1968) who
described high concentrations of NGF as producing
'stunted growth' although he did not observe
destruction. Levi-Montalcini (1965) noted that
neurite extrusion was abolished by high concentrations of NGF, but thought the cells were still
healthy. These observations stress the advantages

Fig. 19.   Another electron micrograph of similar material to that
                shown in Fig. 18. Several neurites are shown in longitudinal
                section, with contents consisting predominantly of ribo-
                somes and distended endoplasmic reticulum. Preparative
                details as in Fig. 18 (x 28,000).

Fig. 20.   A large, flattened neuroblast with long forking neurite, seen
                in a culture stimulated with NGF 100 μgm/ml (x 600).

Fig. 21.   Large sprouting neuroblast seen in a culture stimulated with
                thrombin 20 units/ml (x 600).

Fig. 22.   Phase contrast photograph of a flattened fresh ganglion
                immediately after removal from the 10 day chick. Most of
                the cells are typical large, maturing neuroblasts, but there
                are a few diminutive 'embryonic' cells (lines) (x 600).

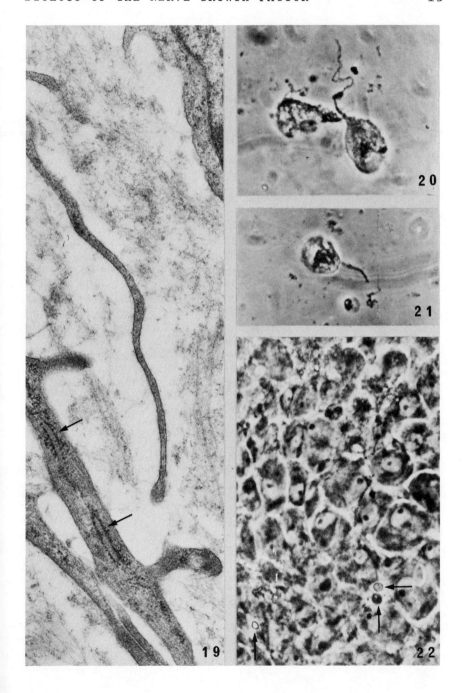

Fig. 23.   Several lysed 'ghosts' of neuroblasts lying on the surface of
                      a ganglion incubated in plasma containing 1% NGF-antiserum
                      (x 500).

Fig. 24.   Extensive lysis of neuroblasts at the surface of, and within
                      a ganglion explanted into plasma containing 1% of secon-
                      dary boosted NGF-antiserum (x 500).

Figs. 25 & 26.   Two photographs showing partially lysed neuroblasts, whose
                      previously extruded neurites are now fragmenting, and
                      whose cytoplasm is incompletely destroyed. From cultures
                      in plasma containing antiserum at 10^{-5} fold dilution (x 500).

Fig. 27.   A group of differentiating neuroblasts, one with neurite,
                      from a culture of 2-day chick neural tube, incubated over
                      the neural tube differentiating band in an electrophoretic
                      gel of mouse submaxillary gland (x 500).

Figs. 28 & 29.   Two further figures from cultures similar to that from
                      which Fig. 27 was taken. Large, partially differentiated
                      neuroblasts are seen together with much smaller cells
                      (x 500).

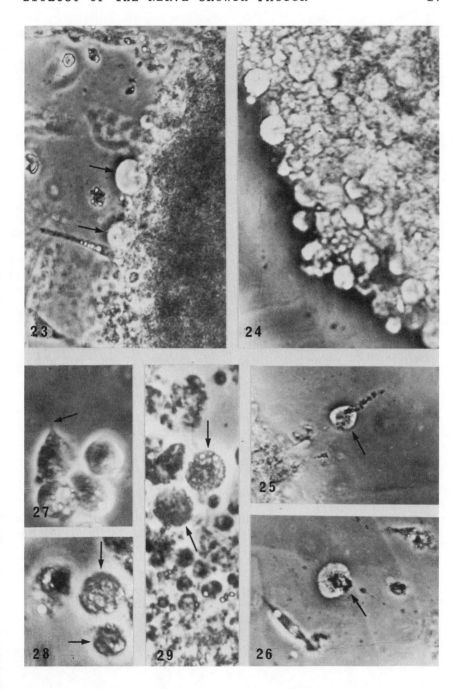

Fig. 30.   A largely homogeneous population of 'embryonic' ganglion
                  cells, which have migrated from a 10 day chick sensory
                  ganglion incubated in Eagle's medium containing 10^{-4} dilu-
                  tion of boosted NGF-antiserum. All the cells shown here
                  are small, with sparse, dense cytoplasm and refractile
                  nucleus. Contrast this cell population with that of the
                  ganglion, as explanted 48 hours earlier (Fig. 22) (x 500).

Fig. 31.   Another field, similar to that seen in the previous figure,
                  containing larger numbers of the diminutive 'embryonic'
                  cells. From a similar culture to Fig. 30 (x 500).

Fig. 32.   This photograph is from a similar culture to the two previous
                  ones, but incubated in even more dilute antiserum (10^{-5}
                  dilution). Here, together with the typical 'embryonic' cells
                  are found small-to-medium neuroblasts — in fact transitional
                  forms between the 'embryonic' cells and typical neuroblasts
                  (x 500).

Fig. 33.   A similar mixture of cells to that in the previous figure is
                  shown here — of interest is the tiny cell, upper left, with
                  sprouted process (arrow) (x 500).

Fig. 34.   Two cells, essentially similar to the 'embryonic' cells seen
                  in earlier figures, but found in a culture incubated with
                  10 µgm/ml of alkaline-treated beta-NGF. Essentially the
                  same de-differentiation has occurred here as with antiserum
                  (x 500).

Fig. 35.   A mixture of 'embryonic' cells and little neuroblasts seen in
                  a culture incubated with alkaline-treated thrombin (equiva-
                  lent of 25 units/ml) (x 500).

Fig. 36.   Another region of a ganglion incubated for 48 hours in
                  Eagle's medium containing 10^{-5} dilution of boosted anti-
                  serum. Portion of the thin-spread ganglion is seen here,
                  with a wide stretch of cell population, almost exclusively
                  composed of very small 'embryonic' cells (x 500).

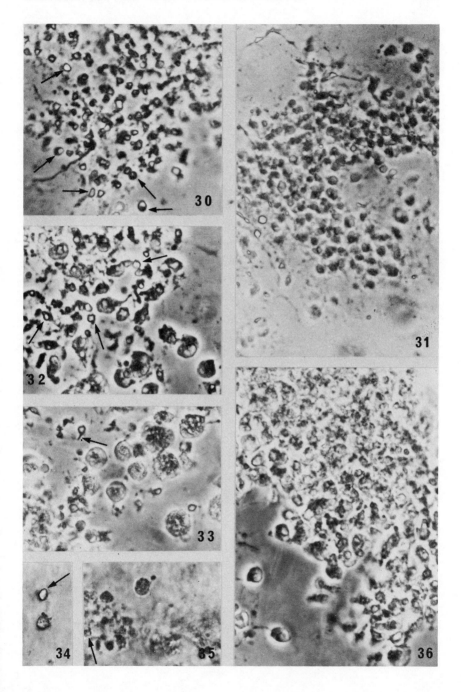

Figs. 37 & 38.   'Woolly' degeneration of neuroblasts incubated in plasma
                    containing trypsin 1 mgm/ml. The surface of the cell
                    appears to be lost, and cytoplasmic organelles appear to
                    be shed (x 500).

Fig. 39.   Less severe degeneration, still readily detectable, is seen
                    in neuroblasts incubated in trypsin 100 µgm/ml (x 500).

Figs. 40 & 41.   Neuroblasts from a culture incubated in plasma containing
                    NGF-alpha, 100 µgm/ml. The cells appear to undergo a
                    degenerative change similar to that seen with trypsin (x 500).

Fig. 42.   Neuroblasts from a culture incubated with separated throm-
                    bin activation products, in equivalent concentration to 25
                    units/ml of thrombin. Here again, a 'woolly' degeneration,
                    similar to that induced by trypsin, appears to occur (x 500).

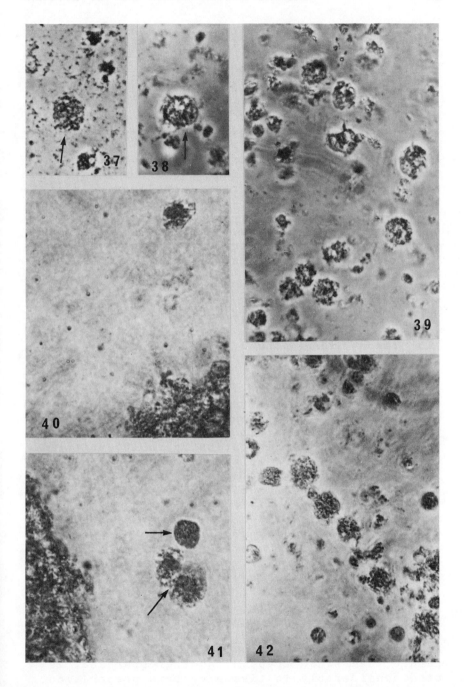

of methods of culture permitting detailed observa-
vation of individual cells.

MEDIA

Whilst carrying out the various experiments
described in the previous section, we tested various media for maintenance of ganglia *in vitro*.
Eagle's basal medium appeared to produce more
energetic migration and growth of neuroblasts than
plasma or serum (Fig. 2 represents control migration in Eagle's medium), and the cells remained
healthy, and growing for as long as we maintained
our cultures-3 to 4 days. Medium 199 was equally
satisfactory although the level of cellular activity was a little lower than for Eagle's basal
medium.

THROMBIN AS A MIMIC OF NGF

Thrombin has proved in our hands to be an
effective mimic of NGF. In concentrations of 5
N.I.H. units/ml of bovine thrombin (Parke Davis),
growth levels obviously in excess of control were
observed (Figs. 5 & 21 represent sprouting induced
by thrombin). There appeared to be a satisfactory
relationship between extent of differentiation of
neuroblasts and concentration up to 100 units/ml,
at which point the same sort of supra-optimal
inhibition was observed as with NGF. We (Hoffman
& McDougall, 1968) showed on electrophoretic gels
that the band responsible for clotting was also
the one over which NGF activity was observed-at Rf
0.36. Human thrombin proved rather more potent
than bovine thrombin, for equivalent coagulating
capacity the NGF activity was five-fold higher.
Although thrombin possesses arginase activity,
in contrast to beta NGF, DFP treatment, which
inhibits clotting activity fails to affect the NGF-
like activity of the preparation, thus indicating
that the NGF activity is not enzymic in character.
Nevertheless, since thrombin is enzymatic in
nature, and since trypsin, another protease, is
used considerably in tissue-culture preparation,
we tested the effects of trypsin on neuroblasts.

Both standard tissue culture preparations such
as Difco Trypsin 1:300 and trebly recrystal-
lized Trypsin were tested, in widely varying concentrations - from 1% to .01%, in serum, plasma,
Eagle's basal medium, and incubating for short
(1 to 2 hour) periods to long (48 hour) periods.
Even in the lowest concentration a characteristic
destructive change was observed (Figs. 37 to 39) in
all media used. The cells appeared to lose their
surface, and the interior organelles began to be
shed. This action persisted even after the enzyme
preparation was boiled for hours, thus indicating
the action was not enzymatic.

* MODIFICATION OF STRUCTURE AND
BIOLOGICAL CONSEQUENCES

In an attempt to examine similarities and
differences between salivary (beta) NGF and thrombin, we subjected both to various chemical procedures. Pronase digestion for 24 to 48 hours of
both beta-NGF and thrombin resulted in 50-100-fold
increase in biological activity *in vitro*. Under
these conditions little of peptide character
would remain. Incubation, either at room temperature or 37°C at pH 10.5 resulted, for both thrombin
and NGF, in a most interesting inversion of their
biological activity. All NGF activity was lost,
and the gel became populated by typical embryonic
cells in large numbers, as described in more detail
in the next section. Thus the differentiating
molecules became dedifferentiating molecules.
Fig. 34 shows a few embryonic cells from a culture
subjected to alkaline treated beta-NGF, while Fig.
35 shows similar cells from a culture treated with
alkalized thrombin. If the alkaline treated thrombin or NGF was then pronase digested, the dedifferentiating activity increased. From this evidence it seems clear that small fragments of the
protein NGF described earlier are the active components, as suggested by the observations of
Angeletti (1968) on heterogeneity of snake venom

* Unpublished work in collaboration with J. Clegg
and M. A. Naughton.

NGF. Schenkein's description of a low MW high
potency NGF also supports this conclusion. Poten-
tation of the activity by pronase digestion, together with reversal of activity by alkaline treatment, point to the active fragments having substantial carbohydrate content.

Greene *et al*., (1969) have considered the
significance of alpha and gamma, the two members
of the 7S NGF which do not behave as NGF when
isolated separately, and have suggested that their
prime function is to protect beta (NGF proper) from
degradation. We have examined alpha in our tissue
culture system, and have found that it is primarily destructive; in concentrations of 10^{-1} to -2
mgm/ml it strips the neuroblast of its' surface,
much in the way trypsin does (Figs. 40 & 41). In
lower concentrations (10^{-3} to -4 mgm/ml) it merely
causes release of small to medium neuroblasts from
the ganglion on to the gel surface. There was
evidence also of possible slight dedifferentiation
effects. We then examined the commercial thrombin
preparation, which because of the method of preparation also contains products released by activation of prothrombin: when separated on DEAE
cellulose one peak showed marked dedifferentiating
and destructive effects (Fig. 42). Thus both
salivary and other forms of NGF are accompanied by
molecules with varied antagonistic biological action.

DISTRIBUTION OF NGF

The demonstration of thrombin, an ubiquitous
protein, as a mimic of NGF casts an interesting
light on studies of distribution of NGF. As
mentioned earlier, Bueker, Shenkein and Bane (1960)
found NGF to be almost ubiquitous, in low concentration. Since thrombin mimics the properties of
salivary NGF so closely, it is likely that a great
deal of the low level activity of NGF detected in
many tissue extracts is attributable to the thrombin inevitably released by the coagulation of blood
in extracted tissues.

On the other hand, the demonstration by Winick

and Greenberg (1965) that NGF could be found
consistently in the axial regions of embryos, and
in the sympathetic chain as it developed, may be
more significant of functional NGF, involved in
initiating the differentiation of the developing
ganglionic system.

ANTISERUM AGAINST NGF

Cohen (1960) first described the preparation
of an antiserum against the Nerve Growth Factor,
using a single dose of Freund's adjuvant together
with NGF injected into rabbits. The resulting antiserum, when mixed with NGF, blocked the latter's
biological action on sensory or sympathetic chick
ganglia *in vitro*. When injected into newborn or
adult mice it produced severe elective destruction
of sympathetic ganglia remaining intact. Levi-
Montalcini and Cohen (1960) reported that injection of this antiserum into newborn mice produced
93% destruction of sympathetic ganglion cells -
the remaining neurons were atrophic, while satellite
cells remained healthy. Levi-Montalcini and
Angeletti (1960) reported that antiserum treatment
of adult mice produced only 60% destruction of
sympathetic ganglion cells. Further studies by
Levi-Montalcini and Booker (1960) demonstrated
drastic reduction of the number of surviving ganglion cells in the sympathetic system of a variety
of mammals treated with the antiserum.

The NGF antiserum is even more selective than
the foregoing section reveals: Vogt (1964) showed
that in newborn rats, NGF antiserum treatment produced near total destruction of the neuronal population of the paravertebral ganglia, but the
prevertebral ones (coeliae, mesenteric) appeared
normal morphologically. Zaimis, Berk and Callingham (1965) confirmed that rats treated at birth
with NGF antiserum had few ganglion cells left in
the paravertebral ganglia, but also showed severe
changes in the coeliac ganglion, with reduction
both of catechol-amine content, and uptake of
tritiated nor-adrenaline in the innervated organs.
Visscher, Lee and Azuma (1965) found no change in

the nor-adrenaline content of brain or adrenal
medulla in NGF antiserum treated animals, suggesting that the adrenergic cells in these sites were
unaffected by the treatment. Klingman (1966)
attempted "Immunosympathectomy" with NGF antiserum *in utero*, in mice of 12 to 17 days gesta-
tion, but obtained only very incomplete destruction of ganglia in the young when born. She
attributed this poor result either to insensitiv-
ity of neuroblasts at the stage treated, or to inability of the antibodies to cross the placental
barrier. Levi-Montalcini and Angeletti (1961)
had earlier shown immunosympathectomy *in utero* to
be ineffective, blamed the placental barrier and
showed that NGF antibody injected into the nursing
mother reached the young via milk.

      Action of NGF Antibody on Neuroblasts in Vitro

     Although NGF antibody was tested and assayed
in vitro in early experiments, there is little
account of its action on ganglion cells. All
earlier studies such as Cohen's (1960) consist of
mixing NGF and antiserum, and observing absence of
neurite halo around explanted ganglion. Sabatini,
Pellegrino and de Robertis (1965) described ultrastructural studies of degenerative changes occurring
in ganglion cells in the first hours after administering antiserum *in vitro* and *in vivo*. They
put forward two alternate hypotheses to explain the
destructive changes they observed: either the
antiserum deprives the neuroblast of some substance
vital for its survival (NGF) or the antiserum re-
acts with some antigen in or on the neuroblast,
with cytotoxic consequences.

     The culture methods we were using are suited
to the study of the fate of individual neuroblasts,
so we proceeded to study the effects of antisera
on neuroblasts migrating on acrylamide gel surfaces (Hoffman, 1970). Antiserum was produced in
rabbits to a purified, active NGF preparation,
using either direct intravenous injection, or
subcutaneous injection together with Freund's
adjuvant. In both instances, 42 days after the

primary immunization, booster doses were given, following a rigorous desensitization procedure, made necessary by the anaphylactogenic character of the preparation. The animals were bled, and sera prepared 11 to 25 days after boosting, then a second boost, one month later produced another series of antisera.

Antisera in plasma or serum. Antisera were added in serial dilution to cultures of 10 to 11 day chick sensory ganglia in plasma or serum. Drastic changes were observed in the neuroblasts on the gel surface: usually in medium containing antiserum as dilute as 10^{-5}, $^{-6}$ in serum, the neuroblasts were lysed in characteristic fashion (Figs. 23 & 24). The internal cytoplasmic contents of these cells disappeared, while the membrane apparently remained intact thus in phase contrast they appeared as bright 'ghosts', reminiscent of the red cell 'ghosts' seen after haemolysis. Further dilution of antiserum usually resulted in incomplete lysis being observed, so that appearances such as Figs. 25 and 26 were common. Column purified fractions of antisera were examined, and when 7S globulin was prepared from a primary antiserum whose potency ran out at dilution 10^{-2}, the purified IgG was potent to dilution 10^{-6} - thus indicating primary sera contain interfering components which block the action of the effective IgG.

This lytic pattern of destruction of neuroblasts by antiserum contrasts sharply with that previously seen after treatment with trypsin, or alpha NGF. In the case of antiserum, an empty membranous bag remains: in the case of trypsin - or alpha - the cell membrane appears to be ruptured, and the contents slowly leached.

Antisera in synthetic media. Since synthetic media appeared to support such energetic growth of neuroblasts, we examined the action of antiserum in synthetic media, both Eagle's basal medium, and Medium 199. Lysis was significantly absent amongst the cells seen on the gel; however, in high concentrations of antiserum in these media (10^{-1}, $^{-2}$)

no typical neuroblasts were seen. In their place
appeared very small cells (Figs. 30 & 31) irregu-
lar in outline, with relatively large refractile
nuclei and a thin, dark rim of cytoplasm. These
cells, when stained, proved to have strongly pyro-
ninophilic cytoplasm, and the electron microscope
revealed the cytoplasm to be packed with *individual*
ribosomes. As the antiserum was further diluted
out, the cell population seen on the gel contained
larger cells grading towards typical neuroblasts
(Figs. 32, 33, 36). At no stage in the dilution
series was lysis or destruction of cells observed.
If ganglia were squashed and observed directly
under phase contrast optics (see Fig. 22) - or
sectioned - it was evident that the cell population on the gel surface was representative of the
rest of the cells in the ganglion. The tiny cells
present in such large numbers after treatment with
high concentration of antiserum, seemed identical
to the occasional tiny cells seen in the ganglia
when first explanted, and to the cells of the
ganglionic anlagen seen in embryos of 2 to 3 days
incubation. These are essentially the undifferen-
tiated embryonic ganglion cells described by such
authors as Pannese (1968). Thus the cells of the
ganglion after 48 hours incubation in synthetic
medium containing antiserum are much smaller than
those found in the ganglion when first explanted.
These cells have become smaller and more embryonic
during the period spent cultured in antiserum-con-
taining medium, just as cells cultivated in medium
containing the antigen become larger and prematurely differentiated.

The contrast between destructive action of
antibody, in the presence of serum, and dedifferentiating action in the absence of serum led to a
search for evidence of specific serum components
involved in lysis. That the effect was not primarily one of complement fixation was indicated by
failure of guinea pig serum (a potent source of
complement), when added to Eagle's solution, to
induce lysis. On the other hand, even 10% fowl
serum in Eagle's solution produced effective lysis,
while partial lysis at low titer occurred in 3%
fowl serum in Eagle's solution. When fowl serum

was electrophoretically distributed in acrylamide
gel, and ganglia layered over a longitudinal slice
of this gel, with Eagle's solution above them,
dedifferentiation occurred in all regions other
than one band, which showed lysis, at Rf 0.47:
traces of lysis occurred at two other points.
Thus a specific serum protein acted as a specific
cofactor to produce lysis.

SPECIFIC ACTION OF NGF ON NEUROBLASTS

Morphology

Both *in vitro* and *in vivo* NGF appears to
induce and accelerate differentiation of sensory
and sympathetic neuroblasts. In injected animals,
more neuroblasts are seen, they are larger, have
more cytoplasmic RNA, and extrude more neurites.
In an electron microscopic study Crain, Benitez
and Vatter (1964) claimed that a specific para-
crystalline organelle appeared in the cytoplasm
of neuroblasts incubated with NGF, but could not
be detected in control ganglia. This was not confirmed in later E.M. studies by Spiegelman (1968),
Levi-Montalcini, Caramia, Luse and Angeletti
(1968) and Hoffman and Burnet (1970, p. 69). In
fact, appearances closely similar to those illus-
trated by Crain *et al.*, can be observed in control
ganglia, and are in fact attributable to highly
oriented ribosome pairs (Hoffman & Burnet, 1970).

The principal changes occurring in NGF treated
neuroblasts are: increase in ribosome content of
cytoplasm, hypertrophy of ribosomal reticulum,
with the accumulation of apparent secretory material in its cisternae, and increase of microfila-
ment content in cytoplasm (Levi-Montalcini, Caramia, Luse & Angelletti, 1968, Hoffman & Burnet,
1970). The distended ribosomal reticulum sacs
extend along the neurites effectively to their
tips; on the whole, filaments and tubules are rare
in these neurites (Figs. 18 & 19) which fail to
show birefringence. We have also seen appearances
suggestive of the formation of neurite-somatic and
neurite-neuritic synapses in these cultures.

The question of the stage of development of
the ganglion cell which is triggered by NGF remains
obscure. Most evidence points to a primarily
differentiating role, which assumes that the action
is on the early, pluripotent embryonic ganglion
cell.

Metabolism

In general, adding NGF to cultures of ganglia
accelerates all anabolic processes other than
DNA synthesis. Glucose utilization is increased
(Cohen 1959), lipid synthesis is markedly increased
(Angeletti, Levi-Montalcini & Calissano, 1968).
Net synthesis of protein rises (Cohen, 1959) as
does turnover of protein (Angeletti, Gandini-
Attardi, Toschi, Salvi & Levi-Montalcini, 1965).
RNA synthesis rises considerably, but DNA synthe-
sis is unaffected.

All of this information is consistent with
the cytological picture - the failure of DNA synthesis to increase supports the interpretation that
the action of NGF is to differentiate the cells
of a pool, in a specific direction, possibly at
the expense of an alternative one, without significant change in the proliferation of stem cells.

Essentiality of NGF

Destruction of neuroblasts by NGF antibody
led Levi-Montalcini and Angeletti (1961) to conclude that NGF supply was vital to the survival of
neuroblasts. This conclusion was reinforced by
their later experiments (Levi-Montalcini &
Angeletti, 1963) which consisted of isolating chick
sensory and sympathetic neuroblasts from ganglia
incubated for one-half hour in 0.5% trypsin.
These cells died rapidly if transferred to, and
incubated in Eagle's solution, even when supple-
mented with 10% serum. However, the addition of
NGF to the medium enabled the cells to survive and
differentiate. Our own experiments (Hoffman &
McDougall, 1968) indicated that sensory neuro-

blasts thrive in synthetic media, if one omits
the trypsin digestion. Trypsin is in very low
concentration destructive of neuroblasts; it is
possible that it strips NGF off the neuroblast,
but the appearance of trypsin treated cells suggests it strips rather more.

ROLE OF NGF IN REGENERATION OF NEURONS

Since NGF increases anabolism generally in
neuroblasts, and especially the synthesis of RNA
and protein, it might well affect the regenerative
capacity of nerve cells after interruption of the
axons. Scott, Guttmann and Horsky (1966) found
that after a crush lesion in peripheral nerves the
protein synthesizing activity in the sensory
ganglion cells of these nerves increased markedly
if NGF was injected. The rate of regeneration of
sensory nerve fibers also rose.

CHEMICAL HETEROGENEITY OF NGF

From the evidence presented here, it may be
concluded that the NGF present in such high concentration in the male mouse submaxillary gland
is only one of the molecular species possessing
this biological activity - NGF is generally defined
in biological, not chemical terms. Thrombin,
ubiquitous wherever trauma and the coagulation of
blood occur, is another substance possessing NGF
activity, with an activity at least as high as
that of many salivary NGF preparations. Further,
although thrombin acts similarly to salivary NGF
in the biological sphere it has obvious chemical
differences, since it is not antigenically cross-
reactive: NGF antiserum fails to neutralize the
NGF-like action of thrombin. It is also evident
that molecules with NGF activity occur in a wide
range of sizes: the 7S NGF has a molecular weight
of 140,000, Cohen's preparation was typically M.W.
44,000, Schenkein's high potency NGF was about
12,000 M.W. while Angeletti described a fragment
of M.W. 5,000 or less. Our own recent preparations
obtained by digestion with pronase, are necessarily

much smaller than these others. Thus a variety
of molecular species, many of them conceivably
available in the organism, may possess NGF
activity.

SITE OF ACTION OF NGF

There is insufficient evidence to permit
more than speculation on the site of action of
NGF on the neuroblast. Levi-Montalcini and
Angeletti (1961) described fluorescence in the
cytoplasm of chick sympathetic ganglion cells
when sections of these ganglia were treated with
fluorescent NGF antiserum. This evidence suggests
that NGF, or another molecule antigenically cross-
reacting with NGF is present in the cytoplasm.
On the other hand, the action of antibodies,
particularly the capacity of 19S macroglobulin to
destroy or dedifferentiate developing neuroblasts,
seems more readily explained by the presence of
NGF on the cell surface, accessible to antibody
molecules. Macroglobulin would not readily enter
the cell. Further, the reversal of differentiation
of neuroblasts by alkaline modified NGF beta, or
thrombin, suggests a form of analogue competition,
with original NGF and its analogue competing for
receptor sites on the cell surface.

It is clear that NGF is not an essential
substance for the survival of the cells of the
ganglion: rather it is essential for their
differentiation, towards which it acts as a trigger. The fact that NGF antibody, or chemically
modified NGF reverse the differentiation process,
tends to suggest that two factors are relevant to
the induction of differentiation by NGF. Firstly,
the molecule must fit a particular receptor site
in order to attach, secondly it must have the
necessary configuration (or charge distribution)
to induce the appropriate changes at the cell
surface, resulting in induction of differentiation
e.g., by "allosteric action". Antibody attaching
to the NGF may well distort configuration sufficiently so that, although the complex can attach,
it is inactivated. Alkaline treatment of NGF may

well achieve the same effect by removing end sugar
residues, and altering charge distribution.

GENERAL ROLE OF NGF IN THE ORGANISM

The various substances which can act as
NGF may perform one role in ontogenesis, and
another in the mature adult animal. Unquestion-
ably some form of NGF is involved in the normal
differentiation of sensory and sympathetic neuroblasts, and in shaping the pattern of development
of the ganglia in the developing embryo. It is
significant that limb bud alterations, induced
experimentally, alter the development of the
relevant sensory, sympathetic and motor neuroblasts, whereas the active tumors, or injected
NGF, alter only sensory and sympathetic elements.
One would like to suggest that other substances,
with analogous action to NGF, participate in the
differentiation of motor neuroblasts. In this
regard the substance described by Adler and
Narbaitz (1965) and investigated by us (Hoffman &
McDougall, 1968) has some relevance. These authors
described a substance demonstrable in mouse submaxillary gland extract, which prematurely differentiated the early chick neural tube. We found
that it was electrophoretically separable from
NGF, and promoted differentiation of certain stages
of neural tube cells into neuroblasts (see Figs.
27, 28 & 29). Such substances may be involved in
the differentiation of neural elements insensitive
to NGF.

The evidence of selectivity of action of NGF
tends to parallel that of NGF-antibody on neuroblasts: thus the cells which are differentiated
by NGF are lysed by its antibody, while neuroblasts insensitive to NGF fail to be lysed by its
antibody. NGF antibody becomes increasingly
selective in action as the nervous system matures:
in the embryo all sympathetic and sensory neuroblasts appear sensitive, in the newborn mammal
only paravertebral sympathetic neuroblasts respond,
and in the adult only about 60% of the cells of
even these ganglia are sensitive. Since the cells

lysed by antibody are also the cells sensitive
to NGF, a simple interpretation would suggest that
receptor sites for NGF on the cell surface become
masked on many of the neurones as they mature,
that NGF no longer sits in these sites, and there
is, therefore, no means of antibody attachment.
A considerable obstacle to such a postulated
mechanism for increasingly limited sensitivity
to NGF is the evidence of Scott, Guttmann and
Horsky (1966) that NGF in the adult still stimulates protein synthesis and axon regeneration in
sensory neurones, which all other work suggested
lost their susceptibility to NGF in the embryonic
stage. Since these cells are still sensitive to
NGF in the adult, thrombin, which will be formed
from prothrombin wherever blood coagulates, i.e.,
in trauma, may well play some part in triggering
the regeneration of sensory neurones.

REFERENCES

ADLER, R., & NARBAITZ, R.   Action of submaxillary
    gland extract on neural tube growth in organ
    culture. *Journal of Embryology and Experi-
    mental Morphology*, 1965, *14*, 281-287.
ANGELETTI, R. H.   Studies on the Nerve Growth
    Factor (NGF) from snake venom: Molecular
    heterogeneity. *Journal of Chromatography*,
    1968, *37*, 62-69.
ANGELETTI, P., CALISSANO, P., CHEN, Y. & LEVI-
    MONTALCINI, R.   Multiple molecular forms of
    the Nerve Growth Factor. *Biochimica et
    Biophysica Acta*, 1967, *147*, 180-182.
ANGELETTI, P. U., GANDINI-ATTARDI, D., TOSCHI,
    G., SALVI, M. L., & LEVI-MONTALCINI, R.   Meta-
    bolic aspects of the effect of Nerve Growth
    Factor on sympathetic and sensory ganglia.
    Biochimica et Biophysica Acta, 1965, *95*,
    111-120.
ANGELETTI, P. U., LEVI-MONTALCINI, R., & CALISSANO,
    P.   The Nerve Growth Factor: Chemical prop-
    erties and metabolic effects. *Advances in
    Enzymology*, 1968, *30*, 51-73.
BLOOD (MULLER), L.   The effect of NGF on dorsal

root ganglia of chick embryos.   PhD thesis,
University of London, 1969.

BUEKER, E. D.   Implantation of tumors in the hind-
limb field of the chick and the developmental
response of the lumbosacral nervous system.
Anatomical Record, 1948, *102*, 369-390.

BUEKER, E. D., SCHENKEIN, I., & BANE, J. L.   The
problem of distribution of a Nerve Growth
Factor specific for spinal and sympathetic
ganglia.   *Cancer Research*, 1960, *20*, 1220-
1228.

COHEN, S.   A nerve growth promoting protein.   In
W. D. McElroy and B. Glass (Eds.), *Symposium
on the chemical basis of development*.   Baltimore: Johns Hopkins Press, 1958, 665-679.

COHEN, S.   Purification and metabolic effects of
a nerve growth promoting protein from snake
venom.   *Journal of Biological Chemistry*,
1959, *234*, 1129-1136.

COHEN, S.   Purification of a nerve growth promoting protein from the mouse salivary gland,
and its neurocytotoxic antiserum.   *Proceedings of the National Academy of Sciences*,
1960, *46*, 302-310.

COHEN, S., & LEVI-MONTALCINI, R.   Purification and
properties of a nerve growth-promoting factor
isolated from mouse sarcoma 180.   *Cancer
Research*, 1957, *17*, 15-20.

COHEN, S., LEVI-MONTALCINI, R., & HAMBURGER, V.
A nerve growth stimulating factor isolated
from sarcomas 37 and 180.   *Proceedings of
the National Academy of Sciences*, 1954, *40*,
1014-1018.

CRAIN, S. M., BENITEZ, H., & VATTER, A. E.   Some
cytological effects of salivary Nerve Growth
Factor on tissue cultures of peripheral
ganglia.   *Annals of the New York Academy of
Sciences*, 1964, *118*, 206-231.

FOPPEN, F. A., LIUZZI, G., & D'AGNOLO, E. D.
Nerve Growth Factor and lipid classes in
sensory ganglia.   *Biochimica et Biophysica
Acta*, 1969, *187*, 414-421.

GREENE, A., SHOOTER, E. M., & VARON, S.   Subunit
interaction and enzymatic activity of the
7S Nerve Growth Factor.   *Biochemistry*, 1969,
8, 3735-3741.

HAMBURGER, V., & KEEFE, E. L. The effects of
    peripheral factors on the proliferation and
    differentiation in the spinal cord of chick
    embryos. *Journal of Experimental Zoology*,
    1944, *96*, 223-242.
HAMBURGER, V., & LEVI-MONTALCINI, R. Prolifera-
    tion, differentiation, and degeneration in
    the spinal ganglia of the chick embryo under
    normal and experimental conditions. *Journal
    of Experimental Zoology*, 1949, *111*, 457-502.
HOFFMAN, H. Immunology of Nerve Growth Factor
    (NGF): The effect of NGF antiserum on
    sensory ganglia *in vitro*. *Journal of
    Embryology and Experimental Morphology*, 1970,
    23, 555-570.
HOFFMAN, H., & BURNETT, E. Ultrastructural changes
    induced by an NGF-like action of thrombin on
    chick neuroblasts. *Australian Conference on
    Electron Microscopy*, Canberra, Australian
    Academy of Sciences, 1970.
HOFFMAN, H., & MCDOUGALL, J. Some biological
    properties of proteins of the mouse sub-
    maxillary gland as revealed by growth of
    tissues on electrophoretic acrylamide gels.
    Experimental Cell Research, 1968, *51*, 485-503.
HOFFMAN, H., NAUGHTON, M. A., MCDOUGALL, J., &
    HAMILTON, E. A. Nerve Growth Factors and
    a thymus inhibitor, separation by tissue
    culture on acrylamide gels. *Nature*, 1967,
    214, 703-705.
KLINGMAN, G. *In Utero* immunosympathectomy of
    Mice. *International Journal of Neuropharma-
    cology*, 1966, 5, 163-170.
LAMONT, M. D., & VERNON, C. A. The migration of
    neurons from chick dorsal root ganglia in
    tissue culture. *Experimental Cell Research*,
    1967, *47*, 661-662.
LEVI-MONTALCINI, R. Chemical stimulation of nerve
    growth. In W. D. McElroy and B. Glass (Eds.),
    Symposium on chemical basis of development.
    Baltimore: Johns Hopkins Press, 1958, 646-664.
LEVI-MONTALCINI, R. Morphological and metabolic
    effects of the Nerve Growth Factor. *Archives
    de Biologie* (Liege), 1965, *76*, 387-417.
LEVI-MONTALCINI, R. The Nerve Growth Factor, its
    mode of action on sensory and sympathetic

nerve cells. *Harvey Lectures*, 1966, 217-258.
LEVI-MONTALCINI, R., & ANGELETTI, P. U. Biological properties of a nerve growth promoting
protein and its antiserum. Fourth International Congress of Neurochemistry, Pergamon
Press, 1960, p. 362-377.
LEVI-MONTALCINI, R., & ANGELETTI, P. U. Growth
control of the sympathetic system by a
specific protein factor. *Quarterly Review of
Biology*, 1961, *36*, 99-103.
LEVI-MONTALCINI, R., & ANGELETTI, P. U. Essential
role of Nerve Growth Factor in survival and
maintenance of dissociated sensory and
sympathetic nerve cells, *in vitro*. *Developmental Biology*, 1963, 7, 653-659.
LEVI-MONTALCINI, R., & BOOKER, B. Destruction of
the sympathetic ganglia in mammals by an
antiserum to a nerve growth protein. *Proceedings of the National Academy of Sciences*,
1960, *46*, 385-391.
LEVI-MONTALCINI, R., CARAMIA, F., LUSE, S. A., &
ANGELETTI, P. U. *In vitro* effects of the
Nerve Growth Factor on the fine structure
of the sensory nerve cells. *Brain Research*,
1968, *8*, 347-363.
LEVI-MONTALCINI, R., & COHEN, S. Effects of the
extract of the mouse submaxillary salivary
glands on the sympathetic system of mammals.
Annals of the New York Academy of Sciences,
1960, *85*, 324-341.
LEVI-MONTALCINI, R., & HAMBURGER, V. Selective
growth stimulating effects of mouse sarcoma
on the sensory and sympathetic nervous system
of the chick embryo. *Journal of Experimental
Zoology*, 1951, *116*, 321-362.
LEVI-MONTALCINI, R., & HAMBURGER, V. A diffusible
agent of mouse sarcoma, producing hyperplasia
of sympathetic ganglia and hyperneurotisation
of viscera in the chick embryo. *Journal of
Experimental Zoology*, 1953, *123*, 233-288.
LEVI-MONTALCINI, R., MEYER, H., & HAMBURGER, V.
In vitro experiments on the effects of mouse
sarcomas 37 and 180 on the spinal and sympathetic ganglia of the chick embryo. *Cancer
Research*, 1954, *14*, 49-57.
PANNESE, E. Developmental changes of the endo-

plasmic reticulum and ribosomes in nerve
cells of the spinal ganglia of the domestic
fowl. *Journal of Comparative Neurology*, 1968,
132, 331-364.

SABATINI, M. T., PELLEGRINO DE IRALDI, A., &
DE ROBERTIS, E. Early effects of an antiserum against the Nerve Growth Factor on
fine structure of sympathetic neurones.
Experimental Neurology, 1965, *12*, 370-383.

SCHENKEIN, I. Nerve Growth Factor of a very
high yield and specific activity. *Science*,
1968, *159*, 640-643.

SCHENKEIN, I., & BUEKER, E. D. Dialyzable co-
factor in nerve growth promoting protein
from mouse salivary glands. *Science*, 1962,
137, 433-434.

SCHENKEIN, I., & BUEKER, E. D. The Nerve Growth
Factor as two essential components. *Annals
of New York Academy of Sciences*, 1964, *118*,
171-182.

SCOTT, D., GUTMANN, E., & HORSKY, P. Regeneration
in spinal neurons: Proteosynthesis following Nerve Growth Factor administration.
Science, 1966, *152*, 787-788.

SPIEGELMAN, I. Ultrastructural changes in neurons
of explanted chick ganglia in response to
Nerve Growth Factor. *Anatomical Record*,
1968, *160*, 432.

VARON, S., NOMURA, J., & SHOOTER, E. M. Subunit
structure of a high molecular weight form
of the Nerve Growth Factor from mouse submaxillary gland. *Proceedings of the National
Academy of Sciences*, 1967, 57, 1782-1789. (a)

VARON, S., NOMURA, J., & SHOOTER, E. M. Reversible
dissociation of the mouse Nerve Growth Factor
protein into different subunits. *Biochemistry*, 1967, 7, 1296-1303. (b)

VISSCHER, M. B., LEE, Y. C. P., & AZUMA, T.
Catecholamines in organs of immunosympathecto-
mized mice. *Proceedings of the Society of
Experimental Biology and Medicine*, 1965,
119, 1232-1234.

VOGT, M. Sources of noradrenaline in the "Immuno-
sympathectomized" Rat. *Nature*, 1964, *204*,
1315-1316.

WEIS, J. S. The effects of Nerve Growth Factor

on the spinal ganglia of *Amblystoma maculatim*. *Journal of Experimental Zoology*, 1969, *170*, 481-488.

WINICK, M., & GREENBERG, R. E. Appearance and localization of a nerve growth promoting protein during development. *Pediatrics*, 1965, *35*, 221-228.

ZAIMIS, E., BERK, L., & CALLINGHAM, B. A. Morphological, biochemical and functional changes in the sympathetic nervous system of rats treated with Nerve Growth Factor antiserum. *Nature*, 1965, *206*, 1220-1222.

THE NERVE GROWTH FACTOR PROTEINS OF THE MOUSE SUBMAXILLARY GLAND

Silvio Varon and E. M. Shooter

Department of Biology, University of
California at San Diego La Jolla,
California and Departments of Genetics
and Biochemistry, Stanford University,
Stanford, California, respectively

The proteins which elicit nerve growth factor NGF activity have been the object of interest and investigation for more than a decade. The discovery of a factor which stimulates differentiation of certain neurons in embryonic sensory and sympathetic ganglia (Levi-Montalcini, 1966) and its characterization as a protein (Cohen & Levi-Montalcini, 1957) were events of very considerable significance in neurobiology and their consequences are still being exploited. Soon after the protein character of NGF was established it was found that very much more NGF activity could be obtained from the adult male mouse submaxillary gland than from the original tumor material (Cohen, 1960) and the gland became the preferred starting material for further investigation. The original method for isolating NGF from this gland was devised by Cohen (1960). His preparation was optimally active at about 15 ng/ml in the *in vitro* plasma clot assay and sedimented at 4.3S. An alternate method was developed by Varon, Nomura & Shooter (1967) after the realization that the size of the NGF protein was critically dependent on pH. This new NGF protein was larger than that in the original preparation, was obtained in larger yield but had the same NGF potency. It was given the name 7S NGF, being defined by both its sedimentation prop-

41

erties and its biological activity. The continued
characterization of 7S NGF and its constituent
subunits revealed that NGF activity was only one
of several activities displayed by the complex.
This emphasized that the 7S complex, as a major
protein of the submaxillary gland, warranted study
in its own right, as well as for its NGF activity.
This paper therefore describes in some detail biochemical studies on 7S NGF and its subunits and
correlates this information with several recent
descriptions of NGF proteins from the submaxillary
gland.

THE 7S NGF COMPLEX

Physical Properties and Composition

Sucrose gradient sedimentation analysis of
the clarified homogenate of the adult male mouse
submaxillary gland reveals a major peak of NGF
activity moving with a sedimentation coefficient
of approximately 7S (Varon *et al.*, 1967). Provided
the pH is kept close to neutrality it is possible
in three relatively simple steps to purify this
material some 40 fold from the homogenate and obtain a preparation whose major component still
sediments at 7S. This preparation has a biological potency similar to that of earlier NGF preparations (Fig. 1). The 7S NGF accounts, surprisingly,
for some 2% of the total submaxillary gland protein.

A typical 7S NGF preparation contains between
2 and 5% of non-7S NGF components with either lower
sedimentation coefficients or differing electrophoretic mobilities to 7S NGF. A number of these
components show peptidase activity against a
variety of N-terminal argininyl dipeptides as
judged by appropriate histochemical staining after
migration in starch gel (A. S. Santachiara-Bene-
recetti-unpublished data). This is perhaps not
surprising since the submaxillary gland is rich in
esterases, peptidases and proteolytic enzymes.
However, the 7S NGF preparations are stable when
stored cold or preferably frozen.

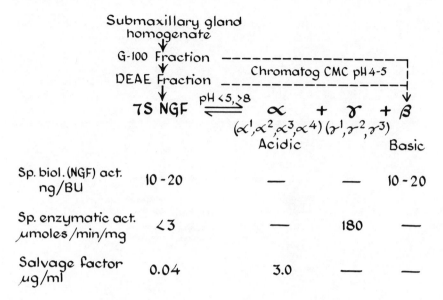

Fig. 1. The isolation and properties of 7S NGF.

The 7S NGF itself migrates as a single broad band in acrylamide gel at pH values between 7 and 8 (Varon *et al.*, 1967; Varon, Nomura & Shooter, 1968; Smith, Varon & Shooter, 1968; Smith, Greene, Fisk, Varon & Shooter, 1969) and focuses in acrylamide gels containing ampholine into a band covering a range of isoelectric points between pH 5.09 and 5.21, with a mean of 5.15 (Fig. 2). These pH values are sufficiently close to the lower pH stability limit of 7S NGF, i.e., approximately pH 5, that continued exposure of the 7S NGF band, after reaching equilibrium at its isoelectric point in the pH gradient, results in its gradual dissociation into subunits. The complete dissociation of 7S NGF produces three types of subunits, α, γ and β which differ markedly in isoelectric points. The yields of these subunits (Varon *et al.*,

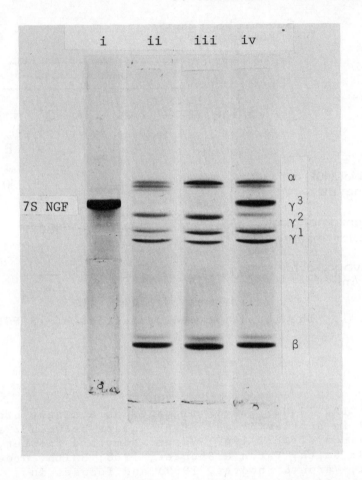

Fig. 2. Isoelectric focusing of 7S NGF and its
subunits. Analyses made in 7-½% acrylamide gels
containing pH 3-10 Ampholine buffer. Migration
for (i) 2 hour at 50 volts and (ii)-(iv) 4 hour
at 100 volts. Stained with Coomassie Blue (i) 7S
NGF, applied near center of gel, (ii) 7S NGF, fresh
preparation, applied at top of gel, (iii) 7S NGF,
stored preparation, applied at top of gel, (iv) 7S
NGF, stored preparation, applied near center and
at top of gel.

1968) together with their similarity in size suggests that 7S NGF contains two each of the α and
γ subunits but only one of the β subunits; however, accurate molecular weight values are needed
before this can be considered proven. Two of
these groups, the α and γ, contain more than one
major component; the individual subunits within
these groups being identified with superscripts
starting with the component of highest isoelectric
point in each instance (Fig. 1). The properties
of the individual α and γ subunits are discussed
in detail in a later section; it is pertinent only
to note here that they can be isolated by ion
exchange chromatography at appropriate pH and that
they share with the other members of the group
certain specific properties. One of these is the
ability to regenerate a 7S NGF species when mixed
with subunits of the other two types in appropriate
amounts (Smith *et al*., 1968). Thus a variety of
7S species can be formed which contain only single
representatives of the α and γ subunit groups
(Fig. 3).

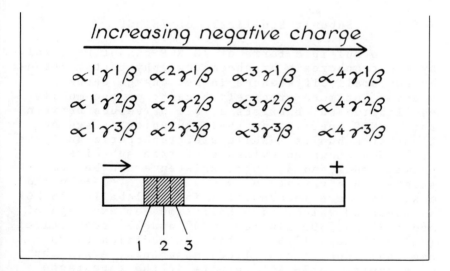

Fig. 3. Multiple forms of the 7S NGF which
possibly occur.

These experiments in turn explain why the dissociation of the 7S NGF preparation produces so many subunits. These preparations contain not one 7S NGF species but at least as many closely related forms as are shown in Fig. 3 and probably more. The only property found so far which differentiates these multiple species, besides subunit composition, is their net charge, the latter being determined by the type of individual α subunit the species contains. Thus the electrophoretically migrating or electrofocused band of a 7S NGF preparation is, because of the multiplicity of species present, relatively broad compared to that of a single protein species and shows a distribution of 7S species, those with the α subunits of highest isoelectric point having the lowest mobility and *vice versa* (Smith *et al.*, 1968). The distribution of species can be seen by serial sectioning of the 7S NGF zone after migration, α^1 containing species are concentrated on the low mobility side (Fig. 3, section 1) and α^4 containing species on the leading edge (Fig. 3, section 3).

Subunit Equilibria of 7S NGF

The multiple forms of 7S NGF cannot be resolved by electrophoresis or chromatography partly because of the small differences in net charge between species but more precisely because of the mobile equilibrium which exists at all pH values between the 7S NGF species and their subunits or aggregations of subunits. While electrophoretic analysis of 7S NGF shows no evidence of free subunits between pH 7 and 8, their existence can be demonstrated in a variety of ways. Thus ^{125}I-labelled α subunits are incorporated into unlabelled 7S NGF at these pH values with half times of exchange of about 30 and 300 minutes at 4° and 27° respectively (Smith *et al.*, 1969). Also the addition of any one individual (unlabelled) α subunit, e.g., the α^2 subunit, to 7S NGF results in the appearance in the excess α subunit pool of the remaining components, in this instance α^3 and α^4 subunits. This result would only be anticipated if all the α subunits in 7S NGF were freely exchangeable with an added excess of any one subunit. It follows, therefore, that 7S NGF is in equilibrium with free α subunits at all pHs and that all the α subunits behave identically in this regard. In contrast ^{125}I-labelled γ and β subunits exchange with their unlabelled counterparts in 7S NGF much more slowly and the other product of the dissociation of 7S NGF near neutral pH must therefore be a complex of γ and β subunits by themselves or with α subunits in lesser amount than exist in 7S NGF. The practical consequences of this mobile equilibrium are that individual 7S NGF species cannot be isolated from the original preparation, nor is it possible to determine whether this preparation contains species with two unlike α or two unlike γ subunits. Since neither individual α nor γ subunits display any differences in their ability to recombine with the remaining two subunit types it is likely that such species do exist. The situation is analogous to that in hemolysates of red cells of an individual heterozygous for an abnormal hemoglobin. It has been shown that these hemolysates do contain hybrid hemoglobins with unlike chains such as $\alpha^A\beta^A\beta^X$ or $\alpha^A\alpha^Y\beta^A$ depending on the locus of the mutation (Guidotti, 1967). However, because of the rapid equilibrium between the $\alpha_2\beta_2$ tetramers and $\alpha\beta$ dimers and the fact that the above hybrids have properties intermediate between those of the two usual hemoglobins found in these hemolysates, $\alpha_2^A\beta_2^A$ plus $\alpha_2^A\beta_2^X$ or $\alpha_2^A\beta_2^A$ plus $\alpha_2^Y\beta_2^A$, any separation process results in the dissociation of the hybrid, the separation of the unlike dimers and their subsequent recombination into species containing only like α or β chains (Guidotti, Konigsberg & Craig, 1963; Guidotti, 1967). Although the 7S NGF equilibria are more complex and the rate of association and dissociation probably somewhat different than for hemoglobin, the end result will be the same, namely that 7S species with unlike α or γ subunits cannot be detected even when present.

Another consequence of the subunit equilibria and of its kinetic parameters is that α subunits can be continuously removed from the 7S complex during slow passage through an anion exchange

material such as DEAE cellulose or Sephadex
(Shooter, Varon & Nomura, 1968). In order to
avoid dissociation by this mechanism and thereby
isolate the native 7S NGF complex, the ion exchange
chromatographic step in the isolation procedure
must be accomplished in a time significantly shorter than the half life of the α subunit exchange at
that particular temperature. Increasing flow
rates some ten fold above normal accomplishes just
this and results in the reproducible elution of
the 7S NGF from DEAE cellulose in a discrete peak
over a narrow range of salt concentration (Varon
et al., 1967). At normal flow rates, significant
amounts of the more acidic α subunits bind to the
resin. As a result 7S NGF no longer elutes in one
peak, and NGF activity is recovered in eluants
of a much wider range of salt concentration as a
variety of other subunit complexes deficient in
α subunits, and residual 7S NGF species are
released from the column. The DNA-dependent RNA
polymerase of E. coli is another example of a protein whose subunit properties are modified by
passage through an ion exchange material; in this
instance one of its subunits, the σ factor, is
separated from the core RNA polymerase enzyme
during chromatography on phosphocellulose (Burgess,
Travers, Dunn & Bautz, 1969).

The demonstration of the dynamic subunit
equilibrium of 7S NGF at neutral pH does not imply
that the 7S complex is unstable under these conditions. The half life of the α subunit exchange is
of the same order as the half life of the tryptophan
synthetase complex (Creighton and Yanofsky, 1966)
suggesting that the rate limiting step in the
exchange is the slow rate at which the 7S complex
dissociates. Moreover a preliminary estimate of
the equilibrium constant of 7S NGF derived from
the sedimentation behavior of ^{125}I-labelled 7S NGF
at low concentration, indicates that it is an
order of magnitude greater than that of tryptophan
synthetase. This stability is also attested to
by the high degree of specificity shown in the
interaction of the three subunit types in 7S NGF.
The 7S complex is regenerated in optimum amounts
from mixtures of the three subunits in proportions

close to those recovered in the initial dissociation of 7S NGF (Shooter & Varon, 1970). Also the
complexes formed between α and β or between γ and
β subunits are much less stable than 7S NGF and
revert to the latter spontaneously when mixed together. The high affinity of the three subunits
for each other is also demonstrated by the fact
that less than 50% of the 7S NGF is lost after
exposure of the supernatant of the submaxillary
gland to a pH sufficiently acidic to completely
dissociate 7S NGF species, followed by dialysis
back to neutral pH to allow recombination. The
recovery would probably be higher still but for
irreversible adsorption of the subunits to the
copious precipitate obtained at acid pH. In any
event, it is clear that a major fraction of the
7S NGF subunits recombine specifically even in the
midst of a large excess of non-7S NGF protein.

The Biological Activities of 7S NGF

Because NGF activity was used as the assay to
follow the isolation of 7S NGF, this was the first
biological activity ascribed to the complex. The
NGF potency of 10-20 ng/BU (Fig. 1) places the
optimal *in vitro* response at a concentration of
approximately 10^{-10} M. Besides producing the typical
fiber halo around embryonic sensory or sympathetic
ganglia, in the usual *in vitro* assay in a plasma
drop (Levi-Montalcini, Meyer & Hamburger, 1954),
7S NGF induces neurite growth in individual neuroblasts migrating on an acrylamide surface (Hoffman,
Naughton, McDougall & Hamilton, 1967; Hoffman &
McDougall, 1968; Hoffman, 1970), and when injected
into newborn mice, the 7S NGF complex results in
a four- to six-fold increase in the size of the
superior cervical ganglia (Varon *et al.*, 1968).
The 7S NGF, therefore, stimulates migration as
well as differentiation of ganglionic neuroblasts
(Hoffman, 1970). Higher than optimal concentrations of 7S NGF in the *in vitro* plasma clot assay
produce less and less fiber outgrowth until finally
no neurite halo is visible. Hoffman (1970) also
noted that in the assay on acrylamide gel less
response is observed at higher NGF concentrations.

However, the effect at the highest concentrations
was to cause cells to clump and disrupt. The
nerve growth factor activity of 7S NGF is a property
of the basic β subunit, both α and γ subunits
being inactive in this regard (Fig. 1).

The second activity displayed by 7S NGF is
that of an esteropeptidase enzyme capable of hydrolyzing esters and to a less extent amides of sub-
stituted or free amino acids, in particular of
arginine (Greene, Shooter & Varon, 1968; Greene,
Shooter & Varon, 1969). Compared to trypsin, it
shows a much higher degree of specificity towards
arginine rather than lysine containing substrates
but unlike trypsin has a very low activity towards
protein substrates such as casein. Only the γ
subunit of the isolated three subunits of 7S NGF
has this enzymatic activity (Fig. 1). Although
under typical conditions of assay 7S NGF displays
a specific activity about one sixth that of the
γ enzyme, it is now clear that this figure does
not represent the true specific activity of the 7S
species. The reasons for believing that the latter
has a very low or even zero activity are discussed
later. A number of enzymes with esteropeptidase
activity have been reported in the mouse submaxillary gland. Gel filtration of extracts of the
male gland resolves these esteropeptidases into
three classes, the 7S complex containing the γ
enzyme, enzymes with molecular weights in the range
60-70,000 and a third class with molecular weight
of 25-30,000 (S. Varon and L. A. Greene, unpublished). Two distinct enzyme forms of the latter
class have been purified and their synthesis shown
to increase in female glands after testosterone
treatment (Calissano & Angeletti, 1968).

The third activity, which is a property of
the acidic α subunits as well as of 7S NGF, has
been termed the "salvage function." This is an
ability to protect embryonic sensory ganglionic
cells during dissociation and recovery from
embryonic ganglia (Varon, 1970). In the absence
of added 7S NGF, trypsin dissociation followed by
washing and aspiration in trypsin-free media results
in the recovery of a reproducible number of large

neuronal and smaller non-neuronal cells from the
ganglia. Addition of increasing amounts of 7S
NGF, particularly to the wash solutions, allows
the recovery of increasing numbers of both type
of cells. The dose-recovery curve has a sigmoid
shape but reaches a plateau at a particular concentration. Therefore, a quantitative measure of
the salvage function can be made by estimating
the concentration required for half maximal effect
(Fig. 1).

THE PROPERTIES OF THE SUBUNITS OF 7S NGF

The β Subunit

The 7S NGF can be dissociated into its component subunits in a variety of ways. These include
exposure to pH 5 or lower or to pH higher than 9
and to 8M urea. The three subunit types are most
readily separated by ion exchange chromatography
initiated at a dissociating pH. The acidic α subunits do not bind to CM-cellulose at pH 4 or 5 and
low salt concentration while the γ subunit group
can be eluted subsequently as a whole at the same
pH by a two- or three-fold increase in salt concentration. The basic β subunit can finally be
eluted at this or at higher pHs by high salt con-
contration (Varon et al., 1968; Smith et al.,
1968). Conversely the β subunit can be isolated
at high pH because, unlike the α and γ subunits,
it does not bind to the strong cationic resin QAE-
Sephadex (Perez, unpublished).

By both procedures the recovered β subunit
accounts for approximately 20% of the 7S NGF protein (by Lowry assay) and 20% of the biological
activity applied to the column. It has therefore
a specific activity (on a weight basis) in the same
range as 7S NGF (Fig. 1). Bearing in mind the
quantitative limitations of the bioassay, it
appears that the biological potency of the β subunit is increased some five-fold in 7S NGF compared
to the free β subunit. The fact that the 7S and
β species can be differentiated in the bioassay
testifies to the stability, partial or complete,

of 7S NGF under the conditions of the bioassay.
The increased potency of the subunit in the 7S
complex may be simply a question of its protection
in the complex by the other two subunits or it
may be based on specific interactions between the
subunits. Like 7S NGF, the β subunit also induces
neurite growth in embryonic neuroblasts on an
acrylamide gel surface (Hoffman, 1970).

In terms of its physical properties the β
subunit sediments at approximately 2.5S in sucrose
gradients but 90% or greater losses of protein and
biological activity occur in these experiments.
The β subunit migrates in a single band in acrylamide gel at pH values both below or above its
isoelectric point. On isoelectric focusing, which
provides the highest resolution for this basic
protein, the preparation shows a major (90-95%
of the total protein) component, a minor component
of slightly lower isoelectric point and a trace
component of slightly higher isoelectric point
(Fig. 2). The isoelectric point of the major
component is greater than pH 9.1 and cannot be
determined in the routine pH gradients established
in acrylamide gel with the pH 3-10 Ampholine solutions since the pH gradient does not exceed 9.1-
9.2 units. In spite of its high isoelectric point
the content of acidic amino acids is somewhat
greater than that of the basic amino acids (Table
I) suggesting that a relatively large number of
the former carry substituent groups such as amide.
The β subunit contains some 5% of carbohydrate in
the form of neutral sugars, glucosamine and galac-
tosamine (Bamburg, unpublished data) and these
residues may also be attached via aspartyl groups.
All the half cysteine residues are present in
disulfide bonds since carboxymethylation of native
β produces no carboxymethylcysteine on subsequent
hydrolysis. No free -SH groups can be detected
either by the nitroprusside reaction or by p-
hydroxymercuribenzoate or Ellman's reagent (Greene,
Varon, Piltch & Shooter, unpublished).

The β subunit elutes from G-50 Sephadex at a
molecular weight approximating to that of trypsin,
i.e. 24,300 Daltons, and after brief exposure to

TABLE I

AMINO ACID COMPOSITION OF
VARIOUS 7S NGF SUBUNITS

Results expressed as residues per 30,000 Daltons

	β(7S NGF)	β(Bocchini *et al.*)	α^2	α^3
Lys	18.9	19	16.9	15.9
His	8.8	9	8.8	8.8
Arg	15.4	16	6.3	6.4
Asp	27.2	25	39.7	38.9
Thr	31.5	30	16.5	16.7
Ser	23.9	23	17.5	18.0
Glu	20.7	19	26.7	26.6
Pro	6.5	5	25.8	26.4
Gly	12.9	12	18.2	20.0
Ala	19.5	19	13.7	13.6
1/2Cys	12.0	10	9.0	8.1
Val	29.9	28	15.5	16.7
Met	2.2$_5$	2	4.7	4.8
Ileu	11.5	11	10.5	10.9
Leu	8.1		28.4	29.3
Tyr	5.1	4	9.8	9.3
Phe	16.2	16	6.0	5.3
Tryp	4.9			

sodium dodecylsulfate (SDS) shows a major migrating
component on SDS-containing acrylamide gels
(Shapiro, Vinuela & Maizel, 1967) corresponding to
a molecular weight of 23,000 Daltons. Continuing
incubation in SDS with or without $\underline{\beta}$-mercaptoethanol
slowly converts this component into a second species
of molecular weight 11-12,000 Daltons. The conversion from the higher to the lower molecular

weight form follows an apparent first order rate
constant with a half life of about 2 hours at 37°.
Dissociation of the native β subunit to components
of approximately 11-12,000 Daltons is also achieved
by gel filtration on Sephadex in the presence of
6M guanidine hydrochloride, by succinylation or by
reduction and carboxymethylation in the presence
of denaturing agents. Since the reduction in
molecular size can be achieved by denaturing agents
in the absence of reducing agents it suggests that
the β subunit comprises two similar chains which
are not held together by disulfide bonds. Each of
these individual polypeptide chains must, therefore,
include three intra-chain disulfide links. That
the chains are probably identical is shown by the
fact that the β subunit still gives a single major
band in isoelectric focusing gels or on ion exchange
chromatography in the presence of 8M urea (Greene
et $al.$, unpublished).

The NGF activity of the 12,000 molecular
weight chains in the presence of SDS or after
reduction and carboxymethylation is very low or
zero. However, the recovery of both β protein and
NGF activity from gel filtration or ion exchange
columns is much improved in the presence of
guanidine hydrochloride or urea, suggesting that
there is much less irreversible adsorption under
these conditions and that the separation of the
two chains by these denaturing agents alone is
reversible. Whether the individual chains are
biologically active cannot be determined from these
results. The recent report (Hoffman, 1970) that
pronase treatment of the β subunit results in a
50-100 fold increase in biological activity as
measured in $vitro$ on acrylamide gel suggests that
not only are the peptide chains in the β subunit
themselves active but that one or more very short
segments of these chains are responsible for the
NGF effect. It should be emphasized at this point
that it may not be entirely valid to assume that
the two methods of assay, using the plasma clot and
an acrylamide surface, will always show stimulation
or neurite growth by the same material. For
example, Hoffman and McDougall (1968) and Hoffman

(1970) find that thrombin, bovine or human, mimics
in many details the NGF stimulation of neuroblast
differentiation on acrylamide surface. This effect
is not observed in the plasma clot assay where
thrombin is also used, admittedly in larger
amounts, to produce clotting. Also, by the acrylamide assay, extracts of submaxillary gland show
two zones of NGF activity and one of these is not
immediately explicable in terms of the known properties of 7S NGF. On the other hand, the complementary use of these two assay systems seems likely
to provide significantly new information on the
NGF effect.

Zanini, Angeletti and Levi-Montalcini (1968)
have described the isolation of a basic NGF protein
which in terms of the method of isolation and the
properties of the final protein suggest that it is
identical to the β subunit of 7S NGF (Shooter &
Varon, 1970). The apparently higher potency,
1 ng/BU, rather than 10-20 ng/BU, is explained by
a change in the definition of the Biological Unit
(BU). Instead of a definition which describes
optimal response as due to a solution containing
1 BU/ml it is now defined as due to 1 BU in the
actual assay. Since the assay uses only 0.05 ml
of an NGF solution, this new definition increases
potencies arbitrarily by an order of magnitude.
The only property of the Zanini *et al.*, (1968)
protein which does not agree with the known
properties of the β subunit is its apparent ability
to dissociate into halves on standing in dilute
solution. The two identical chains in the β
subunit in contrast are only separated with strong
denaturing agents. In a recent paper, Bocchini and
Angeletti (1969) describe the isolation of a basic
protein from an intermediate stage in the isolation
of 7S NGF and again the procedure and the final
properties of the protein suggest that it is the
β subunit. This is confirmed by a comparison of
their amino acid compositions (Table I), by the
similarity of their patterns on isoelectric focusing in acrylamide gel and by the ability of the
new protein to recombine with α and γ subunits to
regenerate 7S NGF. The β subunit can also be iso-

lated from the material, the DEAE fraction, left
after the second stage of 7S NGF isolation (Varon
et al., 1968).

The γ Subunits

The enzymatic activity of the 7S NGF complex
resides in the γ subunits (Greene *et al.*, 1968,
1969). The three individual subunits, γ^1, γ^2 and
γ^3, normally isolated from fresh 7S NGF preparations all have the same specific activity. While
the rate of hydrolysis of typical substrates by
the γ enzyme is linear from the time of addition
to substrate, 7S NGF displays a lag phase before
reaching maximal velocity. The extent of the lag
phase is diminished by incubating the diluted 7S
NGF solution by itself prior to addition of substrate, by high pH or high ionic strength (Greene
et al., 1969). These are effects which would be
anticipated provided that the incubation conditions
produced a shift in the 7S NGF equilibria toward
more subunits and also provided that the only
enzymatically active species are γ subunits which
are dissociated from the 7S NGF complex. The lag
phase would then reflect the time required to
achieve the new dissociation equilibrium and
produce the relevant concentration of "free" γ
subunits. Support for this idea comes from the
fact that the lag phase is restored if incubated
dilute solutions are concentrated or the pH and
ionic strength brought back into the range of 7S
NGF stability. Also, addition of an excess of the
enzymatically inactive subunits, α and β, before
dilution of 7S NGF into the assay system decreases
the observed specific activity of the latter to
about 10% of its value in the absence of those subunits. Since these are conditions which suppress
dissociation of 7S NGF, they measure more accu-
rately the intrinsic specific activity of the 7S
NGF complex. The latter is sufficiently low
(Fig. 1) to suggest that the γ subunit bound in
the 7S complex is inactive. Suppression of the γ
activity requires interaction with both α and β,
either subunit alone having very little effect on

the observed activity of the γ subunits (Greene
et al., 1969). These changes in enzymatic activity
of the γ subunit parallel changes in its physical
properties on aggregation and suggest that the two
are linked. In spite of the significant differences in net charge (or isoelectric points) which
exist between the three individual γ subunits,
7S species reformed from them by recombination with
one given α subunit and the β subunit all have the
same net charge (Smith *et al.*, 1968), showing that
the segments of the γ subunits which differ are
hidden in the recombination process. Whether this
involves a conformational change in the γ subunit
is not yet known.

The differences in electrophoretic mobility
between γ subunits displayed on acrylamide gel
show up also as differences in isoelectric point
(Fig. 2 and Table II) confirming that the former
results at least in part, if not entirely, from
differences in net charge. Whereas fresh γ subunit preparations show three major components,
stored preparations show a decrease in γ^1 and the
appearance of a fourth γ component, γ'. Whether
such changes are produced by the intrinsic enzymatic
activity of the preparation is not yet clear but it
is of interest to note that stored concentrated 7S
NGF preparations which have a very much lower level
of enzyme activity do not show the same changes,
the composition of the γ subunit group remaining
more nearly constant (Fig.2). In contrast the
typical changes in α subunit composition which
occur on storage (see next section) are seen in
both isolated subunit and 7S preparations (Fig. 2).

The association of an esteropeptidase enzyme
with a protein (the β subunit) which stimulates
neuroblast differentiation is an intriguing one
especially since enzymes of this type are themselves
being implicated increasingly in processes to do
with cellular growth and differentiation. Thus
esteropeptidase activity is associated with the
mesenchymal growth factor (Attardi, Schlesinger &
Schlesinger, 1967) while thrombin, itself an enzyme
of this type, has an NGF-like activity. Also the
thymotropic factor present in extracts of mouse

TABLE II

THE ISOELECTRIC POINTS OF 7S NGF
AND THE α AND γ SUBUNITS

Determined from equilibrium positions in acrylamide gels containing Ampholine buffers of appropriate pH ranges.

	α Subunits	γ Subunits
	α^1 4.57	γ^1 5.78
	α^2 4.50 ± 0.09	γ^2 5.60
7S NGF 5.15 ± 0.05	α^3 4.37 ± 0.07	γ' 5.44
	α^4 4.26	γ^3 5.25
	α^5 4.15	

submaxillary gland, and which promotes differentiation of certain lymphocytes, is an esteropeptidase (Hoffman, unpublished). Grossman, Lele, Sheldon, Schenkein and Levy (1969) have recently described the effects of other submaxillary esteropeptidases on the growth of cultured rat hepatoma cells. Of great interest is the recent report (Taylor, Cohen & Mitchell, 1970) that the epidermal growth factor (EGF) can be isolated from mouse submaxillary glands as a 70,000 molecular weight complex containing two subunits. One of these subunits is relatively small and acidic and possesses EGF activity while the other is an esterase with properties very similar to those of the γ subunit. The exact chemical and physiological relationship of these various enzymes to the γ subunit of 7S NGF is unknown but is clearly of interest. It should also be noted that the γ enzyme is a glycoprotein.

The α Subunit

As shown by Varon (1970), the acidic α subunits of 7S NGF, as well as the 7S NGF complex, show salvage properties (Fig. 1); i.e., an increased cell recovery from trypsin-dissociated ganglia. However, the free subunits themselves are considerably less effective in this regard. The salvage effect is noted only for cells from embryonic sensory and sympathetic ganglia over a restricted age range. Hoffman (1970) observed that the α subunits in a similar concentration range caused release of small to medium sized neuroblasts from embryonic ganglia on an acrylamide surface. At higher concentrations these subunits stripped the neuroblasts of their surface, acting in this way like trypsin. It is possible that since both α and 7S NGF are acidic proteins that they function in their salvage role by binding to and inactivating remaining traces of the basic protein trypsin and thereby preventing further cellular damage by this agent. However, the effect may have a more sophisticated origin, because, as with the properties of the other two subunits, aggregation into the 7S complex produces a profound change in efficacy of the subunit (Fig. 1).

The indivdual α subunits display fairly uniform mobility differences in the pH range from 7 to 10.3 (Varon *et al.*, 1968; Smith *et al.*, 1968). A similar uniform distribution is apparent in their isoelectric points (Table II) in the pH range between approximately 4.0 and 4.7. It is unlikely, therefore, that the differences between individual subunits are in amino acid composition. Since the α subunit is a glycoprotein, it seems likely that the differences between individual subunits reside in substituents such as amide groups or amino sugar residues on a common peptide chain or chains. The amino acid composition for two of the major species is sufficiently close to provide some confirmation (Table I). On prolonged storage the less acidic α subunits decrease in amount while the α^4 subunit increases and this change occurs in the 7S complex as well as in the free subunits. It is the type of change antici-

pated from the gradual loss of specific amide or
amino sugar residues and there is precedent for
this in other protein systems. Molecular weight
determinations in SDS gels give a value of about
28,000 for both α and γ chains. The α subunits
contain two chains of unequal size, approximately
18,000 and 12,000 in molecular weight, held together
by disulfide bonds. The individual chains can,
therefore, be isolated and examined only after
reduction with β-mercaptoethanol or dithiothreotol
(Piltch, unpublished). The chain composition
of the γ subunits is apparently more complicated.

CONCLUSION

The 7S complex comprising three different
types of subunits, each with their own particular
biological property, is a major and unusual protein
component of the mouse submaxillary gland. The
differences in the levels of the particular subunit
activities between free and 7S forms and the
masking of the charge differences between γ subunits in the 7S complex suggest that the interactions between the subunits in the complex are
highly specific and stable. A number of other
experiments described in the previous sections
support this view. At least one other growth
factor protein, EGE, is found in the submaxillary
gland in a complex form although in this instance
the isolated complex contains two, rather than
three, different types of subunits. Besides these
two growth factors the gland contains a variety of
esteropeptidases of differing physiological
significance, a number of which effect the differentiation of certain types of cells. The unusual
morphological character of the mouse submaxillary
gland clearly yields substantial dividends in terms
of the characterization of these important biological entities.

If the 7S NGF complex is finally proven to
be a pentamer ($\alpha_2\gamma_2\beta$), it will not be the first
protein with this unfamiliar composition. Arginine
decarboxylase is a large protein containing five
subunits of identical size, each of these subunits

having a molecular weight of 165,000 (Boeker & Snell, 1968). In any event the single β subunit in the 7S NGF complex contains two identical peptide chains and the complex could still, therefore, possess symmetry.

The significance of the multiple forms of 7S NGF in a typical preparation is not understood at the present. They appear in preparations made by entirely different procedures and are also present in a 7S NGF preparation made from a single mouse submaxillary lobe (Smith *et al.*, 1968). Preparations from female glands show the same subunit distribution as do those from female glands after testosterone treatment (Varon, Nomura & Raiborn, unpublished). Whether the number of subunits is a reflection of the number of structural genes controlling 7S NGF synthesis or whether the individual differences are introduced sequentially into three primary gene products can only be answered by further experiments. Finally, the characterization of the cellular receptors for the NGF subunit or indeed for each of the three subunit types will depend upon the development of methods of specifically labelling these proteins.

REFERENCES

ATTARDI, D. A., SCHLESINGER, M. J., & SCHLESINGER, S. Submaxillary gland of mouse: Properties of a purified protein affecting muscle tissue *in vitro*. *Science*, 1967, *156*, 1253-1255.

BOCCHINI, V., & ANGELETTI, P. U. The nerve growth factor: Purification as a 30,000-molecular-weight protein. *Proceedings of the National Academy of Sciences*, 1969, *64*, 787-794.

BOEKER, E. A., & SNELL, E. E. Arginine decarboxylase from *Escherichia coli*. II. Dissociation and reassociation of subunits. *Journal of Biological Chemistry*, 1968, *243*, 1678-1684.

BURGESS, R. R., TRAVERS, A. A., DUNN, J.J., & BAUTZ, E. K. F. Factor stimulating transcription by RNA polymerase. *Nature*, 1969, *221*, 43-36.

CALISSANO, P., & ANGELETTI, P. U. Testosterone

effect on the synthetic rate of two esteropeptidases in the mouse submaxillary gland.
Biochimica et Biophysica Acta, 1968, *156*,
51-58.

COHEN, S. Purification of a nerve growth promoting
protein from the mouse salivary gland and its
neurocytotoxic antiserum. *Proceedings of the
National Academy of Sciences*, 1960, *46*,
302-310.

COHEN, S., & LEVI-MONTALCINI, R. Purification and
properties of a nerve growth-promoting factor
isolated from mouse sarcoma 180. *Cancer
Research*, 1957, *17*, 15-20.

CREIGHTON, T. E., & YANOFSKY, C. Association of
the α and β^2 tryptophan synthetase of
Escherichia coli. *Journal of Biological
Chemistry*, 1966, *241*, 980-990.

GREENE, L. A., SHOOTER, E. M., & VARON, S.
Enzymatic activities of mouse nerve growth
factor and its subunits. *Proceedings of the
National Academy of Sciences*, 1968, *60*,
1383-1388.

GREENE, L. A., SHOOTER, E. M., & VARON, S. Subunit
interaction and enzymatic activity of mouse
7S nerve growth factor. *Biochemistry*, 1969,
8, 3735-3741.

GROSSMAN, A., LELE, K. P., SHELDON, I., SCHENKEIN,
I., & LEVY, M. The effect of esteroproteases
from submaxillary gland on the growth of rat
hepatoma cells in tissue culture. *Experimental Cell Research*, 1969, *54*, 260-263.

GUIDOTTI, G. Studies on the chemistry of hemoglobin. III. The interactions of the $\alpha\beta$
subunits of hemoglobin. *Journal of Biological
Chemistry*, 1967, *242*, 3694-3703.

GUIDOTTI, G., KONIGSBERG, W., & CRAIG, L. C. On
the dissociation of normal adult human hemoglobin. *Proceedings of the National Academy
of Sciences*, 1963, *50*, 774-782.

HOFFMAN, H. Biological significance and action of
the "nerve growth" factor. In R. E. Bowman
and S. P. Datta (Eds.), *Biochemistry of Brain
and Behavior*. New York: Plenum Press, 1970.

HOFFMAN, H., & MCDOUGALL, J. Some biological
properties of proteins of the mouse submaxillary gland as revealed by growth of tissues

on electrophoretic acrylamide gels. *Experimental Cell Research*, 1968, *51*, 485-503.

HOFFMAN, H., NAUGHTON, M. A., MCDOUGALL, J., & HAMILTON, E. A. Nerve growth factor and a thymus inhibitor, separations by tissue culture on acrylamide gels. *Nature*, 1967, *214*, 703-705.

LEVI-MONTALCINI, R. The nerve growth factor, its mode of action on sensory and sympathetic nerve cells. *Harvey Lecture Series*, 1966, *60*, 217-259.

LEVI-MONTALCINI, R., MEYER, H., & HAMBURGER, V. *In vitro* experiments on the effect of mouse sarcoma 180 and 37 on the spinal and sympathetic ganglia of the chick embryo. *Cancer Research*, 1954, *14*, 49-57.

SHAPIRO, A. L., VINUELA, E., & MAIZEL, J. V. Molecular weight estimation of polypeptide chains by electrophoresis in SDS-polyacrylamide gels. *Biochemical and Biophysical Research Communications*, 1967, *28*, 815-820.

SHOOTER, E. M., & VARON, S. Macromolecular aspects of the nerve growth factor proteins. In A. Lajtha (Ed.), *Protein Metabolism of the Nervous System*. New York: Plenum Press, 1970.

SHOOTER, E. M., VARON, S., & NOMURA, J. The nerve growth factor protein and its subunits. *Chimia*, 1968, *22*, 144.

SMITH, A. P., VARON, S., & SHOOTER, E. M. Multiple forms of the nerve growth factor protein and its subunits. *Biochemistry*, 1968, *7*, 3259-3268.

SMITH, A. P., GREENE, L. A., FISK, H. R., VARON, S., & SHOOTER, E. M. Dissociation equilibria in 7S NGF and its subunits. *Biochemistry*, 1969, *8*, 4918-4926.

TAYLOR, J., COHEN, S., & MITCHELL, W. Epidermal growth factor (EGF): Properties of a high molecular weight species. *Federation Proceedings*, 1970, *29*, 670.

VARON, S. The investigation of neural development by experimental *in vitro* techniques. In D. Pease (Ed.), *Cellular Aspects of Neural Growth and Differentiation*. UCLA Forum Med. Sci. No. 14, Los Angeles, California:

University of California Press, 1970, in press.
VARON, S., NOMURA, J., & SHOOTER, E. M. The
    isolation of the mouse nerve growth factor
    protein in a high molecular weight form.
    Biochemistry, 1967, *6*, 2202-2209.
VARON, S., NOMURA, J., & SHOOTER, E. M. Reversible
    dissociation of the mouse nerve growth factor
    protein into different subunits. *Biochemistry*,
    1968, *7*, 1296-1303.
ZANINI, A., ANGELETTI, P., & LEVI-MONTALCINI, R.
    Immunochemical properties of the nerve growth
    factor. *Proceedings of the National Academy
    of Sciences*, 1968, *61*, 835-842.

CEREBRAL SPHINGOLIPIDS IN THE
QUAKING MOUSE

Julian N. Kanfer

Massachusetts General Hospital
Joseph P. Kennedy, Jr. Memorial
Laboratories

Boston, Massachusetts

There are over 300 mutant genes in the mouse
which are characterized by a variety of specific
phenotypic expressions (Green, 1966, pp. 87-150).
The "Quaking" strain of mouse has been extensively
characterized genetically and histologically by
Sidman, Dickie and Appel (1964) and shown to
bear an autosomal recessive gene (qk) which is
responsible for abnormalities in central nervous
system structure and function. Affected animals
can be recognized by the twelfth day pospartum by
an unsteady gait and tremor of the hindquarters.
Tonic-clonic seizures are induced readily by
sensory stimulation in the adult Quaking animal.
The principal neuropathological findings in the
Quaking mice is a generalized deficiency of myelin.

Myelin is a lipid-protein complex which is
deposited by the oligodendroglical cells in a
lamellar array around the axon body (Hirano &
Dimlutzer, 1967). This material is composed of
76% lipid and 24% protein on a dry-weight basis.
The ratios of cholesterol:phospholipid:cerebro-
sides is approximately 2:2:1 (Smith, 1967). Slight
deviations from this gross composition have been
reported from various laboratories. These
differences may be accounted for either by the
species of animals used or the techniques employed
for the isolation of myelin. The presence of

cerebrosides to sulfatides in a molar ratio of 5:1
has been considered by some authors (O'Brien,
1965) to be a chemical marker of myelin. The rate
of lipid deposition in the brain has been chrono-
logically correlated with the histological appearance of myelin (Folch, Casals, Pope, Meath,
LeBarron & Lees, 1959). Since the lipids, especially the sphingolipids, are important chemical
components of myelin our laboratory embarked upon
comparative studies of these compounds in brains
of Quaking and normal mice. These included: 1.
Quantitative determination of lipid content; 2.
In vivo incorporation of radioactive precursors
into lipids; and 3. Estimation of certain "lysosomal acid hydrolase" activities.

MATERIALS AND METHODS

Adult Quaking mutants and their congenic
normal controls (C57BL/6J) were either made available from Drs. Richard Sidman, Harvard Medical
School and Nicole Baumann, Hospital Saltpietre or
purchased from the Jackson Laboratory, Bar Harbor,
Maine.

Lipid Extraction and Hydrolysis

The extraction of brain lipids was carried
out by suitable modification of published procedure (Kanfer & Richards, 1967). The brains
(including the pons and cerebellum) in each group
were pooled, homogenized in seven volumes of
methanol and warmed to 55°C for ten minutes, after
which 14 volumes of chloroform were added and the
mixture was filtered. The filtrates were partitioned according to the procedure of Folch, Lees
and Sloane-Stanley (1957).

The lower phases from the Folch partitioning
procedure containing principally phospholipids,
steroids and sphingolipids were taken to dryness
under N_2 and redissolved in chloroform-methanol
(2:1 v/v) for analysis. The samples were then
hydrolyzed employing the method of Abramson,

Norton and Katzman (1965) in order to remove ester and plasmalogenic lipids. The lower phases were dried under N_2 and treated with methanolic sodium hydroxide (MeOH-1N NaOH 6:1 v/v) for four hours at 37°C. The samples were then subjected to the Folch partitioning procedure and the lower phases were hydrolyzed further with mercuric chloride-acetic acid for two hours at 37°C. Further partitioning of the hydrolyzed lower phases yielded a solution containing almost pure sphingolipids (Abramson et al., 1965; Kanfer, Bradley & Gal, 1967). The samples were reassayed for composition and radioactivity.

Pooled upper phases obtained from the washing procedure containing the ganglioside fraction were dialyzed overnight at 4°C against two changes of de-ionized water.

Chemical Analysis

Sialic acid was assayed directly by the method of Miettinen and Takki-Leuckkainen (1959). Total phosphate was determined by the method of Ames and Dubin (1960). Carbohydrate was assayed by the method of Dubois, Gilles, Hamilton, Rebers and Smith, 1956. Sulfatides were assayed by the method of Kean (1968).

Thin-Layer Chromatography

The ganglioside samples were separated on Silica Gel G precoated plates (Analtech, Inc.) developed in chloroform-methanol-2.5N NH_4OH (60:35:8 v/v/v) (Penick, Meisler & McCluer, 1966). The lower phase lipids were separated on Silica Gel G precoated plates (Analtech, Inc.) employing chloroform-methanol-H_2O (65:25:4 v/v/v) for general analysis and chloroform-methanol (95:5) in order to obtain separation of ceramide from the other lipids. Thin-layer chromatography was also carried out on borate impregnated Silica Gel G plates in order to distinguish between gluco- and galactocerebroside employing both chloroform-methanol-H_2O

(65:25:4 v/v/v) (Young & Kanfer, 1965) and
chloroform-methanol-H_2O-15N NH_4OH (280:70:6:1 v/
v/v/v) (Kean, 1966) as solvent systems. Approximately the same quantities of sample material
were applied to all plates. Authentic samples of
sphingomyelin, galactocerebroside, glucocerebro-
side, sulfatide, ceramide and ganglioside were
employed as standards. The plates were visualized
either by spraying with anisaldehyde and charring
at 110°C or by spraying with the phosphate reagent
of Dittmer and Lester (1964).

N-propanol-ammonia-water (12:1:2) was employed
as the solvent for separation of steroid sulfate
and sulfatide (Moser, Moser & McKhann, 1967).
These studies indicated that all of the radioactivity in each sample was exclusively associated
with sulfatide.

In Vivo Radioactive Precursor Studies

The radioactive lipid precursors employed in
this study were injected in a total volume of 20
microliters as aqueous solutions into the parietal
region of each animal (Kanfer & Richards, 1967).
The compounds used were: $Na_3{}^{32}PO_4$, 8 x 10^5 total
counts administered (specific activity = 100 mc/mM);
glucose-U-^{14}C, 3 x 10^6 total counts administered
(specific activity = 138 mc/mM); and $Na_2{}^{35}SO_4$,
5 x 10^6 total counts administered (specific activity
= 488 mc/mM). Groups of three animals from the
Quaking and controls were sacrificed at one hour,
eight hours, 1, 2, 3, 4, 6 and 8 days following
administration of the isotope. The samples were
treated as above except that each washing solution
contained 0.01M Na_3PO_4 for the $Na_3{}^{32}PO_4$ experiment
and contained 0.01M Na_2SO_4 for the $Na_2{}^{35}SO_4$ experiments.

The lipids in the lower phases from these
experiments were separated on Silica Gel G precoated plates (Analtech, Inc.) developed in chloro-
form-methanol-H_2O (65:25:4). Authentic samples of
sphingomyelin, cerebroside and sulfatide were used
as standards. Spots were visualized with I_2 vapor

and the areas corresponding to cerebroside and sulfatide standards were removed. Weighed aliquots of the gel from the cerebroside area were assayed for total carbohydrate and radioactivity. Attempts to determine sulfatide directly were unsatisfactory due to interference by silica gel in the assay. Therefore, values were used from hydrolyzed lower phase sulfatide in calculating the specific activity of sulfatide in this experiment. Radioactivity was determined in a Packard liquid scintillation counter.

Lysosomal Acid Hydrolases

Homogenates of cerebral tissue were prepared in five volumes of $0.25M$ sucrose-$10^{-3}M$ EDTA and used directly. Preliminary studies employing several of the substrates indicated that neither freeze-thawing, sonification nor the addition of detergents (Sawant, Shibko, Kumta & Tappel, 1964; Sawant, Desai & Tappel, 1964) influenced the amount of detectable enzymatic activity of the homogenate under the conditions employed. Synthetic substrates used in these studies were purchased from the Pierce Chemical Company and included: p-nitrophenyl (PNP) derivatives of alpha-glucoside, beta-glucoside, alpha-galactoside, beta-galactoside, beta-glucosaminide, alpha-L-fucoside, alpha-mannoside and PNP-phosphate in addition to nitrocatechol sulfate. The levels of hydrolytic enzymes, employing these substrates, were obtained by using published procedures (Van Hoof & Hers, 1968). Duplicate aliquots as well as increasing amounts of homogenates were incubated with each substrate.

Boiled enzyme and buffer controls were routinely included in each determination. Preliminary experiments were performed to establish optimum incubation conditions for time, pH and enzyme stoichiometry. Samples were dialyzed overnight in the cold in order to obtain enzyme proportionality with nitrocatechol sulfate.

RESULTS

Compositional Studies

Quantitative analysis of upper phase lipids, as shown in Table I, indicated a negligible increase in gangliosides in the Quaking mice. Quantitative thin-layer chromatography revealed similar patterns of distribution of these complex lipids in both the control and mutant animals.

Analysis of the lower phase lipids after the Folch extraction as shown in Table I, indicated that no significant differences in ester and lipid phosphate values existed between the Quaking mice and their controls. Quantitative thin-layer chromatography indicated no differences in the amounts or distribution of the various phospholipids. However, there was marked decrease in the carbohydrate and sulfatide content in the samples derived from both of the mutant animals when compared to their litter mates. Since the major carbohydrate containing lipids in the brain are the sphingolipids, it was decided to investigate specifically this class of compounds in greater detail.

TABLE I

Comparison of Lipid Composition of Brain of
Quaking and Control Mice*

	Quaking	Controls
Total phospholipid	16.90	18.20
Ganglioside	0.69	0.58
Cerebroside	8.30	15.70
Sulfatide	0.30	2.10
Sphingomyelin	2.20	3.90

* Micromoles/gm. wet tissue weight.

To obtain a pure sphingolipid fraction the mixture was subjected to a mild hydrolytic procedure in order to eliminate ester and aldehyde containing lipids. The results obtained after mercuric chloride-acetic acid treatment and saponification are presented in Table I. In the Quaking animals the amount of carbohydrate-containing lipid (cerebroside) was decreased to a level of 47% that found in the control animals. The concentration of sulfatides was reduced in the mutant animals to 14% of that found in the controls. The lipid phosphate, which represents solely sphingomyelin as determined by thin-layer chromatography was reduced to a level of only 43% of that found in the control animals. These differences were further substantiated by employing thin-layer chromatography. In all solvent systems used, smaller quantities of the sphingolipids were visualized when compared to the control samples.

In Vivo Tracer Studies

As shown in Fig. 1, the Quaking mice are able to incorporate $Na_2{}^{32}PO_4$ into all phospholipids, at nearly the same rate as the control animals. In the normal animals there is a 37% phospholipid turnover after four days. By contrast, in the Quaking animals there is no demonstrable phospholipid turnover. This phenomenon is still apparent after hydrolysis which specifically reflects sphingomyelin metabolism (Fig. 2), as demonstrated by thin-layer chromatography. The specific activity of sphingomyelin from the mutant animals was found to be 72% greater than that from the normal animals eight days after the administration of the isotope.

Since the label from glucose-^{14}C will be incorporated randomly into all carbon atoms of lipids, including glycerol, fatty acid, sphingosine and bases, radioactivity in the unhydrolyzed lower phase should reflect total lipid synthesis. At the earliest experimental time point of one hour the level of radioactivity in the Quaking animals

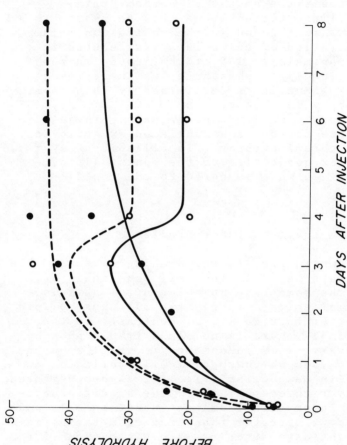

Fig. 1. Rate of incorporation of $Na_2^{32}PO_4$ into total phospholipids of normal and Quaking adult mice. Experimental details are described in the text. Open circles = normal controls; closed circles = Quaking animals; solid line = cpm ^{32}P/micromole P/gram wet weight tissue; broken line = cpm ^{32}P/gram wet weight tissue.

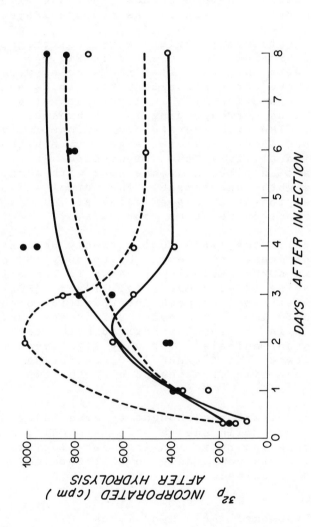

Fig. 2. Rate of incorporation of $Na_2{}^{32}PO_4$ into sphingomyelin of normal and Quaking adult mice. Experimental details are described in the text. Open circles = normal controls; closed circles = Quaking animals; solid lines = cpm ^{32}P/micromole P/gram wet weight tissue; broken line = cpm ^{32}P/gram wet weight tissue.

total lipid is threefold higher than that found in
control animals as shown in Fig. 3. The amount of
label in the mutants gradually declines and by two
days it has almost reached its lowest level. In
contrast the normals have a gradual increase with
a peak at one day and gradual loss by three days.

The data obtained for glucose-U-^{14}C incorporation into cerebrosides is presented in Fig. 4.
These values were obtained after the samples were
treated to remove ester and aldehydric lipids and
subjected to separation by thin-layer chromatography. The bands corresponding to cerebroside
were removed. The carbohydrate and radioactivity
were determined on samples of the gel. The highest
level of radioactivity in the cerebrosides derived
from the mutant animals is at one hour with a rapid
loss by the eighth-hour sample. The normal animals
show a gradual increase to peak value at one day
with a subsequent decrease by four days.

Sulfatide is the lipid most markedly decreased
in the Quaking mouse, the levels being only 18% of
those found in normal animals as shown in Table I.
Studies employing ^{14}C-glucose (Fig. 5) and ^{35}SO$_4$
(Fig. 6) demonstrate that peak incorporation occurs
at three days followed by a polyphasic decay curve
which is found in the samples derived both from
normal and mutant animals. The only significant
difference between the ^{14}C and ^{35}SO$_4$-sulfatide
curves is in the time of appearance of the two
peaks.

Gangliosides are not thought to be a major
component of the myelin sheath. It is significant
that ^{14}C-glucose incorporation into gangliosides
in Quaking mice was comparable to that obtained
with the control animals.

"Lysosomal" Acid Hydrolases

As shown in Table II there is no elevation of
hydrolytic activity but several of these activities
are decreased. It is evident that alpha-mannosidase activity is most severely affected, being

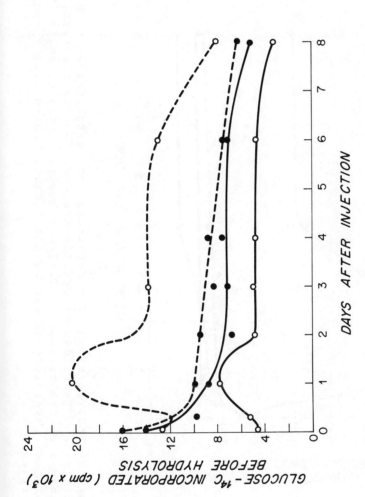

Fig. 3. Rate of incorporation of ^{14}C-glucose into total lipids of normal and Quaking adult mice. Experimental details are described in the text. Open circles = normal controls; closed circles = Quaking animals; solid line = cpm ^{14}C/micromole carbohydrate/gram wet weight tissue; broken line = cpm ^{14}C/gram wet weight tissue.

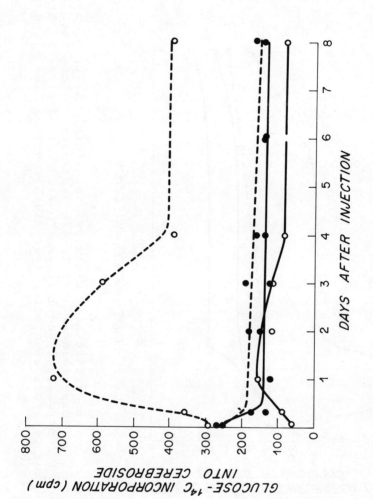

Fig. 4. Rate of incorporation of ^{14}C-glucose into cerebrosides of normal and Quaking adult mice. Experimental details are described in the text. Open circles = normal controls; closed circles = Quaking animals; solid line = cpm ^{14}C/micromole carbohydrate/gram wet weight tissue; broken line = cpm ^{14}C/gram wet weight tissue.

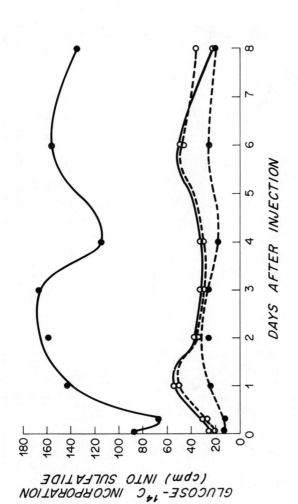

Fig. 5. Rate of incorporation of ^{14}C-glucose into sulfatides of normal and Quaking adult mice. Experimental details are described in the text. Open circles = normal controls; closed circles = Quaking animals; solid line = cpm ^{14}C/micromole sulfatide/gram wet weight tissue; broken line = cpm ^{14}C/gram wet weight tissue.

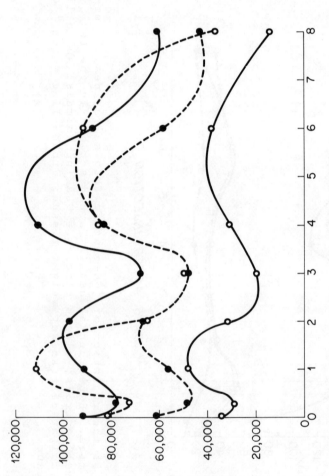

Fig. 6. Rate of incorporation of $Na_2{}^{35}SO_4$ into sulfatides of normal and Quaking adult mice. Experimental details are described in the text. Open circles = normal controls; closed circles = Quaking animals; solid-line = cpm ^{35}S/micromole sulfatide/gram wet weight tissue; broken line = cpm ^{35}S/gram wet weight tissue.

TABLE II

Comparison of Cerebral "Lysosomal" Acid Hydrolase Activities in Quaking and Control Mice

Substrate	Micromoles Substrate Cleaved/Gr. Fresh Weight Tissue/Hour*	
	Control	Quaking
PNP Alpha-Glucoside	2.130 ± 0.081	1.610 ± 0.099
PNP Beta-Glucoside	4.290 ± 0.312	3.620 ± 0.573
PNP Alpha-Galactoside	1.384 ± 0.056	1.110 ± 0.011
PNP Beta-Galactoside	2.722 ± 0.044	1.960 ± 0.285
PNP Beta-Glucosaminide	0.835 ± 0.081	0.847 ± 0.039
PNP Alpha-Mannoside	1.020 ± 0.006	0.336 ± 0.059
PNP Phosphate	29.790 ± 1.425	28.890 ± 1.923
PNP L-Fucoside	1.260	0.975
Nitrocatechol Sulfate	78.720 ± 0.887	47.880 ± 0.327

Except for p-nitro-phenyl beta-glucosaminide, which was present at four micromoles, all the other substrates were at 1.5 micromoles. In addition, each incubation mixture contained 500 micromoles of acetete buffer pH 3.6 for PNP beta-glucosaminide, PNP alpha-galactoside, PNP beta-galactoside; 500 micromoles of acetate buffer pH 4.5 for PNP alpha-glucoside, PNP beta-glucoside, PNP alpha-mannoside, PNP alpha-fucoside, nitrocatechol sulfate; 500 micromoles acetate buffer pH 5.5 for PNP phosphate; 100 and 200 microliters of homogenate in a total volume of 1.1 ml. and was incubated at 37°C with shaking in air for two hours. At that time the tubes were chilled in ice, 1 ml. of 2M NH₄OH was added and the insoluble material removed by centrifugation. The absorption of PNP was determined at 420 nanometers and nitrocatechol at 515 nanometers in a Zeiss spectrophotometer.

* Values represent means ± S.E.

reduced to one third of control values. Incubation mixtures containing aliquots of homogenate
from both the normal and Quaking animal gave addi-
tive results. This would argue strongly against
the possibility of an inhibitor in the mutant
animal. The reduction in activities towards other
substrates is less marked.

DISCUSSION

The cerebrosides and sulfatides are present
in high concentration in myelin and are generally
accepted as lipid markers of this structure (Smith,
1967; Cuzner & Davison, 1968). The Quaking mouse
is a mutant characterized by a myelin deficiency.
It is noteworthy that no diminution of the gangliosides was observed in these mutants. The gangliosides are not usually associated with myelin,
rather these sphingolipids are found to be concentrated at nerve endings (Norton & Autilio, 1966;
Lapetina, Soto & DeRobertis, 1967; Spence & Wolfe,
1967). A decrease in total galactolipids (galactocerebroside and sulfatide) has been reported in
the brains of Quaking mice by Baumann, Jacque,
Pollet and Harpin (1968). This same group of
investigators have reported a significant decrease
of alpha-hydroxy fatty acids, which are found in
high concentration in the cerebral sphingolipids
(Jacque, Harpin & Baumann, 1969). These studies
of the cerebral lipid composition of the mutants
correlates well with the observed histological
changes. The decreased cerebroside, sulfatide and
sphingomyelin content reflects the paucity of
myelin.

The *in vivo* investigations demonstrate that th
Quaking mouse can incorporate radioactive precursor
into sphingomyelin, cerebroside and sulfatide and
were undertaken in an attempt to explain the documented decreased cerebral sphingolipid content in
Quaking mice (Green, 1966, pp. 87-150; Sidman *et
al.*, 1964; Hirano & Dimlutzer, 1967). The most
facile explanations for such an observation would
be either an inability to biosynthesize these compounds or an increased catabolism of these lipids.

The experiments described in this paper demonstrate: a.   The mutant animals have the capacity to incorporate radioactivity into lipids at a rate nearly equal to normals; b.   Excessive turnover was not evident; c.   Under the conditions of the experiment no turnover of sphingomyelin was observed in the mutant animals.

Several possible explanations can be invoked to reconcile these apparently contradictory observations: 1.   A deficiency of myelin may facilitate the entry of radioactive precursors into cells which could result in an increase in the specific activity of intracellular pools of a given isotope. In this situation it is conceivable that even with a low rate of synthesis, the product could have a higher specific activity.   This contention is not supported by finding of normal levels of ganglioside content and incorporation in the mutant animals; 2.   The experiments were not carried out for a sufficiently long period of time to demonstrate increased breakdown in the mutant animals.   Arguing against this is published data indicating turnover times of three to six days for cerebral sphingolipids (Kishimoto, Davies & Radin, 1965; Freysz, Bieth & Mandel, 1969); 3.   In the adult mouse the radioactive precursors are believed to be incorporated into both myelin and non-myelin components.   The concept that myelin constituents are turned over at a slower rate than the non-myelin components has been advanced.   Therefore, in the normal animals the bulk of the lipids which have become labeled would be non-myelin compounds.   In the mutants, which have a myelin deficiency, a large portion of the isotopes may be directed into myelin constituents in an attempt to maintain a minimum level consistent with life.   This pool of radioactive lipid may have a slower rate of turnover than the non-myelin pool.   Further experiments are required to examine this possibility in detail; 4.   A membrane fraction which resembles myelin has been described which is present in young developing rats, but is absent from adults.   The lipid fraction of this "early" myelin resembles cellular membranes rather than mature myelin (Banik & Davison, 1969).   It is possible that this is the

material into which the radioactive precursors are
incorporated in the Quaking animals.

The biphasic turnover typical of all control
curves in this investigation has been observed in
similar *in vivo* incorporation studies of ^{14}C-
hexoses into rat galactolipids (Radin, Martin &
Brown, 1957; Burton, Garcia-Bunuel, Golden & Bal-
four, 1963) and ^{35}SO$_4$ into rat sulfatides (Davison
& Gregson, 1962). This observation suggests that
two pools exist for sphingolipids, one with rapid
turnover and the other with slow turnover.

To evaluate the possibility of altered catabolic activity a study was carried out to quanti-
tate the level of certain "lysosomal" acid hydrolases. Altered hydrolytic enzyme levels have been
reported in several inborn metabolic errors (Hsia,
1966, p. 121).

It is evident from Table II that no increased
hydrolytic activity was detected but rather that
several enzymes were decreased. Bowen and Radin
(1969) in an examination of several hydrolytic
enzymes in young Quaking mice did not detect any
differences in hydrolytic activity towards galactose cerebroside, PNP beta-glucoside, PNP beta-
galactoside or nitrocatechol sulfate. These
authors did not report upon alpha-mannosidase
levels in their studies.

Attenuated levels of hydrolytic enzyme activities have been demonstrated in the sphingolipidoses (Brady, 1966) and glycogen storage diseases
(Hers, 1965). These pathological conditions are
characterized by the accumulation of specific compounds in the organs of affected individuals.

The nature of the relationship in Quaking
mouse cerebral tissue between decreased myelin
content, sphingolipid content and lowered alpha-
mannosidase activity is a matter of speculation.
The simplest explanation would be that the organism
reduces the level of enzymes in response to substrate reduction, i.e., enzymatic activity is
inducible. This would stand in contrast to the

accumulation of substrate with decreased catabolic enzyme activity as seen in the sphingolipidoses. An example of altered levels of lysosomal enzyme activity has been provided by Kampine, Kanfer, Gal, Bradley and Brady, 1967, who demonstrated increases in splenic and hepatic glucocerebrosidase and sphingomyelinase in experimentally-induced erythro-cytorrhexasis. In addition, hepatic lysosomal hydrolase activities increase during starvation of rats (Desai, 1969).

Recently a storage disorder related to Hurler's syndrome, which has been termed mannosi-dosis, has been reported in which a low molecular weight substrate composed of glucosamine and mannose accumulates (Ockerman, 1969a). A decrease in mannosidase activity has been observed in this condition (Kjellman, Gamstrop, Brune, Ockerman & Palmgren, 1969). It is of interest to note that a mannose-containing glycoprotein has been iso-lated from brain tissue (Dibenedetta, Brunngraber, Whitney, Brown & Aro, 1969).

The striking decrease of alpha-mannoside activity seen by us would suggest that there may be a specific localization of such linkages in myelin macromolecules. Mannose has not thus far been detected in cerebral lipid, however, a recent publication has reported the incorporation of radioactive mannose from GDP mannose into a lipid fraction by brain tissue (Katz & Barondes, 1969).

The results of these enzymatic studies would suggest that there is no lysosomal defect in Quaking mice. A general observation in disorders characterized by the accumulation of a biological material is a decrease in a specific hydrolytic enzyme coupled with a non-specific increase in other activities (Van Hoof & Hers, 1968). This increase may be a compensatory mechanism by the organism to an unfavorable intracellular accumu-lation of material.

Independent *in vitro* studies from two labora-tories have documented the inability of Quaking brain to catalyze the condensation of sphingosine

and galactose to form psychosine (Neskovic, Nussbaum & Mandel, 1969; Friedrich & Hauser, 1970), a
presumed precursor of galactose cerebroside. In
addition, Quaking animals apparently lack the
ability to catalyze the biosynthesis of galactose
cerebroside from ceramide and galactose (Morrell,
P., personal communication). It is tempting to
speculate that the inability to biosynthesize
galactose cerebroside is the basic enzymatic defect
in these mutants. However, our *in vivo* studies
would suggest that radioactive precursors can be
incorporated into the cerebral sphingolipids in
the Quaking animals.

Since myelin is 70% lipid the major emphasis
has been on biochemical studies designed to investigate the metabolism of cerebral lipids. However,
it is possible that the basic defect is the
inability to synthesize required proteinaceous
material or an inability to assemble lipid-protein
complexes of myelin.

For the sake of completeness of discussion,
studies on another neurological mutant, the
"Jimpy" mouse, will be described. This animal is
also characterized by a deficiency of myelin.
This mutation is sex-linked and fatal, the animal
rarely survives past thirty days of age. In addition lipid laden droplets have been reported to
be present in the brain and these animals have
been likened to sudanophilic leucodystrophy which
occurs in humans (Sidman, Dickie & Appel, 1964).
Studies on the cerebral lipid content has indicated
a deficit of galactolipids and certain phospholipids in the Jimpy mouse (Galli & Galli, 1969;
Nussbaum, Neskovic & Mandel, 1969; Hogan, Joseph
& Schmidt, 1970). The content and pattern of
distribution of gangliosides in these mutants
appears unchanged (Kostic, Nussbaum & Mandel, 1969).
These mutant animals are unable to catalyze the
synthesis of psychosine *in vitro* (Neskovic, Nussbaum & Mandel, 1969) and have a decreased ability
for the incorporation of radioactive galactose
into galactolipid *in vivo* (Galli, Kneebone & Paoletti, 1969). The level of 2', 3' cyclic nucleotide 3' phosphohydrolase, a myelin marker enzyme

(Kurihara & Tsukada, 1968) has been demonstrated
to be severely depressed in Jimpy animals (Kurihara, Nussbaum & Mandel, 1969).

ACKNOWLEDGEMENTS

Supported in part by PHS grant NB-08994-01
from the National Institute of Neurological Diseases and Stroke; and National Multiple Sclerosis
Society grant 566A1.

REFERENCES

ABRAMSON, M. B., NORTON, W. T., & KATZMAN, R.
    Study of ionic structures in phospholipids by
    infrared spectra. *Journal of Biological
    Chemistry*, 1965, *240*, 2389-2395.
AMES, B. N., & DUBIN, D. T.   The role of polyamines
    in the neutralization of bacteriophage deoxy-
    ribonucleic acid. *Journal of Biological
    Chemistry*, 1960, *235*, 769-775.
BANIK, N. L., & DAVISON, A. N.   Enzyme activity
    and composition of myelin and subcellular
    fractions in the developing rat brain. *Bio-
    chemical Journal*, 1969, *115*, 1051-1062.
BAUMANN, N. A., JACQUE, C. M., POLLET, S. A., &
    HARPIN, M.   Fatty acid and lipid composition
    of the brain of a myelin deficient mutant,
    the "quaking" mouse. *European Journal of
    Biochemistry*, 1968, *4*, 340-344.
BOWEN, D. M., & RADIN, N. S.   Hydrolase activities
    in brain of neurological mutants: cerelro-
    side, galactosidase, nitrophenyl galactoside,
    hydrolase, nitrophenyl glucoside hydrolase
    and sulphatase. *Journal of Neurochemistry*,
    1969, *16*, 457-460.
BRADY, R. O.   The sphingolipidoses. *New England
    Journal of Medicine*, 1966, *275*, 312-318.
BURTON, R., GARCIA-BUNUEL, L., GOLDEN, M. & BAL-
    FOUR, Y.   Incorporation of radioactivity of
    D-glucosamine-1-C14, D-glucose-1-C14, D-
    galactose-1-C14 and DL-serine-3-C14 into rat
    brain glycolipids. *Biochemistry*, 1963, *2*,
    580-585.

CUZNER, M. L., & DAVISON, A. N.   The lipid compo-
     sition of rat brain myelin and subcellular
     fractions during development. *Biochemical
     Journal*, 1968, *106*, 29-34.
DAVISON, A. N., & GREGSON, N. K.   The physiological
     role of cerebron sulphuric acid (sulphatide)
     in the brain. *Biochemical Journal*, 1962, *85*,
     558-568.
DESAI, I. D.   Regulation of lysosomal enzymes. I.
     Adaptive changes in enzyme activities during
     starvation and refeeding. *Canadian Journal
     of Biochemistry*, 1969, *47*, 785-790.
DIBENEDETTA, C., BRUNNGRABER, E. G., WHITNEY, G.,
     BROWN, B. D., & ARO, A.   Compositional pat-
     terns of sialofucohexo-samenoglycans derived
     from rat brain glycoproteins. *Archives of
     Biochemistry and Biophysics*, 1969, *131*, 404-
     413.
DITTMER, J. C., & LESTER, R. C.   A simple, specific
     spray for the detection of phospholipids in
     thin-layer chromatograms. *Journal of Lipid
     Research*, 1964, 5, 126-127.
DUBOIS, M., GILLES, K. A., HAMILTON, J. K., REBERS,
     P. A., & SMITH, F.   Colorimetric method for
     determination of sugars and related substances.
     Analytical Chemistry, 1956, *28*, 350-356.
FOLCH, J., CASALS, J., POPE, A., MEATH, J. A.,
     LEBARRON, F. N., & LEES, M.   Chemistry of
     myelin development.   In S. R. Korey (Ed.)
     Biology of Myelin. New York: Hoeber-Harper
     Publ., 1959.
FOLCH, J., LEES, N., & SLOANE-STANLEY, G. H.   A
     simple method for the isolation and purifica-
     tion of total lipides from animal tissues.
     Journal of Biological Chemistry, 1957, *226*,
     497-509.
FREYSZ, L., BIETH, R., & MANDEL, P.   Kinetics of
     the biosynthesis of phospholipids in neurons
     and glial cells isolated from rat brain cortex.
     Journal of Neurochemistry, 1969, *16*, 1417-1424.
FRIEDRICH, V. L., JR., & HAUSER, G.   Psychosine
     and lactosylceromide biosynthesis in brain,
     spinal cord and peripheral nerve homogenates
     of Quaking mice. *Federation Proceedings*,
     1970, *29*, Abstract 924, 410.
GALLI, C., & GALLI, D. C.   Cerebroside and sulpha-

tide deficiency in the brain of "Jumpy Mice,"
a mutant strain of mice exhibiting neurological symptoms. *Nature*, 1969, *220*, 165-166.

GALLI, C., KNEEBONE, G. M., & PAOLETTI, R.   An
inborn error of cerebroside biosynthesis as
the molecular defect of the Jumpy Mouse brain.
Life Sciences, 1969, *8*, 911-918.

GREEN, M. C.   Mutant genes and linkages.   In E. L.
Green (Ed.) *Biology of the Laboratory Mouse*
(2nd Ed.).   New York, New York: McGraw-Hill,
1966, pp. 87-150.

HERS, H. G.   Inborn lysosomal diseases. *Gastro-
enterology*, 1965, *48*, 625-633.

HIRANO, A., & DIMLUTZER, H. M.   A structural
analysis of the myelin sheath in the central
nervous system. *Journal of Cell Biology*,
1967, *34*, 555-567.

HOGAN, E. L., JOSEPH, K. C., & SCHMIDT, G.   Composition of cerebral lipids in murine sudanophilic leucodystrophy.   The Jumpy mutant.
Journal of Neurochemistry, 1970, *17*, 75-83.

HSIA, D. Y.   Detection and treatment of inborn
errors of metabolism associated with mental
deficiency.   In G. J. Martin and B. Kisch
(Eds.), *Enzymes in Mental Health*.   Philadelphia, Pennsylvania: J. B. Lippencott, Co.,
1966.

JACQUE, C. M., HARPIN, M. L., & BAUMANN, N. A.
Brain lipid analysis of a myelin deficient
mutant, the "Quaking" mouse. *European Journal
of Biochemistry*, 1969, *11*, 218-224.

KATZ, M., & BARONDES, S. H.   Incorporation of
mannose into mouse brain lipid. *Biochemical
and Biophysical Research Communications*, 1969,
36, 511-517.

KAMPINE, J. P., KANFER, J. N., GAL, A. E., BRADLEY,
R. M., & BRADY, R. O.   Response of sphingolipid hydrolases in spleen and liver to
increased erythrosytorhexis. *Biochemica et
Biophysica Acta*, 1967, *137*, 135-139.

KANFER, J. N., & RICHARDS, R. L.   Effect of puromycin on the incorporation of radioactive
sugars into gangliosides *in vivo*. *Journal
of Neurochemistry*, 1967, *14*, 513-518.

KANFER, J., BRADLEY, R., & GAL, A. C.   Effect of
puromycin on the incorporation of erythro

DL-(3H) sphingosine into sphingolipids. *Journal of Neurochemistry*, 1967, *14*, 1095-1098.

KEAN, E. L. Separation of gluco- and galactocerebrosides by means of biorate thin-layer chromatography. *Journal of Lipid Research*, 1966, *7*, 449-452.

KISHIMOTO, Y., DAVIES, W. E., & RADIN, N. S. Turnover of the fatty acids of rat brain gangliosides, glycerophosphatides, cerebrosides and sulfatides as a function of age. *Journal of Lipid Research*, 1965, *6*, 525-531.

KJELLMAN, B., GAMSTROP, I., BRUN, A., OCKERMAN, P., & PALMGREN, B. Mannosidosis: A clinical and histopathologic study. *Journal of Pediatrics*, 1969, *75*, 366-373.

KOSTIC, D., NUSSBAUM, J. L., & MANDEL, P. A study of brain gangliosides in "Jumpy" mutant mice. *Life Sciences*, 1969, *8*, 1135-1143.

KURIHARA, T., NUSSBAUM, J. L., & MANDEL, P. 2', 3', cyclic nucleotide 3'-phosphohydrolase in the brain of the "Jumpy" mouse, a mutant with deficient myelination. *Brain Research*, 1969, *13*, 401-403.

KURIHARA, T., & TSUKADA, Y. 2', 3'-cyclic nucleotide 3'-phosphohydrolase in the developing chick brain and spinal cord. *Journal of Neurochemistry*, 1968, *15*, 827-832.

LAPETINA, E. G., SOTO, E. F., & DEROBERTIS, E. DE. Gangliosides and acetylcholinesterase in isolated membranes of the rat-brain cortex. *Biochemica et Biophysica Acta* (Amst.), 1967, *135*, 33-43.

MIETTINEN, T., & TAKKI-LUUKKAINEN, I. T. Use of butyl acetate in determination of sialic acid. *Acta Chemica Scandinavica*, 1959, *13*, 856-858.

MORRELL, P. Personal communication.

MOSER, H. W., MOSER, A. B., & MCKHANN, G. M. The dynamics of a lipidosis. Turnover of sulfatide, steroid sulfate and polysaccharide sulfate in metachromatic leukodystrophy. *Archives of Neurology*, 1967, *17*, 494-511.

NESKOVIC, N. M., NUSSBAUM, J. L., & MANDEL, P. Enzymatic synthesis of psychosine in "Jimpy" mice brain. *Federation of European Biochemical Societies*, Letters, 1969, *3*, 199-201.

NESKOVIC, N., NUSSBAUM, J. L., & MANDEL, P. Etude
    de la galactosyl-sphingosine transferase du
    cerveau de souris mutante "Quaking." *Comptes
    Rendus, Academie des Sciences*, 1969, *269*,
    1125-1128.
NORTON, W. T., & AUTILIO, L. A. The lipid compo-
    sition of purified bovine brain myelin.
    Journal of Neurochemistry, 1966, *13*, 213-222.
NUSSBAUM, J. L., NESKOVIC, N., & MANDEL, P. A
    study of lipid components in brain of the
    "Jimpy" mouse, a mutant with myelin defic-
    iency. *Journal of Neurochemistry*, 1969, *16*,
    927-934.
O'BRIEN, J. S. Stability of the myelin membrane.
    Science, 1965, *147*, 1099-1107.
OCKERMAN, P. Mannosidosis: Isolation of oligo-
    saccharide storage material from brain.
    Journal of Pediatrics, 1969, *75*, 360-365.
PENICK, R. J., MEISLER, M. H., & MCCLUER, R. H.
    Thin-layer chromatographic studies of human
    brain gangliosides. *Biochemica et Biophysica
    Acta*, 1966, *116*, 279-287.
RADIN, N., MARTIN, F., & BROWN, J. Galactolipide
    metabolism. *Journal of Biological Chemistry*,
    1957, *224*, 499-507.
SAWANT, P. L., DESAI, I. D., & TAPPEL, A. L. Fac-
    tors affecting the lysosomal membrane and
    availability of enzymes. *Archives of Bio-
    chemistry and Biophysics*, 1964, *105*, 247-253.
SAWANT, P. L., SHIBKO, S., KUMTA, V. S., & TAPPEL,
    A. L. Isolation of rat-liver lysosomes and
    their general properties. *Biochemica et
    Biophysica Acta*, 1964, *85*, 82-92.
SIDMAN, R. L., DICKIE, M. M., & APPEL, S. H.
    Mutant mice (quaking and jimpy) with defi-
    cient myelination in the central nervous
    system. *Science*, 1964, *17*, 309-311.
SMITH, M. E. The metabolism of myelin lipids.
    Advances in Lipid Research, 1967, *5*, 241-278.
SPENCE, M. W., & WOLFE, L. S. Gangliosides in
    developing rat brain. Isolation and composi-
    tion of subcellular membranes enriched in
    gangliosides. *Canadian Journal of Biochem-
    istry*, 1967, *45*, 671-688.
VAN HOOF, F., & HERS, H. G. The abnormalities of
    lysosomal enzymes in mucopolysacclaridoses.

European Journal of Biochemistry, 1968, 7, 34-44.

YOUNG, O. M., & KANFER, J. N.   An improved separation of sphingolipids by thin-layer chromatography.   *Journal of Chromatography,* 1965, *19,* 611-613.

THE EFFECTS OF ENDOCRINE, SYNAPTIC AND NUTRITIONAL INPUTS ON CATECHOLAMINE-CONTAINING NEURONS

Richard J. Wurtman

Massachusetts Institute of Technology

Cambridge, Massachusetts

The catecholamine norepinephrine is probably utilized as a neurotransmitter by a small but important fraction of the neurons in the brain (Wurtman, 1966). The cell bodies of most of these neurons are localized within the brain stem; their terminals are present in high concentrations within the structures of the limbic system and the septo-hypothalamo-mesencephalic continuum (Dahlström & Fuxe, 1965). The medial forebrain bundles may contain ascending and descending multisynaptic noradrenergic systems in addition to the "classical" monosynaptic pathways identified by histo-chemical fluorescence techniques.

Essentially, all of the norepinephrine present in central neurons is probably synthesized *in situ* from circulating tyrosine; the rate-limiting step in this synthesis appears to be the meta-hydroxylation of the phenolic amino acid to form L-dihydroxyphenylalanine (DOPA). Norepinephrine can be bound within characteristic synaptic vesicles, released into the synaptic cleft as a result of nerve stimulation (after which its action is terminated by reuptake into the presynaptic neuron, 0-methylation or possibly, deamination) or destroyed within the neuron through the action of monoamine oxidase (MAO) (Wurtman, 1966).

Brain norepinephrine turnover has been examined by several techniques. These include: 1. Measuring the rate at which ^{3}H-norepinephrine accumulates in brains of animals given ^{3}H-tyrosine systemically ("synthesis rate") (Zigmond & Wurtman, 1970); 2. Measuring the disappearance of brain ^{3}H-norepinephrine taken up by catecholaminergic neurons following its injection into the lateral cerebral ventricle or cisterna magna (Glowinski & Baldessarini, 1966); 3. Following the decline in brain norepinephrine content among animals given α-methyl para-tyrosine, an inhibitor of tyrosine hydroxylase (Wurtman, Anton-Tay & Anton, 1969); or 4. Following the increase in brain norepinephrine levels in animals treated with inhibitors of MAO. All four approaches have severe disadvantages: Brain ^{3}H-tyrosine levels vary in a complex manner after systemic administration of the amino acid and ^{3}H-amino acid molecules present within noradrenergic neurons cannot be distinguished from those in other neurons or in glia; brain ^{3}H-catecholamine levels continue to reflect both synthesis and turnover of the amine for a long time after ^{3}H-tyrosine administration; hence, both rates are probably underestimated by this procedure. Exogenous ^{3}H-norepinephrine does not become localized uniformly and uniquely within norepinephrine-containing cells. The last two methods disturb the steady state, and erroneously assume that norepinephrine turnover rates are independent of synthesis even when synthesis is inhibited and vice versa. The analysis of brain norepinephrine turnover is further complicated by the fact that brain norepinephrine behaves as though it were partitioned into several distinct metabolic pools (which cannot yet be assigned to specific subcellular loci). The disappearance of a molecule of ^{3}H-norepinephrine from the brain could reflect a physiologically useful event (i.e., its release into the synaptic cleft) or simply destruction of the excess amine within the terminal of the presynaptic nerve by MAO (Wurtman, 1966).

The levels of norepinephrine within brain cells and the rates at which the catecholamine is synthesized and turns over are influenced by three types of stimuli: two of these, nutritional and hormonal factors, reach the neuron via the circulation; the third, synaptic inputs from other neurons, is presumably mediated by neurotransmitter substances.

NUTRITIONAL INPUTS

There is abundant evidence that perinatal malnutrition influences the development and the biochemical composition of the brain (Scrimshaw & Gordon, 1968). We have observed that brain norepinephrine levels are markedly depressed in weanling rats whose mothers were given a protein-deficient diet (8% vs. 24% to control animals) during pregnancy and the weaning period (Shoemaker & Wurtman, 1970). Tyrosine hydroxylase activity in such brains is not depressed, suggesting that the decrease in brain norepinephrine accumulation reflects a block in synthesis caused by inadequate supplies of its amino acid precursor or some other nutritional factor. It seems possible that impairments in the functional activity of central catecholaminergic neurons are responsible for some of the behavioral sequellae of protein malnutrition.

ENDOCRINE INPUTS

There is abundant pharmacological evidence that central noradrenergic neurons play a special role in the control of pituitary function (Wurtman, 1970). We have examined the effect of gonadectomy on the turnover of brain norepinephrine. Following its uptake from the cerebrospinal fluid, brain ^{3}H-norepinephrine disappears more rapidly in castrated and oophorectomized rats than in control animals (Anton-Tay & Wurtman, 1968). Since gonadectomy does not depress brain norepinephrine levels, it seems likely that brain norepinephrine synthesis must also be elevated. This hypothesis has been supported by studies using ^{3}H-tyrosine. The endocrine mechanism by which gonadectomy modifies brain norepinephrine metabolism appears to involve a direct action of

FSH, the pituitary hormone that is secreted in excessive amounts by castrated animals (Anton-Tay, Pelham & Wurtman, 1969). Hypophysectomy does not increase the turnover of brain norepinephrine, and this procedure blocks the response of the brain to gonadectomy. Moreover, injections of FSH reproduce the effect of gonadectomy in intact or hypophysectomized-gonadectomized animals.

NEURAL INPUTS

Several laboratories have shown that transection of the medial forebrain bundle (MFB) is followed by a decline in norepinephrine levels in the ipsilateral telencephalon (Heller, Seiden & Moore, 1966). It is not certain whether this decrease reflects the interruption of the mono-synaptic pathway described above, with the consequent loss of noradrenergic nerve terminals in the telencephalon, or whether it results from a "trans-synaptic effect," i.e., from impaired norepinephrine synthesis in noradrenergic neurons whose cell bodies lie distal to the transection. (Studies on peripheral sympathetic ganglia suggest that the loss of nerve impulses from the spinal cord causes a decrease in norepinephrine synthesis in postganglionic neurons. The MFB lesion could simply be causing a type of "central decentralization.")

We have observed a clear trans-synaptic effect on norepinephrine levels among animals subjected to transection of one or both olfactory bulbs (Pohorecky, Zigmond, Karten & Wurtman, 1969). Following this lesion, norepinephrine levels in the ipsilateral telencephalon decline, as does the ability of the telencephalon to take up ^{3}H-norepinephrine from the cerebrospinal fluid. Since the olfactory projections in the rat are entirely uncrossed, these changes can be explained by a simple loss of noradrenergic nerve endings coming from cell bodies in the olfactory bulbs. In contrast, norepinephrine levels in the brain stem *rise* following olfactory bulb transection. This effect could result only from the

loss of a trans-synaptic input which acts normally
to depress norepinephrine levels (possibly, but not
definitely, an "inhibitory" input which also
suppresses norepinephrine synthesis). The bulb
lesion frees the midbrain and the medulla from this
input.

In spite of the limitations inherent in the
techniques currently available for examining the
effects of physiological inputs on central catecholaminergic neurons, these neurons still provide a
very useful system for approaching the general
problem of how such inputs modify brain function.

REFERENCES

ANTON-TAY, F., & WURTMAN, R. J. Norepinephrine:
Turnover in rat brains after gonadectomy.
Science, 1968, *159*, 1245.

ANTON-TAY, F., PELHAM, R. W., & WURTMAN, R. J.
Increased turnover of ^{3}H-norepinephrine in rat
brain following castration or treatment with
ovine follicle-stimulating hormone. *Endocrinology*, 1969, *84*, 1489-1492.

DAHLSTRÖM, A., & FUXE, K. Evidence for the existence of monoamine neurons in the central
nervous system. II. Experimentally induced
changes in the intraneuronal amine levels of
bulbo-spinal neuron systems and IV. Distribution of monoamine nerve terminals in the
central nervous system. *Acta Physiologica
Scandinavica*, 1965, *64*, Supplement 247, 1-87.

GLOWINSKI, J., & BALDESSARINI, R. J. Metabolism of
norepinephrine in the central nervous system.
Pharmacological Reviews, 1966, *18*, 1201-1238.

HELLER, A., SEIDEN, L. S., & MOORE, R. Y. Regional
effects of lateral hypothalamic lesions on
brain norepinephrine in the cat. *International
Journal of Neuropharmacology*, 1966, 5, 91-101.

POHORECKY, L. A., ZIGMOND, M. J., KARTEN, H., &
WURTMAN, R. J. Enzymatic conversion of
norepinephrine to epinephrine by the brain.
*Journal of Pharmacology and Experimental
Therapeutics*, 1969, *165*, 190-195.

SCRIMSHAW, N. S., & GORDON, J. E., (Eds.). *Malnutrition, Learning and Behavior*. Cambridge: M.I.T., 1968.

SHOEMAKER, W. J., & WURTMAN, R. J. Effect of perinatal undernutrition on development of brain catecholamines in the rat. *Federation Proceedings*, 1970, *29*, 496.

WURTMAN, R. J. *Catecholamines*. Boston: Little, Brown & Co., 1966.

WURTMAN, R. J. Brain catecholamines and the control of secretion from the anterior pituitary gland. In J. Meites (Ed.), *Hypophysiotropic Hormones of the Hypothalamus: Assay and Chemistry*. Baltimore: Williams & Wilkins, 1970.

WURTMAN, R. J., ANTON-TAY, F., & ANTON, S. On the use of synthesis inhibitors to estimate brain norepinephrine synthesis in gonadectomized rats. *Life Sciences*, 1969, *8*, 1015-1022.

ZIGMOND, M. J., & WURTMAN, R. J. Daily rhythm in the accumulation of brain catecholamines synthesized from circulating ^{3}H-tyrosine. *Journal of Pharmacology and Experimental Therapeutics*, 1970, *172*, 416-422.

DRUG INDUCED ALTERATIONS IN BRAIN
BIOSYNTHETIC ENZYME ACTIVITY--A MODEL
FOR ADAPTATION TO THE ENVIRONMENT BY THE
CENTRAL NERVOUS SYSTEM

Arnold J. Mandell

Department of Psychiatry
University of California at San Diego

La Jolla, California

INTRODUCTION AND BACKGROUND

Neurochemistry in a way similar to other areas
of biochemistry has come to the time in its history
in which the simple outlining of metabolic paths
has for the most part been completed. Enzymology
in the classical sense (elucidation of kinetics,
co-factor requirements, and characteristics of
more or less purified enzymes) has been superceded
by a concern for how such complex and interrelated
activities are regulated. Regulation would seem
to be of utmost importance in understanding the
brain, which on one hand must be exquisitely sensitive to subtle environmental alterations and at
the same time cannot allow itself to move too far
away from a homeostatic or compensated state. It
would seem more specifically that the brain,
involved principally with information processing,
must be able to regulate the rate of biosynthesis
and degradation of intercellular messengers.
Several metabolic systems can be considered to
belong to this class of messengers. These are
conservatively called "putative" neurotransmitters.
They include substances with such well established
reputations for central nervous system action as
acetylcholine in addition to such compounds as
norepinephrine, serotonin, dopamine, histamine,
glutamic acid, glycine, GABA and even such an

97

esoteric and little known compound as imidazole
acidic acid. Requirements for status as a
significant neurotransmitter have been listed and
argued by a number of authors (reviewed by Mandell
& Spooner, 1968). Ability to alter nerve cell
excitability in amounts comparable to those present
in tissue, available mechanisms for its release
correlated with events in nerve cell excitability,
mechanisms for degradation within a time consistent
with a neural event time base and other such
criteria have been listed. In all such discussions
it is generally agreed that there should be present
finely tuned mechanisms for the control of the
synthesis, release and inactivation of such compounds in order for the neural system to have
codifying information processing capacity. Following this line of argument, therefore, our laboratory
decided that to focus on the regulation of the
biosynthesis of neurotransmitter systems might be
one way in which we could get our hands on an
aspect of information storage in the brain. That
is, we speculated that if some sort of exterior
influence impinged on the brain for a significant
period of time and the brain encoded this in a way
which included modulating its excitability in
specific systems in order to adapt to this impingement, perhaps this alteration could be characterized. We would then have a model with which to
begin to explore one way in which the brain encodes
information. This is one line of argument that
led us to our current series of studies relating
long-term drug action to the specific activities
of rate limiting, neurotransmitter biosynthetic
enzymes.

Another important influence suggesting that
alterations in the specific activity of enzymes
might be found in the brain as the result of
impingement of drugs or intercellular messengers
is the large body of data relating the actions of
hormones on enzymes involved with carbohydrate and
amino acids metabolism in the liver (reviewed by
Mandell & Rubin, 1965, pp. 42-54). This material
followed the now classical work by Knox and his
co-workers (Knox, Auerbach & Lin, 1956) demonstrating the substrate and hormonal induction

of tryptophan pyrolase and tyrosine transaminase
in the liver. It became tempting to speculate
that such hormonal messengers might alter brain
cell metabolism in some adaptive way as well.
Informal reports from the laboratories of a number
of neurochemists from the middle fifties to very
recent years have indicated that there were
attempts to influence the specific activity of
brain enzymes by the use of the glucocortocoids
(H. Waelch, personal communication, 1965). Except
for a very recent report by McEwen and his coworkers (Azmitia & McEwen, 1969), however,
steroid influence on brain enzymes has been unde-
pendable, evanescent or negative. It occurred to
us that perhaps an approach using hormones whose
action was principally that of altering nutrition-
ally important metabolic systems such as gluconeo-
genesis were not relevant. A myriad of studies
have shown that even in cases of rather severe
malnutrition, very little in the way of protein
mobilization occurs in the brain. It is as though
the brain will not be treated as a nutritional
reservoir and therefore will not be influenced by
those hormones activated during circumstances of
nutritional extremes. It makes sense from an
adaptational point of view that the organ whose
major responsibility it is to find food could ill-
afford to be impaired by its deficiency. It is
much more productive to view the brain as having
to adapt to impingement having to do with
excitability; overwhelming stimulation at one
extreme and exquisitely subtle information at the
other. It was therefore no surprise to us when
early studies of isotopically labelled neurotransmitter pools revealed that such things as electroshock treatment, behaviorally stressing circumstances, drugs influencing central excitability
and electrical stimulation increased disappearance
rates of neurotransmitters (Costa, 1969, pp. 11-35).
Using this relatively crude *in vivo* technique with
the assumption of a steady state and a single
compartment, conclusions were made that the
increased disappearance rate of the labelled
neurotransmitter pool reflected an increased rate
of biosynthesis as well as degradation. The
increase in biosynthesis might result from either

active site alteration or an increase in the amount
of the rate limiting biosynthetic enzyme. In one
such series of studies involved with norepinephrine
biosynthesis, Udenfriend and his group gathered
evidence that norepinephrine is a negative feedback regulator of its own biosynthesis by competing
for pteridine co-factor at the active site of the
rate limiting enzyme, tyrosine hydroxylase (Udenfriend, Zaltzman-Nirenberg & Nagatsu, 1965).
Another mechanism for the regulation of neurotransmitter biosynthesis has been suggested by a
series of recent experiments by Weiner and his
group (Alousi & Weiner, 1966) and Axelrod and his
group (Mueller, Thoenen & Axelrod, 1969). Using
peripheral noradrenergic systems such as the *vas*
deferens and the adrenal, these groups have
demonstrated an increase in specific activity of
tyrosine hydroxylase following either electrical
stimulation or the administration of drugs altering
noradrenergic system excitability. These increases
in specific activity were sensitive to the action
of drugs which are inhibitors of protein synthesis.
Changes in tyrosine hydroxylase have not been
demonstrated in the central nervous system previous
to the work of our laboratories (Mandell, Morgan &
Oliver, 1970).

In the recent several months, we have initiated a group of studies making use of the chronic
administration of drugs which influence biogenic
amine metabolism in the brain and assays of
biosynthetic enzymes involved with neurotransmitter
systems. About a year ago we reported an increase
in chick brain tyrosine hydroxylase specific
activity following the administration of amphetamine (Mandell, Morgan & Oliver, 1970). In recent
months we have demonstrated changes in brain
choline acetylase and tyrosine hydroxylase as a
result of chronic administration of drugs (Mandell
& Morgan, 1970a; Mandell & Morgan, 1970b). The
following constitutes a report of our recent
experiments directed toward the elucidation of
control mechanisms involved with biosynthesis of
neurotransmitters with particular emphasis on
changes in specific activities of biosynthetic
enzymes. The first group of studies are

phenomenological demonstrations of alterations in
choline acetylase, tyrosine hydroxylase and tryptophan hydroxylase as a result of chronic drug
administration, specifically reserpine and amphetamine. The second group of studies we will report
relate to the evidence we have gathered thus far
that the alterations in enzymes which we have
observed in response to drugs appear to begin in
the cell body and via axoplasmic flow the new
enzyme appears to migrate to the nerve endings.
The third study reported is some preliminary
evidence that cyclic-AMP may be involved in the
adaptational change to drugs by these neurotransmitter biosynthetic enzymes. We will conclude
with a model for the enzymatic adaptation of neural
systems to chronic drug inpingement. This may be
the beginning of the derivation of a model for the
understanding of the development in neural systems
of tolerance and withdrawal reactions to drugs.
It emphasizes pre-synaptic enzymatic changes.

METHODS AND RESULTS

In the first experiments, two-week-old White
Leghorn chicks were injected intraperitoneally
with reserpine, (5 mg./kg. b.i.d.) for three days.
Six hours after the last injection of reserpine,
the animals were sacrificed and the brains
homogenized with 3.0 cc. of 0.32 M sucrose at 4°
centrigrade. Enzyme assays for brain choline
acetyltransferase were carried out using the
radio-chemical assay of Schrier and Shuster (1967).
Protein determinations were done using the method
of Lowry, Rosebrough, Fan and Randell (1951).
Reserpine treatment resulted in a rise in brain
choline acetyltransferase activity in all areas
studied. The rise reached statistical significance
in the mid-brain and the cerebral hemispheres
(Fig. 1). Enzyme activity is expressed as mμM of
acetylcholine synthesized per milligram of protein
per hour under standard assay conditions. The
time course of the increase in the specific
activity of choline acetyltransferase following a
single injection of reserpine is depicted in
Table I. Note that the acetylase reached a stable

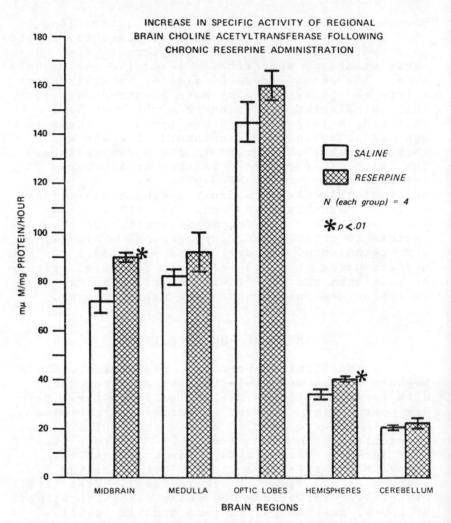

Fig. 1.   Choline acetyltransferase activity in
various areas in the brain six hours after the last
injection of reserpine (5 mg./kg.) given twice a
day for three days.   Enzyme activity is expressed
as mμM of acetylcholine synthesized per milligrain
of protein per hour.   Each bar represents the mean
± S.E.M. (brackets) of four observations.   Every
area indicates a reserpine induced increase over
the saline injected controls.   The changes in the
midbrain and hemisphere reach significance.

TIME COURSE OF RESERPINE INDUCED INCREASE
IN BRAIN CHOLINE ACETYLTRANSFERASE

Hours After Reserpine	% of Final Spec. Act.	Number of Animals
0	82 ± 2%	3
3	91 ± 3%	3
6	84 ± 2.6%	3
9	85 ± 4.1%	3
12	101.5 ± 2.3%	3
48 hours; q 12 h (Chronic)	100 ± 3%	5

Table I. Time course of the increase in the specific activity of brain choline acetylase activity following a single injection of reserpine (5 mg./kg.). The level achieved at 48 hours following chronic administration was made equal to 100%. Note that this level is achieved in 12 hours following one injection.

level in 12 hours. This is the same as that seen
in 48 hours following treatment with reserpine.
A recent study in our laboratory making use of
optic lobes replicated these findings. Fig. 2
summarizes a replicative study of optic lobe
choline acetyltransferase specific activity
following reserpine given with the same dose and
time course reported in the previous experiment.
An alteration of adrenal tyrosine hydroxylase in
response to reserpine has been previously reported
by Mueller *et al.* (1969). Their work and that of
others has suggested that reserpine, by altering
norepinephrine binding, leads to an increase in
norepinephrine biosynthesis probably from both a
reduction in chronic feedback inhibition by
norepinephrine as well as new enzyme synthesis.
Increases in specific activity of brain choline
acetylase have not been previously reported. Martel
and Weiner (1970) have found that rat brain choline
acetylase was reduced by actinomycin D in six hours,
suggesting that these enzymes may turn over rather
quickly. In an effort to see if this change was
due to drug induced alterations in brain excitability or specific to reserpine, a similar experiment was carried out making use of the chronic
administration of amphetamine. In the amphetamine
experiments, the "acute" animals received one
injection of 10 milligrams/kg. or saline and were
sacrificed six hours later. The "chronic" animals
received an injection every twelve hours for five
days and were sacrificed five days later. In
these experiments the optic lobes were studied
since this is the area of the highest endogenous
choline acetyltransferase activity. Fig. 3 shows
the mean of the specific activities of optic lobe
choline acetyltransferase following the acute
injection of saline and methadrine (10 mg./kg.)
and the chronic administration of methadrine
(10 mg./kg. twice a day for five days). Each bar
represents the mean and standard error of the mean
values from six animals. The increase of the acute
group just failed to reach significance. The
chronic group was significantly higher than the
saline control. In the repetition of this experiment, six animals were studied per group comparing
the chronic methadrine optic lobe values with the

OPTIC LOBE
CHOLINE ACETYLTRANSFERASE ACTIVITY
AFTER DRUGS

DRUG	SPECIFIC ACTIVITY*	N
SALINE	136.8 ± 3.6	6
RESERPINE	153.5 ± 2.8	6

Fig. 2. A replicative experiment to study the effect of reserpine administration (under the same dose and time conditions of the previous experiment)
on the specific activity of choline acetyltransferase in the area of highest
base line activity, the optic lobes. Activity is expressed as mμM/mg.
protein/hour. The difference is significant at the p < .01 level.

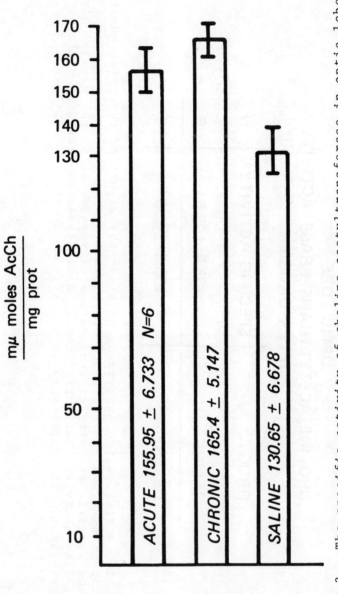

Fig. 3. The specific activity of choline acetyltransferase in optic lobe following the acute and chronic administration of methadrine, 10 mg./kg., twice a day. The control group consisted of six chicks injected with 50 μl of saline, twice per day. Note the elevation of the specific activity following the acute and chronic administration of methadrine. The chronic methadrine values are significantly higher than the saline controls (p < .01).

optic lobes from animals receiving saline. There
was a significant difference (p < .01). Saline
values equaled 136.8 ± 3.6 versus methadrine values
of 152.3 ± 5.4 mμM AcCh per milligram protein per
hour. Thus it appears that two rather diverse
drugs, reserpine and amphetamine, increase the
specific activity of choline acetyltransferase.
In addition to re-uptake binding of choline as a
synaptic regulator of functional neurotransmitter
level as has been reported by Potter (1970), it
may be that relatively rapid increases and decreases
in the amount of the biosynthetic enzyme, choline
acetyltransferase is a significant regulator of
synaptic chemistry in the brain's cholinergic
systems in the same way that these two regulatory
mechanisms function in concert to regulate the
amount of biogenic amine neurotransmitter.

To generalize from our studies of drug induced
changes in choline acetyltransferase as an important
neurotransmitter biosynthetic enzyme, we have begun
to investigate the effects of agents influencing
nervous system excitability on tyrosine hydroxylase, the rate limiting biosynthetic enzyme in the
synthesis of norepinephrine. In these experiments
two-week-old White Leghorn chicks were injected
intraperitoneally with methadrine (10 mg./kg.
twice a day for two days), reserpine (5 mg./kg.
twice a day for two days) and 6-hydroxydopamine
(200 mg./kg. once a day for two days). Six hours
after the last injection of methadrine and reserpine and 24 hours after 6-hydroxydopamine, the
animals were sacrificed and the adrenals were
removed and homogenized in pairs with 2.0 cc of
0.25 M sucrose at 4° Centrigrade. Tyrosine
hydroxylase was assayed by the method of Mussachio,
Julen, Kety and Glowinski (1969). Fig. 4 is a
summary of our initial findings. Methadrine
treatment resulted in more than 100% increase of
tyrosine hydroxylase activity over saline treated
controls. This change returned to control levels
within five days. Reserpine resulted in as marked
an increase in tyrosine hydroxylase activity as
did amphetamine. This has been attributed by
Mueller *et al.* (1969) to reserpine induced
increase in preganglionic cholinergic activity,

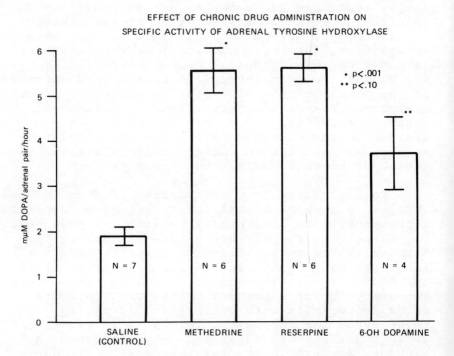

EFFECT OF CHRONIC DRUG ADMINISTRATION ON
SPECIFIC ACTIVITY OF ADRENAL TYROSINE HYDROXYLASE

Fig. 4. Increase in adrenal tyrosine hydroxylase activity following the chronic administration of drugs altering adrenergic neurotransmission. Each bar represents the mean ± S.E.M. (brackets) of the indicated number of observations. The dose and time parameters of each drug are indicated in the text. The alterations induced by methadrine and reserpine reach significance. 6-hydroxydopamine increases tyrosine hydroxylase but the change fails to reach statistical significance.

either as a compensatory autonomic reflex phenomena
or originating from reserpine effects on central
brain systems. 6-hydroxydopamine, reported to be
incorporated into synaptic vesicles leading to
damage of the nerve endings, resulted in an
increase in adrenal tyrosine hydroxylase. This
latter change failed to reach statistical significance. The same kind of change in tyrosine
hydroxylase activity with three drugs of rather
diverse modes of action is of interest. The most
economical explanation is that the increase in
enzyme activity is a non-specific concommitant of
increases in peripheral sympathetic outflow resulting either from peripheral or central activation.
Mueller *et al*. (1969) have noted that the three
drugs they have used to increase tyrosine hydroxylase (reserpine, phenoxybenzamine and 6-hydroxy-
dopamine) interfere in various ways with the
post-ganglionic noradrenergic effector, leading to
a reflex increase in pre-ganglionic activity.
They have prevented this increase (and the
concommitant increase in tyrosine hydroxylase) by
section of the pre-ganglionic sympathetic trunk.
Our finding that chronic amphetamine treatment
leads to an increase in adrenal choline acetyltransferase as seen in Fig. 5 may suggest that one
source of the activation leading to the increase
in adrenal tyrosine hydroxylase (in addition to a
direct action on the adrenal) may be via an
increase in the choline acetyltransferase in the
cholinergic pre-ganglionic fibers. The drug-
induced increases in tyrosine hydroxylase activity
could be inhibited by cycloheximide and actinomycin-
D pretreatment. From this, Mueller *et al*. (1969)
have concluded that the increase in activity was
due to the synthesis of new enzyme.

     In our studies of adrenal choline acetyl-
transferase responses to chronic methadrine
administration, it was discovered that there were
some inconsistencies in the time course of the
changes in this enzyme when compared with that in
brain. These irregularities led to our next
experiments in which methadrine was given (10
mg./kg. twice a day) for six days to one-week-old
White Leghorn chicks. Six animals were sacrificed

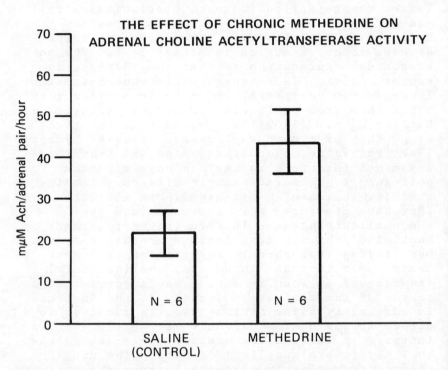

Fig. 5. Increase in adrenal choline acetyltransferase induced by the chronic administration of
methadrine. Each bar represents the mean ± S.E.M.
(brackets) of six observations. Dose and time are
indicated in the text. This increase just fails
to reach statistical significance. See text.

at each of seven times: 0, 6, 12, 24 and 48 hours,
4 days and 6 days. Assays for adrenal choline
acetyltransferase, adrenal tyrosine hydroxylase
and brain stem choline acetyltransferase were
carried out using previously indicated methods.
Fig. 6 shows that whereas brain stem choline
acetyltransferase varies only slightly during the
entire course of the methadrine treatment, adrenal
choline acetyltransferase does not achieve its
highest level until 48 hours. Since choline
acetyltransferase is pre-ganglionic in the adrenal,
we speculated that the alternative explanations
for this difference in amphetamine effect on
choline acetyltransferase in the brain stem and
the adrenal was either due to a differential rate
of the influence of amphetamine on the specific
activity of the enzyme in the two organs or that
the recently elucidated phenomena of axoplasmic
flow of newly synthesized protein might be operating
(Barondes & Samson, 1965). That is, new choline
acetyltransferase synthesized in response to
methadrine treatment might have its origins in the
cell body and require two days to migrate down the
axon to the pre-ganglionic nerve ending in the
adrenal. One of the standard ways to test such a
hypothesis is through the administration of
inhibitors of protein synthesis after the stimulus
invoking new protein synthesis has been delivered.
Once the new protein is synthesized in the cell
body, the inhibitor of protein synthesis would not
interfere with its passage down the axon. If
there was a differential rate of response in
synthetic process itself, the protein inhibitor
would prevent the delayed rise. Because the time
course of this phenomena would require several
days of chronic methadrine administration in order
to obtain this result, it became clear that it was
impossible to use inhibitors of protein synthesis
for this period of time without making the animal
very sick. Deductions from such studies would be
complicated. As an alternative to this experiment,
homogenates from pooled adrenals from saline and
methadrine treated animals were fractionated sub-
cellularly and the various fractions assayed for
choline acetyltransferase activity (Gray and
Whittaker, 1962). Fig. 7 is a display of the

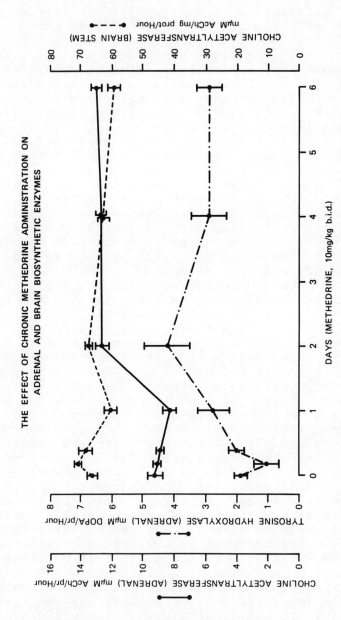

Fig. 6. The specific activities of brain and adrenal choline acetyltransferase and adrenal tyrosine hydroxylase during the twice-a-day administration of methadrine, 10 mg./kg. Note that the adrenal choline acetylase takes two days to reach its peak. See text.

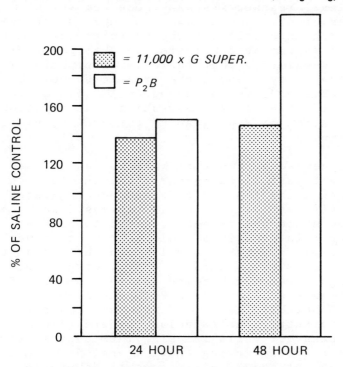

Fig. 7. The amount of enzyme activity expressed as % of control following 24 and 48 hours of twice-a-day methadrine administration. Each bar represents the values from 16 pooled adrenals. The P_2B fraction is reported to contain nerve endings. Note the delayed rise in this fraction. See text.

results of this experiment. After 24 hours of
methadrine treatment, the 11,000 X G supernatant
and P_2B fraction containing nerve endings were
both moderately elevated over the saline control
values and the increase for both fractions were
relatively similar. At 48 hours, the time at
which (Fig. 6) the adrenal choline acetyltransferase level reached its peak, one can see a
continued rise in the 11,000 X G supernatant value
but a far greater rise in the nerve ending fraction
(P_2B). This can be considered another piece of
evidence suggesting that there is axoplasmic flow
of choline acetyltransferase from nerve cell bodies
to the nerve endings in the adrenal. The enzyme
appears to arrive in the adrenal two days following
the initiation of a program of chronic stimulation
with stimulant drugs.

The next experiment to be reported is the
most recent part of our program to elucidate the
underlying mechanisms in drug induced increases in
the specific activity of brain enzymes. We used a
substance which has been speculated to play a
significant informational role in the inner work-
ings of cells and particularly when responding to
extra-cellular messengers. We are, of course,
referring to what Sutherland called the "second
messenger system," cyclic-AMP (Sutherland,
Robison & Butcher, 1968). Using rats implanted
with intraventricular cannulae, we are able to
observe behavior while infusing them over several
hours in a freely moving field (Segal & Mandell,
1970). We infused 23 micrograms of dibutyrl-
cyclic-AMP over a three-hour period. Twenty-four
hours later the caudate nucleus (chosen because of
its proximity to the ventrical into which cyclic-
AMP was being infused) was studied for enzyme
levels of tyrosine hydroxylase, choline acetyltransferase, acetylcholine estrase and monoamine
oxidase. In our previous experiments (only some
of which were reported today), the first three
enzymes have increased at one or another times in
response to central nervous system agents. Monoamine oxidase has consistently failed to respond
to a wide variety of agents influencing central
nervous system excitability. Fig. 8 shows that

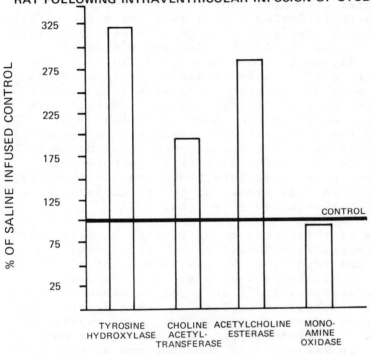

SPECIFIC ACTIVITY OF ENZYMES FROM CAUDATE NUCLEUS OF
RAT FOLLOWING INTRAVENTRICULAR INFUSION OF CYCLIC-AMP

Fig. 8.   The specific activities of four brain
enzymes expressed as % of saline control 24 hours
following the infusion of 23 micrograms of cyclic-
AMP over three hours.   See text.

tyrosine hydroxylase, choline acetyltransferase
and acetylcholine esterase increase in specific
activity 24 hours after the infusion of cyclic-
AMP. Monoamine oxidase does not change. This
enzymatic pattern of response is similar to that
which we have seen in response to drugs. It is
interesting to note that intraventricular infusion
of cyclic-AMP appears to produce many of the same
behavioral responses that we have reported
previously following the infusion of norepinephrine
intraventricularly in this experimental situation
(Segal & Mandell, 1970). Greengard's recent
report (Miyamoto, Kuo & Greengard, 1969) of the
stimulation of protein kinase in brain by cyclic-
AMP when taken in conjunction with this finding
suggests the possibility that some sort of derepression following the phosphorylation of a
histone (or a similar mechanism) may be responsible
for the synthesis of new enzymes in response to
drugs. We are in the process of repeating the
experiments using various brain regions in order
to establish this phenomena before exploring its
many mechanistic ramifications.

We have recently begun to look at serotonin
biosynthesis in connection with this work. Making
use of the tryptophan hydroxylase assay of Ichiyama,
Nakamura, Nishizuka and Hayaishi (1968), we have
demonstrated a significant, 35% increase in brain
stem tryptophan hydroxylase in response to two
injections of reserpine, twelve hours apart. It
appears that brain tryptophan hydroxylase may
respond to reserpine in the same way as tyrosine
hydroxylase.

DISCUSSION

We have reported the responses of choline
acetyltransferase, tyrosine hydroxylase and
tryptophan hydroxylase to the chronic administration
of drugs altering central nervous system excitability. If one can conceive of neurotransmitter
systems as functioning to modulate excitability,
and that the response of the nervous system to
excitability inducers is a compensation to dampen

out such effects, one might speculate that adaptive
changes in excitability in the brain might occur
by the mechanisms which we (on the basis of too
little data) have outlined in the next figure.
Taking our cue from Greengard's work with protein
kinase, Fig. 9 shows the impingement of an
excitatory drug ("speed") directly or indirectly
(via potentiating the action of a neurotransmitter)
setting off an increase in the second messenger
system, cyclic-AMP. This can be accomplished by
an increase in adenyl cyclase or a decrease in the
phosphodiesterase. We would speculate that the
next step would be the activation of a protein
kinase followed by the phosphorylation of a histone,
the derepression of a DNA or RNA (post-tran-
scriptional new-protein synthesis) and a resulting
increase in a group of enzymes related to neurotransmitter biosynthesis. Following the synthesis
of these new enzymes (such as choline acetyltransferase, tyrosine hydroxylase, or tryptophan
hydroxylase) they are transported down the axon to
the nerve endings where they increase neurotransmitter biosynthesis. Recent work by Potter (1970)
in the cholinergic system and Kopin's group
(Sedvall, Weise & Kopin, 1968) in the adrenergic
system suggest that functional neurotransmitter
is newly synthesized neurotransmitter. These
groups relegate the storage forms of neurotransmitter to a secondary role either as an ancillary
system or a sluggish second system. If functional
neurotransmitter is newly synthesized neurotransmitter, then nerve ending rate limiting biosynthetic
enzyme becomes an important regulatory influence
in synaptic physiology. For example, in the case
of choline acetyltransferase in response to "speed,"
an increase in nerve ending choline acetyltransferase might lead to the increasing biosynthesis
of acetylcholine in significant areas. It is of
note that acetylcholine when injected into certain
parts of the brain produces sleep and particularly
REM sleep (George, Haslett & Jenden, 1964). It
is of interest that the post-amphetamine sedation
is characterized by a high density of REM sleep
(Kramer, Fischman & Littlefield, 1967). If we
may be permitted to add speculation on top of
speculation, perhaps the amphetamine tolerance

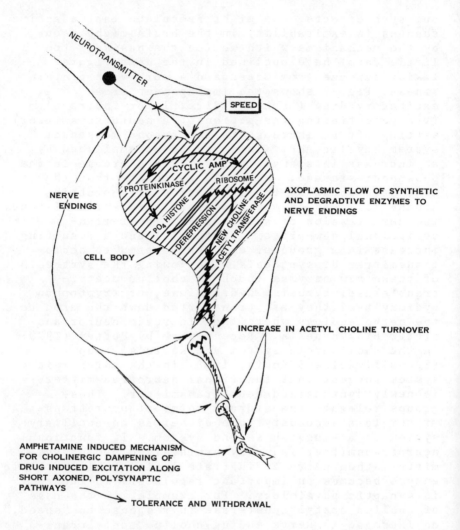

Fig. 9.   A model summarizing some of the speculated
mechanisms by which a neural system via neurotransmitter biosynthetic enzyme synthesis adapts
(and dampens) excitatory drug activation.   The
drug, "speed", sets off a cyclic-AMP dependent
mechansim for new enzyme protein synthesis;
following which the new enzyme migrates down the
axon where it functions to increase the synthesis
of (inhibitory--?) compensatory neurotransmitters.
See text.

and post-amphetamine depression is due to a
compensatory increase in choline acetyltransferase
and a resulting increase in functional acetylcholine
at significant nerve endings.

We must quickly acknowledge that we have taken
liberties with too little data in grand theoretical
style. It is, however, exciting to us that we are
coming to a time in neurochemistry when we are
able to study regulation and when we can begin to
think in meaningful metabolic adaptational terms
such that much of the material we have learned
from cellular regulation in more general mammalian
systems will now be applicable to the brain. This
kind of work suggests the possibility that we have
found a mechanism in brain analagous to "enzyme
induction" as demonstrated in other mammalian
cellular systems. Could it be that this or a
similar mechanism might be responsible for certain
aspects of learned and remembered adaptational
patterns in the brain?

REFERENCES

ALOUSI, A., & WEINER, N. The regulation of nore-
    pinephrine synthesis in sympathetic nerves:
    Effects of nerve stimulation, cocaine and
    catecholamine-releasing agents. *Proceedings
    of the National Academy of Sciences*, 1966, *56*,
    1491-1496.
AZMITIA, E. C., & MCEWEN, B. S. Corticosterone
    regulation of tryptophan hydroxylase in the
    midbrain of the rat. *Science*, 1969, *166*,
    1274-1276.
BARONDES, S. H., & SAMSON, F. Axoplasmic transport.
    Neurosciences Research Progress Bulletin, 1967,
    5, 307-419.
COSTA, E. Turnover rate of neuronal monoamines:
    pharmacological implications. In A. Cerletti
    & F. J. Bore (Eds.), *The Present Status of
    Psychotropic Drugs*, New York: Excerpta Medica
    Foundation, 1969.
GEORGE, R., HASLETT, W. L., & JENDEN, D. J. Choli-
    nergic mechanisms in sleep. *International
    Journal of Neuropharmacology*, 1964, *3*, 541-552.

GRAY, E. G., & WHITTAKER, V. P. The isolation of
    nerve endings from brain: an electron-
    microscope study of cell fragments derived by
    homogenization and centrifugation of cell
    fragments. *Journal of Anatomy*, 1962, *96*,
    79-88.
ICHIYAMA, A., NAKAMURA, S., NISHIZUKA, Y., &
    HAYAISHI, O. Tryptophan-5-hydroxylase in
    mammalian brain. *Advances in Pharmacology*,
    1968, *6*, 5-17.
KNOX, W. E., AUERBACH, V. H., & LIN, E. C. C.
    Enzymatic and metabolic adaptations in animals.
    Physiological Review, 1956, *36*, 164-254.
KRAMER, J. C., FISCHMAN, V. S., & LITTLEFIELD, D. C.
    Amphetamine abuse: Patterns and Effects of
    high doses taken intravenously. *Journal of
    the American Medical Association*, 1967, *201*,
    305-309.
LOWRY, O. H., ROSEBROUGH, N. J., FAN, A. L., &
    RANDELL, R. J. Protein measurements with the
    Folin phenol reagent. *Journal of Biological
    Chemistry*, 1951, *193*, 265-275.
MANDELL, A. J., & MORGAN, M. Amphetamine induced
    increase in tyrosine hydroxylase and choline
    acetyltransferase activity. *Nature*, 1970,
    in press.
MANDELL, A. J., & MORGAN, M. Increase in regional
    brain choline acetyltransferase activity
    induced with reserpine. *Communications in
    Behavioral Biology*, 1970, in press.
MANDELL, A. J., MORGAN, M., & OLIVER, G. W. The
    effects of *in vivo* administration of anti-
    depressant and stimulant drugs on the specific
    activities of brain tyrosine hydroxylase and
    indoleamino-N-methyltransferase. In M. Katz
    & T. William (Eds.). *NIMH Workshop on the
    Biology of Depression*, Washington, D. C.,
    Government Printing Office, 1970.
MANDELL, A. J., & RUBIN, R. T. Enzyme induction
    and the psychosomatic hypothesis. In *Stress
    and Adaptation*, Forest Hospital Symposium
    Series, Des Plaines, Illinois: Forest Hospi-
    tal Foundation, 1965.
MANDELL, A. J., & SPOONER, C. E. Psychochemical
    research studies in man. *Science*, 1968, *162*,
    1442-1453.

MARTEL, P., & WEINER, N.   Choline acetyltransferase
    and acetylcholine levels in rat brain: Effect
    of actinomycin-D. *Science*, 1970, in press.
MIYAMOTO, E., KUO, J. F., & GREENGARD, P.   Adeno-
    sine-3, 5-monophosphate-dependent protein
    kinase from brain. *Science*, 1969, *165*, 63-65.
MUELLER, R. A., THOENEN, H., & AXELROD, J.   Inhi-
    bition of trans-synaptically increased tyrosine
    hydroxylase activity by cycloheximide and
    actinomycin-D. *Molecular Pharmacology*, 1969,
    5, 463-469.
MUSSACHIO, J. M., JULEN, L., DETY, S. S., &
    GLOWINSKI, J.   Increase in rat brain tyrosine
    hydroxylase activity produced by electro-
    convulsive shock. *Proceedings of the National
    Academy of Sciences*, 1969, *63*, 1117-1119.
POTTER, L. T.   Synthesis, storage and release of
    (^{14}C) acetylcholine in isolated rat diaphragm
    muscles. *Journal of Physiology*, 1970, *206*,
    145-166.
SCHRIER, B. K., & SHUSTER, L.   A simplified radio-
    chemical assay for choline acetyltransferase.
    Journal of Neurochemistry, 1967, *14*, 977-985.
SEDVALL, G. C., WEISE, V. K., & KOPIN, I. J.   The
    rate of norepinephrine synthesis measured *in
    vivo* during short intervals; influence of
    adrenergic nerve impulse activity. *Journal
    of Pharmacology and Experimental Therapeutics*,
    1968, *159*, 274-282.
SEGAL, D., & MANDELL, A. J.   Behavioral activation
    of rats during intraventricular infusion of
    norepinephrine. *Proceedings of the National
    Academy of Sciences*, 1970, in press.
SUTHERLAND, E. W., ROBISON, G. A., & BUTCHER, R. W.
    Some aspects of the biological role of adeno-
    sine-3, 5-monophosphate (cyclic-AMP).
    Circulation, 1968, *3*, 279-306.
UDENFRIEND, S. D., ZALTZMAN-NIRENBERG, P., &
    NAGATSU, T.   Inhibitors of purified beef
    adrenal tyrosine hydroxylase. *Biochemical
    Pharmacology*, 1965, *14*, 837-845.

STEROID HORMONE INTERACTION WITH
SPECIFIC BRAIN REGIONS

Bruce S. McEwen, Richard E. Zigmond,
Efrain C. Azmitia, Jr. and Jay M. Weiss

The Rockefeller University

New York, New York

I. INTRODUCTION

One aim of the burgeoning field of neurobiology is to elucidate the role of basic cellular
mechanisms common to all cell types in the neural
control of behavior and of endocrine and other
vegetative functions. This is a formidable task,
considering the enormous complexity of the brain
and there is no one single approach which will
provide all the answers. In fact, the diversity
of disciplines and research strategies, some of
which are represented in this symposium, is one of
the attractive features of the field. We have
chosen to focus on the role of the cell nucleus in
the regulation of cellular events in the brain,
since this organelle contains the genetic information from which virtually all cellular processes
ultimately take their form. We have also chosen to
examine the action of steroid hormones on brain
biochemistry, since there are at least two good
reasons for this choice related to our interest in
brain cell nuclei. First, the action of steroid
hormones on many target tissues in the body involves
the activation of genes leading to increased RNA
and protein synthesis. Second, there exist in the
cell nuclei of these target tissues macromolecules,
probably proteins, which bind the steroid hormones
in a stereospecific linkage; the exact function of

123

these molecules is unknown but they are of a type
which may well control the activity of the genome.
The demonstration of such steroid-binding macromolecules in brain cell nuclei provides us with a
relatively simple and sensitive detection mechanism
with which to explore the kinds of hormones which
may be effective and the regions of the brain in
which they may be most likely to regulate gene
activity. There is another important reason for
choosing hormones for the study of brain biochemistry: considerable evidence from neuroendocrinology and behavioral endocrinology indicates that
steroid hormones do act directly on the brain to
control the secretion of appropriate trophic
hormones and to influence the appropriate behavior.

It is the purpose of this paper to review the
literature which supports the view that hormones
act at the level of cell nuclei and that hormones
also influence neural processes, and to summarize
our progress to date in looking for steroid binding
to cell nuclei in selected regions of the brain.
We shall also indicate the kinds of biochemical,
neuroendocrinological and behavioral consequences
which have been observed from hormone action in
these and other brain regions.

II.   DO HORMONES ACT DIRECTLY ON THE BRAIN?

The most direct answer to this question has
been provided by experiments in which the implantation of a tiny amount of crystalline steroid in a
discrete region of the brain duplicates the effects
of that steroid administered systemically in larger
doses. Implants of cholesterol and other inactive
steroids are used to control for artifacts due to
the cannula or to a nonspecific steroid effect.
Estradiol-17β implanted in a slender cannula in the
preoptic region and anterior hypothalamus of ovariectomized female rats, induces behavioral estrus
and suppresses the release of gonadotrophic hormone
from the pituitary (Lisk, 1967). The dose is
insufficient to produce effects in peripheral endocrine target organs, such as the uterus, and so the
effect is a purely local one in the brain. Similar

experiments have been reported in which implants of corticosteroids in various brain regions suppress the release of ACTH from the pituitary (see Section V, C).

Another means of measuring responses of cells in the brain to hormones is by recording the electrical responses of single neurons. This technique has been applied to show responses of single units in discrete brain regions to the administration of steroid hormones such as estradiol (Lincoln & Cross, 1967), progesterone (Komisaruk, McDonald, Whitmoyer & Sawyer, 1967), testosterone (Pfaff & Pfaffmann, 1969), cortisol (Slusher & Hyde, 1969) and dexamethasone (Steiner, Ruf & Akert, 1969). In the last three studies, effects have been produced with local administration (including iontophoretic application) of hormones to the surfaces of neurons.

Another indication of the action of steroid hormones on the brain is the effect of adrenal steroids on the threshold to seizures elicited by electroshock. This literature, reviewed by Woodbury (1958), indicates that steroids which affect electrolyte metabolism, such as desoxycorticosterone, increase the threshold, while steroids which affect carbohydrate metabolism, such as cortisol, decrease the threshold. Corticosterone, which is relatively ineffective in this test by itself, tends to counteract the effects of both mineralo- and glucocorticoids on brain excitability, a result which has led Woodbury to call this steroid the "regulatory" or "normalizing" hormone of the adrenal cortex. Measurements of the EEG and of changes in the electrolyte balance in the brain indicate that these effects on excitability are undoubtedly direct and are not solely caused by changes in peripheral nerve excitability.

Because of such cases in which steroid hormones in the general circulation directly influence neural processes, it is reassuring to find that radioactive steroid hormones placed in the general circulation do enter the brain rapidly and with ease. This has been clearly demonstrated in

numerous autoradiographic and biochemical studies
on estradiol uptake (Michael, 1965; Attramadal,
1965; Eisenfeld & Axelrod, 1965; Kato & Villee,
1967; Pfaff, 1968a; Stumpf, 1968), testosterone uptake (Pfaff, 1968b; McEwen, Pfaff & Zigmond, 1970b,
1970c), progesterone uptake (Raisinghani, Dorfman, Forchielli, Gyermek & Geuther, 1968; Seiki,
Miyamota, Yamashita & Kotani, 1969), cortisol uptake (Eik-Nes & Brizzee, 1965), aldosterone uptake
(Cameron, Tolman & Harrington, 1969) and corticosterone uptake (McEwen, Weiss & Schwartz, 1969,
1970). Our own studies showed that, within the
physiological range of corticosterone doses, the
amount of radioactive steroid in the brain
increases almost linearly with the dose (McEwen
et al., 1969). This means that as the blood level
of corticosterone changes (as with stress or with
diurnal variations), the amount of hormone in the
brain also changes. There are certain important
exceptions to this rule of proportionality between
blood and brain concentrations of hormone, namely,
that in certain brain regions there is, in addition
to the proportional uptake, a limited-capacity
binding mechanism for endogenous levels of both
estradiol and corticosterone (Eisenfeld & Axelrod,
1965; Kato & Villee, 1967; McEwen et al., 1969,
1970a). The identification of these limited-
capacity binding sites is the subject of our
research which will be summarized in Sections IV
and V.

     The biochemical consequences of the interaction
of steroid hormones with the brain have received
relatively little attention, but there are many
fragmentary bits of information which indicate the
kind of biochemical processes which are under
hormonal control. These studies, which will be
considered in detail in Sections IV and V, involve
at least five major approaches: 1. Measurements
of changes in the size of nucleoli and nuclei in
neurons of affected brain regions; 2. Autoradiographic and microchemical studies of RNA metabolism
3. Changes in the turnover of biogenic amines by
biochemical and histological procedures in relation
to the hormonal state; 4. Changes in fluxes of
electrolytes across cell membranes in. the brain;

and 5.   Changes in enzymatic activity resulting
from an altered hormonal state.

III.   A MECHANISM OF STEROID-HORMONE ACTION
BASED ON STUDIES ON NON-NERVOUS TARGET TISSUES

Recent substantial progress in the understanding of basic mechanisms by which steroid hormones
affect hormone-sensitive tissues has centered
around the role of alterations in genomic activity
in the form of increased RNA and protein synthesis.
From these studies it would seem that steroids
might act on the brain in a similar fashion,
inducing changes in genomic activity in cell nuclei
which lead to different levels of key enzymes and
other proteins that are responsible for altered
neural activity. Although the exact molecular
events leading to such steroid-induced genomic
changes are not presently known for any hormone-
sensitive cell, it seems extremely likely that the
binding of the particular steroid hormone to a
stereospecific binding protein in the cytoplasm and
cell nucleus of the target cell plays a central
role. Such binding proteins, which have now been
found in at least four different steroid hormone-
target tissue systems, represent precisely,
specifically programmed products of the differentiation of each tissue. The detection of such
molecules seems to us to be a sensitive and
relatively simple means of exploring the complexity
of the brain for hormone-sensitive regions. Before
discussing our own experiments, let us briefly
consider the process of hormone binding and action
on non-nervous, hormone-sensitive tissues.

The most thoroughly studied example of this
kind of hormone action is that of estrogen on the
uterus. Estradiol-17β interacts first with protein
macromolecules in the cytoplasm which have a sedimentation coefficient of 8S (for review, see Jensen,
Suzuki, Numata, Smith & DeSombre, 1969). The
complex moves to the nucleus, where the hormone
becomes associated with a 5S macromolecule which
may well be a piece of the cytoplasmic 8S molecule
with some nuclear material attached (Jensen *et al.*,

1969).   The nuclear 5S molecule is extracted from
the nuclei by 0.3 M up to 1.0 M KCl (King & Gordon,
1967).   The end result of radioactive estrogen
administration is that 8S molecules in the cytosol
disappear and estrogen-labelled 5S molecules appear
in the nucleus (Shyamala & Gorski, 1969).   The
process of converting 8S cytosol binding to 5S
nuclear binding is very sensitive to temperature
and does not occur readily at 0°C, while 8S binding
does take place at this temperature (Jensen, Suzuki,
Kawashima, Stumpf, Jungblat & DeSombre, 1968).   The
biosynthetic responses to estrogen administration
begin in the nucleus with enhanced RNA polymerase
activity and increased RNA production, and later
appear in the cytoplasm as increased protein synthesis, resulting in the growth in mass and number of
uterine cells and increased cell function (Hamilton,
1968).   Jensen's group has incorporated these events
into a model of what they call "induced derepression" in which the estrogen stimulates the movement
into the nucleus of a protein-hormone complex which
combines with a repressor of gene function in the
nucleus and thereby activates specific regions of
the genome (Jensen *et al.*, 1969).

Recent evidence (Szego & Davis, 1967) for a
rapid effect of estradiol on cyclic AMP formation
in the uterus need not be interpreted as contradict-
ing a nuclear action.   Rather, the two processes are
probably complementary, with the cyclic AMP increasing the penetration of essential precursors, such
as amino acids, into the uterus (Griffin & Szego,
1968) and the estrogen acting at the nuclear
level to activate the genome.

The interaction of testosterone with androgen-
sensitive tissues, such as the prostate, also
involves hormone-binding to cell nuclei.   The
hormone which is bound is not testosterone, but
rather a metabolite, dihydrotestosterone (Bruchovsky
& Wilson, 1968b; Fang, Anderson & Liao, 1969;
Mainwairing, 1969; Unhjem, 1970).   A number of
androgen-sensitive tissues, including prostate,
seminal vesicles (Bruchovsky & Wilson, 1968a) and
the brain (Jaffe, 1969), contain the enzyme responsible for reducing testosterone to dihydrotestos-

terone. Hormone-binding macromolecules have been
demonstrated in the cytosol of prostate and seminal
vesicles (Fang *et al.*, 1969; Stern & Eisenfeld,
1969). Their relationship to the nuclear-binding
protein is not known, except for the fact that both
proteins have similar sedimentation coefficients
(in apparent contrast to the uterus) and similar
preference for dihydrotestosterone as opposed to
other steroids (Fang *et al.*, 1969). The nuclear-
binding protein is solubilized from prostatic cell
nuclei by salt concentrations of 0.4 M up to 1.0 M
(Bruchovsky & Wilson, 1968b; Fang *et al.*, 1969;
Mainwairing, 1969). The consequences of testosterone administration on biosynthesis in the prostate
are very similar to the events which occur in the
uterus following estrogen administration: Increased
RNA polymerase activity and nuclear RNA synthesis
(Liao, Leininger, Sagher & Barton, 1965; Barton &
Liao, 1967) followed by increases in cytoplasmic
protein synthesis and cellular growth and function
(Williams-Ashman, 1965). Probably the most compelling evidence for associating the binding of
dihydrotestosterone with these functional changes
is that agents such as cyproterone and progesterone,
which prevent androgens from inducing these changes
in the prostate and seminal vesicles, also antago-
nize the binding of dihydrotestosterone to the
cytosol and nuclear macromolecules (see Fang *et
al.*, 1969; Stern & Eisenfeld, 1969).

Aldosterone is another steroid hormone which
induces cellular changes at the nuclear level and
at the same time binds to macromolecules in the
kidney and toad bladder and a variety of other
tissues as well, including brain (Bogoroch, 1969;
Cameron *et al.*, 1969; Swaneck, Highland & Edelman,
1969). The available evidence indicates that there
are both cytoplasmic and nuclear macromolecules
which bind aldosterone and which have similar sedimentation coefficients and specific preference for
aldosterone as opposed to other steroids (Swaneck
et al., 1969). The kidney nuclear aldosterone-
binding protein is extracted from cell nuclei by 0.1
M Tris buffer (Swaneck *et al.*, 1969) and thus may
be less tightly bound to the kidney nuclei than the
estradiol- and dihydrotestosterone-binding proteins

are bound to their respective nuclear types. The
consequences of aldosterone action upon the kidney
involve increased RNA and protein synthesis
(Fimognari, Fanestil & Edelman, 1967) and increased
activity of the sodium- and potassium-activated
ATPase (Jorgenssen, 1969). The strongest evidence
for associating hormone-binding with genomic activation rests on the fact that analogues of aldosterone which mimic the action of aldosterone in
increasing sodium transport also bind to nuclear
aldosterone-binding protein, while other analogous
steroids which are inactive on sodium transport do
not bind (Swaneck et al., 1969).

Yet another steroid-like molecule, Vitamin D,
possesses a very similar story to that described
above for the three steroid hormones. This substance increases the transport of calcium from the
lumen of the intestine into the intestinal mucosa
and appears to do so by stimulating RNA and protein
synthesis leading to the formation of a more effective transport system (Norman, Haussler, Adams,
Myrtle & Roberts, 1969; DeLuca, 1969). Cell nuclei
isolated from chick intestinal mucosa possess a
protein which binds a metabolite of Vitamin D
(DeLuca, 1969; Haussler & Norman, 1969; Lawson,
Wilson, Barker & Kodicek, 1969). The binding protein is solubilized from chromatin by 0.2 M salt
(Haussler & Norman, 1969). There is very little
evidence thus far that would directly link binding
and action of the Vitamin D metabolite, although
DeLuca (1969) has reported that the rate of RNA
synthesis by intestinal mucosa chromatin isolated
from Vitamin D-treated rats is greater than that by
chromatin isolated from untreated, vitamin-deficient
rats.

IV.   SUMMARY OF ESTRADIOL UPTAKE
      AND ACTION IN THE BRAIN

A.   Uptake and Retention

Beginning with the autoradiographic investigations of Michael (1965), Attramadal (1965) and Pfaff

(1968a) and the biochemical studies of Eisenfeld
and Axelrod (1965) and of Kato and Villee (1967),
it has become evident that the female sex hormone,
estradiol-17β, enters the brain from the blood, concentrates particularly in cells of the hypothalamus
and preoptic region and is retained by these cells
in the face of decreasing blood levels. Estradiol
can also be found in other brain regions in lower
amounts, though its rate of disappearance from
these regions more closely parallels its rate of
disappearance from the blood. Thin-layer chromatography and recrystallization indicate that one or
two hours after injection most of the estradiol in
the hypothalamus is unmetabolized. Other biochemical experiments have revealed that the retention process in the hypothalamus has a more limited
capacity for estradiol than that in the cerebral
cortex, i.e., it can be saturated by unlabelled
hormone injected prior to, or concurrently with, the
labelled hormone at doses which do not change the
concentration of radioactivity in cerebral cortex.
Furthermore, other steroids, such as estradiol-17α
and testosterone, do not appreciably saturate the
retention mechanism, indicating that the retention
process is highly specific for estradiol-17β.
^{3}H-Estradiol is also not removed by a subsequent
injection of unlabelled estradiol. The possible
physiological significance of these saturation
experiments has been shown in recent experiments by
McGuire and Lisk (1968) and by Kato, Inaba and
Kobayashi (1969). These workers have found that in
an intact, cycling female rat the hypothalamus takes
up more tritiated estradiol during diestrus than
during proestrus. Measurements of endogenous
estrogen have shown that the peak of estradiol in
the blood is during proestrus, thus suggesting that
the endogenous estradiol can partially saturate the
estradiol retention mechanism.

Stumpf (1968) and, more recently, Anderson and
Greenwald (1969) have presented elegant autoradiographic evidence for the concentration of estradiol
in brain cells in the preoptic area, hypothalamus
and amygdaloid region--areas of the brain which have
been implicated by other experiments in the control

of female sexual behavior and gonadotrophic secretion. Both groups found localization in the nucleus
preopticus medialis, nucleus preopticus suprachiasmatis, nucleus arcuatus, pars lateralis of the
nucleus ventromedialis and the medial amygdaloid
nucleus. These workers were not able to find
labelled cells in the nucleus suprachiasmatis,
nucleus supraopticus or in the hippocampus.

Work in our laboratory using subcellular
fractionation techniques (Zigmond & McEwen, 1970)
showed that estradiol concentrates in cell nuclei,
isolated in a highly purified state from the
preoptic-hypothalamic region, and also concentrates
in nuclei from an area including the amygdala and
overlying cortex (Table I). Correcting for nuclear
yield, approximately 43% of the labelled steroid
can be accounted for in the nuclei from the
preoptic-hypothalamic area, while 31% is found in
the amygdaloid sample. Other regions of the brain
have lower nuclear concentrations of estradiol
(Table I), which may nevertheless indicate meaningful binding sites (Zigmond & McEwen, 1970). Competition experiments with estradiol-17α and testosterone showed that at low doses only the natural
steroid suppresses nuclear binding, while at doses
of 1 mg both estradiol-17α and estradiol-17β compete
successfully, although testosterone does not
compete. The time course of nuclear binding of
the hormone indicates that estradiol is retained in
the nuclei for up to four hours after an intraperitoneal injection of the radioactive steroid.
This retention of ^{3}H-Estradiol by cell nuclei from
the preoptic-hypothalamic area against a decreasing
blood concentration shows a considerable amplification of the same phenomenon seen on a tissue
level. A similar amplification is seen for
saturation experiments: whereas 1 mg of unlabelled
estradiol reduces radioactive uptake at the tissue
level by about 60%, it completely prevents the
uptake of radioactive hormone by the isolated cell
nuclei. Therefore, we are led to believe that, in
the hypothalamus as in the uterus, a major site of
estradiol retention is the cell nucleus.

TABLE I

Regional Concentration of Radioactivity in Brain Cell Nuclei of Ovariectomized Female Rats Two Hours After Injection of 0.6 μg Estradiol-6, 7-^{3}H

Brain Region	Number of Animals	Radioactive Concentration in Cell Nuclei CPM/mg Protein ± SEM	Concentration Ratio N/WH*
Preoptic Region plus Hypothalamus	18	2094 ± 342	12.9 ± 0.5
Amygdala with Overlying Cortex	5	868 ± 155	5.7 ± 0.9
Hippocampus	6	221 ± 59	1.9 ± 0.6
Cerebral Cortex	6	112 ± 17	0.8 ± 0.2
Olfactory Bulbs	2	54 (70, 38)	0.65 (0.8, 0.5)

* Whole homogenate of region.
Procedural details may be found in Zigmond and McEwen (1970).

Eisenfeld (1969) has studied *in vitro* binding of ^{3}H-Estradiol to macromolecules in soluble, high speed supernatant (cytosol) fractions from various organs. The distribution of these molecules seems to follow the same pattern as the distribution of nuclear binding sites--the highest concentration occurs in the uterus and anterior pituitary, followed by the hypothalamus, cortex and plasma, in that order. Estradiol binding to hypothalamic supernatants can be blocked by adding unlabelled estradiol to the medium, but not by adding a hundred times as much progesterone or testosterone. The binding is significantly reduced by chymotrypsin treatment but not by DNase or RNase. It is interesting to note that Eisenfeld's findings, like our own, show estradiol binding substances to be present in all parts of the brain rather than only in the hypothalamus.

These results on estradiol binding by brain cell nuclei and soluble macromolecules in the cytosol closely resemble results on estrogen binding in the uterus, although the relationship of the cytoplasmic and nuclear binding in the brain is not yet known. It does, however, seem likely that the mode of estradiol binding in the hypothalamus and in the uterus may be very similar. Whether the macromolecules which bind the hormone in these two tissues are the same or different remains to be determined.

B.   Biochemical Aspects of Estradiol Action on the Brain

Studies on biochemical changes in the brain during the estrous cycle, following ovariectomy, and after estrogen replacement therapy indicate that alterations do occur, ranging from changes in RNA metabolism to changes in enzyme activity and in catecholamine turnover. Belajev, Korotchkin, Bajev, Golubitsa, Korotchkina, Maksimovsky and Davidovskaja (1967) reported that hypothalamic neurons contain more RNA and incorporate more ^{14}C-adenine into RNA during diestrus than during estrus. Since estrogen levels rise during the period (proestrus) which lies between diestrus and estrus, this result may be due to a suppression by estrogen of RNA production in the hypothalamus. The observation by Lisk and Newlon (1963) that implantation of crystalline estradiol into the arcuate nucleus results in a decrease in nucleolar volume in that area is consistent with the observation of the Russian workers, since the nucleolus contains large amounts of RNA which are exported to the cytoplasm (see DuPraw, 1968, pp. 495-497), and changes in nucleolar size have been correlated with changes in RNA content of neurons (Edstrom & Eichner, 1958). In the whole hypothalamus of the deermouse, Eleftheriou and Church (1967) found increases of RNA content per unit of tissue weight during proestrus and estrus, compared with diestrus. Whether the deermouse is different from the rat, or whether other regions of the hypothalamus show increased RNA synthesis which overcomes the decreases in other regions, remains to be discovered. In this study and that of the Russian workers, the role of estradiol as opposed to that of other humoral factors has not been established.

The enzyme monoamine oxidase, which inactivates biogenic amines, has been found to vary in the hypothalamus during the phases of the estrus cycle in the female rat (Kamberi & Kobayashi, 1970). The enzyme activity is higher during proestrus and estrus than during diestrus. This cyclic variability occurs in the hypothalamus, especially in the median eminence and to a lesser extent in the amygdaloid complex but not in the cerebral cortex. These findings parallel our observations (see above) on the degree of estrogen binding to cell nuclei from the hypothalamus, amygdala and cortex, but there is no other evidence at this time to link the two observations.

A number of laboratories have reported changes in the levels or turnover rates of hypothalamic amines accompanying changes in circulating gonadal hormones. Anton-Tay, Pelham and Wurtman (1969) reported an increase in the disappearance of injected ^{3}H-norepinephrine from the hypothalamus

and midbrain of the rat after ovariectomy, which,
in view of unchanged levels of norepinephrine,
seems to indicate an increase in synthesis of the
amine and its release or metabolism. Additional
experiments using hypophysectomized rats suggested
that the increased turnover is due to an increase
in release of FSH. Coppola (1969), using different methods, found an increase in both pool
size and turnover of total hypothalamic catecholamines associated with increased rates of gonadotrophin secretion. Injections of either estrone or
progesterone into an ovariectomized female return
these measures to values found in intact rats. It
is not clear whether Coppola's results can also be
attributed to a direct action of pituitary hormones

Fuxe, Hokfelt and Nilsson (1969) have studied,
by fluorescence microscopy, the effects of ovariectomy and hormone injection on a group of dopamine
containing neurons whose terminals are in the
median eminence and whose cell bodies are mainly
in the arcuate nucleus. Although they found no
changes in dopamine levels, they did find changes
in depletion of the amine after the injection of a
synthesis blocker. After ovariectomy the rate of
depletion drops to the lowest rate found during a
normal estrous cycle. Injections of estradiol or
testosterone markedly accelerate the rate of depletion. This effect is highly specific, since
injections of large doses of progesterone, dexamethasone or hydrocortisone have only slight effect
on these neurons and injections of estradiol and
testosterone have no effect on another group of
dopamine nerve terminals located in the nigro-
neostriatum. These investigators have obtained
similar results by measuring the disappearance from
the median eminence of injected ^{3}H-dopamine. Since
hypophysectomy produces an effect in the same
direction as ovariectomy, these results seem to be
caused by a direct action of estrogen rather than
of pituitary hormones.

In a number of the biochemical studies noted
above, the confounding effects of changes in
gonadal steroids and pituitary gonadotrophins
have not been separated. Also there is a need

for studies using RNA and protein synthesis inhibitors, to establish whether changes in enzyme activity or catecholamine turnover are due to actions
of hormones at the nuclear level. However, these
results together with those presented in the next
two sections do suggest biochemical actions of
estradiol, perhaps directly on the genome, in
precisely those areas of the brain which show the
highest hormone retention, the preoptic-hypothalamic
area and the amygdala.

C. Neuroendocrinological and Behavioral Correlates

Much of the motivation for studying the localization in the brain of peripherally injected
radioactive estradiol stems from implantation work
which has attempted to localize areas of the brain
involved in the stimulation of estrous behavior and
in the feedback control of gonadotrophin secretion.
These experiments have demonstrated that implants
of crystalline estradiol into the preoptic area
stimulate female sexual behavior without affecting
pituitary release of LH or FSH (Lisk, 1967).
Implants in the median eminence-arcuate nucleus
region inhibit the release of gonadotrophin by the
pituitary (Davidson, 1969).

There is some evidence that implants directly
into the pituitary gland are also effective in
inhibiting gonadotrophin secretion (Davidson, 1969).
Under certain conditions estrogen may also have
a stimulatory effect on the pituitary gland.
However, whether this action is a direct one and
what the precise conditions are under which estrogen
stimulates rather than inhibits the pituitary have
not yet been determined (Davidson, 1969).

A number of workers have found that the amygdala is also involved in the regulation of pituitary
hormone secretion in adult rats, although there is
some disagreement as to whether the effect of the
amygdala is primarily stimulatory or inhibitory
(Eleftheriou & Pattison, 1967; Velasco & Taleisnik,
1969). Lesions of the amygdaloid region in young
rats have been shown to cause precocious puberty.

Again there is disagreement over the interpretation
of the results, some workers feeling the lesion
has removed a stimulatory structure, others holding
that it results in electrochemical stimulation of
an inhibitory area (Critchlow & Bar-Sela, 1967).
In both young and adult animals, the influence of
the amygdala seems to be through the hypothalamus
by way of the stria terminalis (Critchlow & Bar-
Sela, 1967; Velasco & Taleisnik, 1969).

The amygdala is also implicated as an area of
estrogen sensitivity. Tindal, Knaggs and Turvey
(1967) evoked a lactogenic response in rabbits
after implanting estradiol into the amygdala and
stria terminalis but not after implanting it into
the pyriform cortex or other areas of the brain,
suggesting that estrogen-sensitive neurons in the
amygdala may participate in the regulation of
pituitary prolactin release. In contrast to these
results on pituitary control, the importance of
the amygdala in the control of sexual behavior is
still unclear. Lesions in the entorhinal cortex
and the amygdala produce hypersexuality in female
rabbits reminiscent of the syndrome observed by
Klüver and Bucy when they removed the temporal
lobes of male monkeys (see Sawyer, 1967). Lesion
experiments on the cat suggest that it may be the
overlying cortical area rather than the amygdala
which is involved (see Sawyer, 1960).

Schally, Bowers, Carter, Arimura, Redding and
Saito (1969) have begun experiments on the
biochemical mechanism of estrogen inhibition of
pituitary secretion. Although the data are not
yet as clear cut as in the better-studied case of
feedback by thyroid hormones, the work does show
that the inhibitory effect can be abolished by
injections of actinomycin D and may depend on RNA
synthesis. Similar experiments on the mechanism
of estrogen stimulation of behavior have not been
reported.

In studying the biochemical mechanisms underlying the physiological and behavioral effects of
estradiol as well as those of other steriod
hormones, a number of complications should be

borne in mind. First, a single hormone may have
different effects in nearby cell groupings, so that
a large tissue sample may include cell groupings
in which the hormone has opposite or at least
different biochemical effects. For example, the
stimulation of estrous behavior by estradiol in the
preoptic region may involve different biochemical
changes than those which lead to the inhibition of
gonadotrophin secretion in the nearby arcuate
nucleus-median eminence region. Second, hormones
such as estradiol have different effects at different stages of development: estradiol induces
a state of permanent vaginal estrus if given to a
newborn rat (Whalen, 1968), initiates precocious
puberty and stimulates gonadotrophin secretion in a
prepuberal rat (Davidson, 1969) and stimulates
estrous behavior while inhibiting gonadotrophin
secretion in the adult female (Davidson, 1969).
Third, the effects of an injected hormone may
depend on the hormonal state of the animal prior
to injection. For example, Everett (1948) has
shown that in a five-day cycling rat, an injection
of estradiol benzoate on Day 2 but not on Day 3
will advance ovulation by twenty-four hours.

D. Developmental Aspects of Sex Hormone Action on the Brain

     During the first five days of a rat's life,
testosterone has an "organizing effect" on the
brain (Whalen, 1968). If a male rat is castrated
during this period, he will develop a feminine
cyclical pattern of gonadotrophin output as an
adult. A female injected with testosterone pro-
pionate during the same period will develop a
masculine acyclical pattern of pituitary gonadotrophin secretion. These changes in the female are
not due to effects on the ovary or the pituitary
(Segal & Johnson, 1959) and they can be produced
by implanting small amounts of testosterone
directly into the brain, though the sites from
which acyclicity can be produced are not highly
localized (Wagner, Erwin, Critchlow, 1966; Nadler,
1968).

Androgen injections into neonatal females and neonatal castration of males also interferes with the development of the normal adult sexual behavior (Whalen, 1968), but the locus of this effect is not yet clear. Attempts to localize the behavioral action of testosterone on neonatal females with brain implants have been unsuccessful, since the implants needed to decrease the feminine behavior of a female rat were so large that physiologically significant quantities of the steroid entered into the general circulation (Nadler, 1968). Another problem which must be considered is that the lower level of masculine behavior in neonatally castrated male rats may be due to failure of peripheral sensory organs to develop adequately (Whalen, 1968; Mullins & Levine, 1969).

The biochemical consequences of this early androgen action have recently received some attention from Shimada and Gorbman (1970). They found evidence for a species of RNA in the adult forebrain of female rats treated neonatally with testosterone, which was not present in the untreated female controls. There were no differences in the RNAs present in the hindbrain. These long-lasting changes suggest that neonatal androgen activates in a permanent fashion certain genes which are normally inactive in female animals. A comparable study on normal and neonatally castrated male rats has not yet been reported.

The neonatal androgen effect is a situation in which caution must be exercised in interpreting the physiological and behavioral significance of biochemical results (see Section III, B above). One explanation that has been proposed for the constant physiological estrus and decreased lordosis behavior resulting from a neonatal injection of androgen is that these animals have impaired binding capacity for estradiol and therefore are "insensitive" to estradiol (e.g., Flerko, Mess & Illei-Donhoffer, 1969). A number of investigators have in fact found decreased retention of estradiol in the uterus, pituitary and hypothalamus (Flerko et al., 1969; McGuire & Lisk, 1969; McEwen & Pfaff, 1970). Anderson and Greenwald (1969) and Zigmond

and McEwen (unpublished results) have found
decreased nuclear binding in the hypothalamus.
Aside from the central problem of establishing the
functional significance of hormone binding, these
findings do not explain why, for instance, both
androgen-sterilized females and normal females
will show male mounting behavior when injected with
estradiol (Pfaff and Zigmond, 1970). Methods will
have to be developed to separate these diverse but
perhaps concurrent effects of a single hormone.

V.   SUMMARY OF CORTICOSTERONE UPTAKE
AND ACTION IN THE BRAIN

A.   Uptake and Retention

Having been successful in finding stereospecific, limited-capacity retention of estradiol
in regions of the female rat brain which are known
to be involved in the estradiol-sensitive regulation
of female sexual behavior and gonadotrophin
secretion, we decided to use this approach for a
completely different hormonal system, the pituitary-
adrenal axis. We shall discuss below, in Part C,
the evidence that corticosteroids influence neural
processes leading to ACTH secretion through a
direct action upon certain regions of the brain.

The first experiments were conducted with
adrenalectomized rats because we reasoned that, if
there were corticosterone retention sites in the
brain, the endogenous level of corticosterone
might saturate such sites and thus make their
detection impossible. In these early experiments
we measured the concentration of radioactivity per
milligram of tissue in nine regions of the brain
and compared it to the concentration of radioactivity in the blood. Fig. 1 summarizes some of
these results for corticosterone uptake and for
patterns of uptake of estradiol in ovariectomized
female rats and testosterone in castrated male
rats. The pattern of corticosterone uptake is
quite different from that of the two sex hormones,
as shown by a nonsignificant rank order correlation

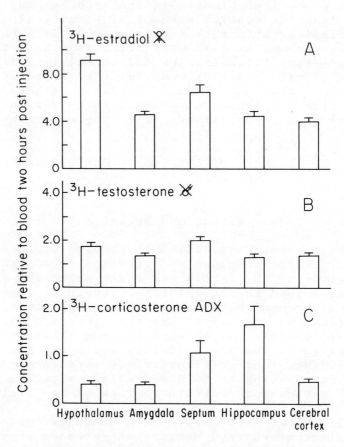

Fig 1.   Uptake of three steroid hormones by rat
brain regions after an intraperitoneal injection of
0.5 to 0.7 µg of labelled steroid: ³H-estradiol
by ovariectomized females, ³H-testosterone by
castrated males, ³H-corticosterone by adrenalectomized males.   Data are expressed as the concentration of radioactivity per milligram tissue divided
by the concentration of radioactivity per milligram
of blood.   For procedural details and original data,
see McEwen *et al.*, 1969, McEwen *et al.*, 1970a,
1970b and McEwen & Pfaff, 1970.

(McEwen *et al.*, 1970b). The two structures with the highest uptake of radioactivity injected as corticosterone are the septum and the hippocampus. Thin-layer chromatography of the radioactive material extracted from the hippocampus two hours after intraperitoneal injection revealed that more than 70% had the R_f of authentic corticosterone (McEwen *et al.*, 1969).

Compared with that of an adrenalectomized rat, the hippocampus of an animal with intact adrenals showed a lower concentration of ^{3}H-corticosterone, suggesting that the retention process can be saturated by physiological levels of the hormone (McEwen *et al.*, 1969). In order to study further the saturability and to examine the stereospecificity of the retention process, we conducted a series of competition experiments with various unlabelled steroid hormones (McEwen *et al.*, 1969). Adrenalectomized rats given 3 mg of corticosterone 30 minutes before the radioactive steroid showed a reduced uptake in hippocampus and a tendency toward reduction in the septum. Comparable doses of dexamethasone and cortisol were also effective in reducing uptake in these two brain structures. No significant effects of competition were noted in other brain regions in these tissue-uptake experiments. We concluded from these competition experiments that there is in hippocampus, and possibly also in septum, a limited-capacity retention mechanism for corticosterone and that stress levels of corticosterone in normal rats are able to saturate the hippocampal, but may not be able to saturate the septal, concentration mechanism. This saturable retention process is superimposed on a less specific exchange of radioactive hormone between the blood and brain which is unaffected by large doses of unlabelled hormone. This latter uptake process is quite uniform throughout the brain, as indicated by the nearly equal concentrations of radioactivity in all regions of the brain in animals saturated with unlabelled hormone.

One of the most powerful ways by which we could characterize the retention of corticosterone by the hippocampus was to associate it with

particular cell organelles or macromolecules. On
performing cell fractionation experiments (McEwen
et al., 1970a) like those described for estradiol
(Section IV, A), we found that a very high concentration of radioactivity, injected as corticosterone
one hour before sacrifice, occurred in purified
cell nuclei isolated from the hippocampus (Table
II). This nuclear concentration was around seven
times the concentration of radioactivity in the
whole homogenate of hippocampus and more than 90%
of the nuclear radioactivity migrated with the R_f
of corticosterone in thin-layer chromatography.
Ten percent of the radioactivity in the hippocampus
was recovered in the purified nuclear fraction;
correcting for the fact that we isolated only 36%
of the nuclei, this means that around 28% of the
radioactivity in the hippocampus is associated with
cell nuclei. This figure assumes that none of the
corticosterone was lost from nuclei during the
isolation procedure; if some hormone was lost, as
is likely due to the many steps necessary to purify
nuclei, this figure could be even higher. To show
that radioactivity did not accumulate in hippocampal nuclei after homogenization and during the
isolation, we mixed radioactive corticosterone with
an unlabelled homogenate of hippocampus. The
nuclei that we had isolated had almost no counts in
them. The time course of corticosterone binding
to hippocampal cell nuclei showed maximum binding
from thirty minutes to two hours after an intraperitoneal injection of hormone and then a rapid
decline of binding between two and four hours
(McEwen *et al.*, 1970a).

When we isolated nuclei from other brain
regions of adrenalectomized rats, we found some
concentration of radioactive corticosterone which
could not be regarded simply as an artifact. In
all brain regions that we examined, the nuclear
concentration of radioactivity exceeded that in the
whole homogenate. These results are presented in
Table II. The concentration in hippocampal nuclei
is the highest, but the concentration in nuclei
from the amygdala and cerebral cortex is also quite
high. The hypothalamus, midbrain plus brain stem
and cerebellum all have lower concentrations. In

TABLE II

Regional Concentration of Radioactivity in Brain Cell Nuclei of Adrenalectomized Male Rats One Hour after Injection of 0.7 μg Corticosterone-1, 2-³H

Brain Region	Number of Animals	Radioactive Concentration in Cell Nuclei CPM/mg Protein ± SEM	Concentration Ratio N/WH*
Hippocampus	10	8310 ± 1824	6.8 ± 1.1
Amygdala with Overlying Cortex	7	2323 ± 505	3.9 ± 0.4
Cerebral Cortex	3	986 ± 356	2.5 ± 0.4
Hypothalamus	7	733 ± 149	1.7 ± 0.2
Midbrain plus Brain Stem	3	591 ± 173	1.4 ± 0.3
Cerebellum	3	416 ± 109	1.0 ± 0.1

* Whole homogenate of region.
Procedural details may be found in McEwen *et al.* (1970a).

the case of the hypothalamus, competition and
mixing experiments of the type described below for
the hippocampus have revealed that the nuclear
uptake in this region must be taken seriously.
Thus, the nuclear isolation experiments succeeded,
where the tissue uptake experiments failed, in
revealing that many regions of the rat brain besides
the hippocampus have some limited-capacity nuclear
sites for the retention of corticosterone.
Unfortunately, the septum is too small to permit
routine nuclear isolation and we have not yet
examined nuclear binding in this region.

We investigated the saturability of the
nuclear binding process and in doing so we obtained
some indication of the high degree of specificity
of this system for the corticosterone structure.
First, we found very little radioactive corticosterone in nuclei isolated from the hippocampus of
rats with their adrenals intact, thus indicating
a saturation by endogenous steroid (McEwen *et al.*,
1970a). Second, a saturating dose of unlabelled
corticosterone administered to adrenalectomized
rats before the radioactive steroid almost
completely abolished the nuclear concentration of
radioactive hormone. In both of these experiments,
the effect of competing corticosterone at the
nuclear level is to abolish almost completely
the concentration of radioactive hormone, while at
the tissue level the competing hormone reduces the
concentration of radioactivity to the level
observed in other brain regions (McEwen *et al.*,
1969, 1970a). This is further indication that we
are dealing with a limited-capacity retention
process in cell nuclei superimposed on a more
general entry of steroid into the brain tissue. We
obtained some indication of the specificity of the
nuclear binding process for corticosterone when we
administered radioactive cortisol and radioactive
cholesterol to adrenalectomized rats. In neither
case was the concentration of radioactivity in
purified hippocampal nuclei more than 0.2% of that
in the whole hippocampal homogenate. We then
performed competition experiments with several
corticosteroids in an attempt to block hippocampal
nuclear accumulation of radioactive corticosterone

in adrenalectomized rats. We found that at a dose
of 3 milligrams, most corticosteroids such as
cortisol, dexamethasone and desoxycorticosterone
reduced nuclear uptake of radioactive corticosterone
almost as well as corticosterone itself (McEwen *et
al.*, 1970a). However, when we lowered the dose to
0.5 mg, only corticosterone competed significantly
for nuclear binding (Table III). From the
structures of these steroids, it would seem that
the specificity of the hippocampal nuclear binding
sites lies in the presence of hydroxyl groups at
carbons 11 and 21 and the absence of an hydroxyl
group at carbon 17 or hindering groups in carbon 18.
Further examination of this specificity under more
carefully controlled conditions must await the
isolation of the binding factor and the development
of an *in vitro* binding assay.

In our initial subcellular fractionation
experiments (McEwen *et al.*, 1970a), we also examined the concentration of radioactivity in two
cytoplasmic fractions of the hippocampus. The high-
speed pellet, consisting of cytoplasmic organelles
and membranes, had a low concentration of radio-
activity--around 0.5 relative to the whole homo-
genate--and we have not studied it further. The
high-speed supernatant or cytosol, consisting of
soluble components of the tissue, contained around
30% of the radioactivity and possessed a concentration per milligram protein two to three times that
in the whole homogenate. In view of the reports
that cytosol of the uterus, prostate and kidney
contains macromolecules capable of binding estradiol,
testosterone and aldosterone (see Section III), we
have examined the hippocampal cytosol for similar
binding macromolecules. To do this, the cytosol
from the hippocampus of adrenalectomized rats
labelled *in vivo* was passed over columns of Sephadex
G25 in order to separate macromolecules from free
steroids. Of the radioactivity in the hippocampal
cytosol, 55 ± 5% was bound to the macromolecular
fraction with a mean concentration per microgram of
protein of 1.64 ± .17. In other brain regions, we
observed less binding (hypothalamus: 27 ± 7%,
cerebral cortex: 39 ± 7%, amygdala: 39 ± 5% and
lower concentrations per microgram protein (0.55 ±

TABLE III

Competition *in vivo* for Binding of ^{3}H-Corticosterone by Other Steroids in Rat Hippocampus

Steroid	Nuclear Binding % Control	Cytosol Binding % Control
Corticosterone	21*	6*
Deoxycorticosterone	94	16*
Aldosterone	67	39*
Cortisol	119	37*
Dexamethasone	119	25*
Progesterone	146	64
Cholesterol	113	112

* Significantly different from control (p < .05, or greater). Competing hormones were injected into adrenalectomized male rats at a dose of 0.5 mg 30 minutes before administering 0.7 μg ^{3}H-corticosterone. Animals were sacrificed one hour after isotope injection.

.10, 0.97 ± .13 and 0.82 ± 0.6, respectively).
This distribution of cytosol binding parallels the
distribution of nuclear binding sites (McEwen *et
al.*, 1970a). Moreover, the smaller percentage of
bound hormone in the cytosol of hypothalamus
compared to hippocampus suggests the presence of
different concentrations in each structure of
saturable binding factors.

       Competition *in vivo* with 0.5 mg doses of a
number of unlabelled hormones reduced the percentage
of radioactivity bound to the nuclear fraction and
lowered the concentration of radioactivity bound
per microgram of protein (Table III). All the
corticosteroids which we tested competed significantly for binding in the hippocampal cytosol, but
progesterone and cholesterol did not compete. Since
these experiments were conducted under the same
conditions, and in many cases on the same tissue
samples, as the nuclear competition experiments, it
would seem that the cytosol-binding macromolecules
have a lesser specificity for corticosterone than
those in the hippocampal cell nuclei.

    B.   Indications of the Biochemical Action of
              Corticosteroids on the Brain

       At the present time it is not possible to give
a coherent picture of the biochemical effects of
corticosteroids on the brain, rather only to indicate a number of findings which provide us with an
incentive for further research. Let us begin with
the hippocampus where we have found the largest
concentration of binding factors. Mühlen and
Ockenfels (1969) have described histologically the
cellular changes occurring in this region after
administration of cortisol to guinea pigs. Nuclei
and nucleoli of pyramidal neurons undergo a
striking increase in size, changes which in other
situations have been shown to be due to enhanced
RNA synthesis (Edstrom & Eichner, 1958). These
authors have observed similar changes in nucleus
infundibularis, nucleus suprachiasmatis and nucleus
paraventricularis thalami. They have also described
a paradoxical effect of the hormone on some cells

in all four regions; namely, pycnosis and cell
death. Although it is possible that the dose of
hormone is so high as to be toxic, they did also
find a tendency for this same phenomenon to appear
after exposing the untreated guninea pigs to a
severe stress. This phenomenon brings to mind the
action of corticosteroids in suppressing cell
function by inhibiting protein and RNA synthesis in
lymphocytes (Kidson, 1967), but is extremely
puzzling for the brain, where such cell destruction
cannot be replaced by regeneration.

Corticosteroids appear to regulate the
activities of certain brain enzymes. DeVellis and
Inglish (1968) have reported that the enzyme
glycerol phosphate dehydrogenase in the rat brain is
under the control of corticosteroids. Enzyme in all
parts of the brain appears to be affected. In a
more recent report, DeVellis and Inglish (1969)
indicate that cultured, cloned glial cells synthesize this enzyme under control of cortisol,
corticosterone or aldosterone. In the same cell
line, lactic dehydrogenase is increased by
epinephrine but not by corticosteroids. Corticosteroids such as cortisol also appear to be
important in the induction of glutamine synthetase
in embryonic chick retina in tissue culture (Moscona
& Pidington, 1966).

There seems to be an important relationship
between the adrenal cortical hormones and the
metabolism of serotonin in the rat brain, which
would appear to be mediated by corticosteroid
regulation of the enzyme tryptophan hydroxylase in
the midbrain of the rat (Azmitia & McEwen, 1969;
Azmitia, Algeri & Costa, 1970). The midbrain is
the locus of the raphe nucleus, site of the neuron
cell bodies which produce serotonin (Dahlström &
Fuxe, 1964). Tryptophan hydroxylase is one of two
enzymes responsible for converting tryptophan to
serotonin and is believed to be rate-limiting in
the conversion (Lovenberg, Jequier & Sjoerdsma,
1968). These studies began with the observation
that tryptophan hydroxylase activity decreased in
the midbrain of rats following bilateral adrenalectomy (Azmitia & McEwen, 1969). Subsequent

measurements of the conversion of labelled
tryptophan to serotonin *in vivo* showed a marked
reduction in the midbrain and brain stem of adrenalectomized animals compared to sham-operated normals
(Azmitia, Algeri & Costa, 1970). Further studies
of the tryptophan hydroxylase activity indicated
that intraperitoneal administration of corticosterone increased the activity of tryptophan hydroxylase within four hours and this increase could be
blocked by intracranial administration of a protein
synthesis inhibitor (Azmitia & McEwen, 1969). More
recently, we found that four types of stressors
(cold stress, ether stress, intraperitoneal
injection of saline and foot shock) increase the
activity of tryptophan hydroxylase in the midbrain.
The percent increase in enzyme activity produced by
each procedure and the percent increase in
corticosterone blood level at the time of sacrifice
are summarized in Table IV, Section A. Adrenalectomized rats failed to show an increased enzyme
activity when exposed to two of these stress procedures (foot shock and cold stress) (Table IV,
Section B), and we surmise that the adrenal glands
and presumably the adrenal steroids are responsible
for the increase in tryptophan hydroxylase activity
observed in the intact rats. We believe that
these results may indicate a major pathway by which
the biosynthesis of serotonin is maintained during
severe and prolonged exposure to stress. Except
for the dependence on *de novo* protein synthesis,
we do not, however, have any indication of the
cellular mechanism by which this control is
exercised.

Another approach to the biochemical action
on the brain of the adrenal steroids has involved
estimating the sodium and potassium ion distribution within brain cells and in the extracellular
fluid and determining the flux of ions between
these two compartments. These studies, reviewed
by Woodbury (1958), have shown that adrenalectomy
leads to decreased intracellular potassium and
increased sodium concentrations and a decreased ion
flux; mineralocorticoids such as aldosterone and
deoxycorticosterone reverse these changes and
restore these parameters to normal. Glucocorticoids

TABLE IV

Effect of Various Stressors on Tryptophan Hydroxylase Activity
in the Midbrain of the Rat

Stressor	Duration	Number of Animals	Percent Δ Tryptophan Hydroxylase*	Percent Δ Corticosterone* in Blood
A. Adrenal glands intact				
Cold (4°C)	5 hours	5	+ 69.0†	+ 97†
Ether	7 exposures/ 3 days	5	+ 19.6‡	+ 105†
Foot shock	7 exposures/ 3 days	5	+ 20.5‡	+ 107†
Saline injection, daily/ i.p.	16 days	8	+ 20.0†	- - -
B. Adrenal glands removed 5 to 7 days previously				
Cold (4°C)	5 hours	5	- 21.7†	0
Foot shock	7 exposures/ 3 days	5	- 5	0

* Elevation over control levels at sacrifice.
† $p < .01$, Student's t-test
‡ $p < .05$, Student's t-test
For procedural details, see Azmitia and McEwen (1969).

such as cortisol and corticosterone are relatively
ineffective. The mechanism by which the mineralocorticoids promote pumping of sodium out of brain
cells may be related to the stimulation by aldosterone of the sodium and potassium stimulated ATPase
in the kidney and toad bladder (Section III) and
deserves further study. In this connection,
Swaneck *et al*. (1969) reported some tendency of
radioactivity injected as aldosterone to accumulate
in brain cell nuclei, and we have made similar
observations (Zigmond & McEwen, unpublished).

C.   Neuroendocrinological and Behavioral Effects
        of Corticosteroids

        We would ultimately like to relate the bio-
chemical action of corticosterone on the brain to
the physiological role of corticosterone in
regulating ACTH secretion and in influencing neural
activity related to behavior. In this section we
shall describe some of the evidence that corticosterone does appear to have such regulatory
effects.

        In discussing regulation of ACTH secretion
we shall first consider the effects of physiological levels of the natural hormone, which in the rat
is corticosterone. In the rat the effects of
elevated and reduced corticosterone levels, within the physiological range, are consistent with
the negative feedback by the steroid on basal ACTH
release, but stress-induced ACTH secretion may not
be subject to such negative feedback. Elevated
corticosterone blood levels, such as are produced
by a single ether stress or by an injection of 3
mg/kg of the hormone, lead to a transient reduction
lasting from two to four hours, of basal or resting
corticosterone levels (Zimmerman & Critchlow, 1969).
This inhibition does not extend to the corticosterone secretion evoked by a second ether stress
(Zimmerman & Critchlow, 1969), although the effect
of other stressors has apparently not been tested.
Reduced corticosterone levels, such as are produced
by unilateral adrenalectomy, lead to the compensatory hypertrophy and hyperfunction of the other

adrenal (Mangili et al., 1966). Bilateral adrenalectomy leads to a delayed increase in pituitary
ACTH levels and prolonged hypersecretion of ACTH
(Vernikos-Daniellis, 1965). Furthermore, ACTH
secretion to mild stressors is enhanced by bilateral
adrenalectomy (Mangili et al., 1966), indicating
increased reactivity of the pituitary or of brain
regions controlling the pituitary in the absence
of circulating corticosterone.

Effects of corticosteroids on the sensitivity
of the adrenal cortex and pituitary have been
reported and are reviewed by Mangili et al. (1966).
However, they are not sufficient by themselves to
account for the negative feedback effects described
above. What regions of the brain may be involved
in these regulatory effects? The hypothalamus is
by far the best-studied region, due to its
proximity to the pituitary and to its content of
neurons which produce the corticotropin releasing
factor (CRF) which is carried to the adenohypophysis
by the portal blood system (McCann & Dhariwal,
1966). Implantation of corticosteroids in the basal
hypothalamus has been shown to inhibit both basal
and stress-induced corticosterone secretion
(Mangili et al., 1966), and it remains to be seen
if the binding sites for corticosterone which we
have found in the hypothalamus (see above)
have any role in this phenomenon. The most
potent agent which affects the hypothalamus in
this way, both by implantation and by systemic
injection, is the synthetic corticosteroid
dexamethasone (Mangili et al., 1966). This steroid
most probably acts on those cells which produce
CRF, blocking its synthesis (Hedge & Smelik, 1969).
Only very high doses of the natural hormone in the
rat, corticosterone, have been shown to block
stress-induced corticosterone secretion when
injected systemically (Smelik, 1963; Hodges &
Jones, 1964). One possible, but by no means
certain, conclusion from these results is that
the effects of dexamethasone on the hypothalamus
in blocking stress-induced ACTH release are not
relevant to the normal physiological mechanism by
which corticosterone regulates ACTH secretion in
the rat.

Other regions of the limbic system also play an important role in regulating both the resting and stress-induced release of ACTH, and there is now good evidence that corticosteroids influence basal corticosterone levels by acting on these extra-hypothalamic structures. Lesion experiments and electrical stimulation through chronically-implanted electrodes have indicated that the hippocampus, septum, midbrain reticular formation and amygdala are all involved in the regulation of ACTH secretion via pathways which feed into the hypothalamus (Mangili *et al*., 1966). Lesion studies have also suggested that the cerebral cortex, not considered part of the limbic system, has an inhibitory influence over ACTH release (Mangili *et al*., 1966). This is interesting in view of our demonstration of corticosterone binding factors in the cortex.

A few studies have been reported for several of these extra-hypothalamic regions in which implantation of tiny amounts of corticosteroid has changed the basal secretion of ACTH. Knigge (1966) reported that implantation of cortisone in the hippocampus of rats increased basal corticosterone plasma levels, while implantation in the amygdala decreased basal corticosterone secretion. Neither kind of implant affected the increase in corticosterone blood levels evoked by ether stress. Kawakami *et al*. (1968) reported comparable studies on rabbits, in which implants of corticosterone in the hippocampus also increased basal corticosterone production, while implants in the amygdala decreased basal corticosterone production. Slusher (1966) has reported that implantation of cortisol in the hippocampus of rats increases the morning plasma levels of corticosterone (which normally are low) and decreases those in the afternoon (when the diurnal peak normally occurs), thus in effect abolishing the diurnal rhythm. Slusher (1966) reported similar effects of cortisol implants in the midbrain. The midbrain has a small amount of corticosterone binding factors (see above), and it is also the part of the brain in which we have demonstrated corticosterone regulation of tryptophan hydroxylase activity. In this connection, local injections of serotonin in hippocampus, amygdala, midbrain and septum have been shown to alter ACTH secretion (Naumenko, 1969).

Thus, the picture we are able to draw at the present time indicates that corticosteroid action in the extrahypothalamic regions of the rat and rabbit brain deal with the regulation of basal (and possibly diurnal) secretion of ACTH. In line with this conclusion is the fact that the corticosteroid-binding phenomenon which we have described for the hippocampus occurs at low levels of circulating corticosterone, within the range of basal blood levels found during the diurnal cycle.

In discussing her implantation experiments, Slusher (1966) noted that the effects of corticos-teroids at the level of the hippocampus and midbrain may involve ". . . mechanisms related not only to the pituitary adrenal activity but also to other behavioral, neural and physiological phenomena." This interesting idea is finding support in studies of the influence of ACTH and adrenal steroids on fear-motivated behavior which are being conducted in a number of laboratories including our own. Recent progress in this field is summarized in a recent symposium (de Wied & Weijnen, 1970). Our own studies (Weiss, McEwen, Silva & Kalkut, 1970) have shown that adrenalectomized rats and hypophy-sectomized rats given ACTH are more fearful in conditioned avoidance situations than intact rats or untreated hypophysectomized animals. This and the fact that adrenalectomized rats also show greater ACTH release to mild stressors than intact rats (Mangili *et al.*, 1966) hints at the duality suggested by Slusher by showing that increased behavioral and pituitary-adrenal reactivity go hand in hand when corticosteroids are absent from the circulation.

VII.   SUMMARY AND CONCLUSIONS

In this paper we have described the association of two steroid hormones, estradiol and corticos-terone, with specific, regionally-localized binding

sites in brain cell nuclei. We have attempted to
justify the search for such binding sites in terms
of a model of regulation of genomic activity in cell
nuclei by steroid-binding macromolecules, a model
which is finding widespread support from studies
of steroid-hormone action on many target tissues.
We have summarized the (so far, rather limited)
evidence for the direct action of steroid hormones
on biochemical processes in the brain in a search
for clues as to the link between steroid hormone
action on cell nuclei and the behavioral and
physiological consequences of the hormone action.
And we have described the probable nature of these
consequences, that is, the regulation of certain
behavioral processes and the feedback control of
pituitary tropic hormone secretion.

     It is important that we also summarize the
limitations of this approach, so that the reader
will not be misled by statements which may have
seemed overly optimistic. First, we do not believe
that we have in nuclear binding the only mechanism
of action of these hormones on the brain. Electrophysiological evidence (Section II) would tend to
suggest a direct action of some steroids on the
excitability of the nerve cell membrane. Moreover,
the presence in hippocampus of cytoplasmic binding
of corticosterone having a different specificity
for corticosteroids than the nuclear sites suggests
an independent cytoplasmic role for the hormone.
Second, we cannot, nor can anyone, state with
complete assurance that binding of hormone to
specific "receptors" in cell nuclei represents an
action by which genes are derepressed. In Section
III, we summarized the evidence which exists and
we believe it to be most compelling but still incomplete. An alternative view, that the hormone
binding might represent an inactive or storage form
of the hormone, should not be overlooked; but if
this were the correct explanation, it would be
remarkable indeed that cell nuclei in specific
regions of the brain and in other hormone-sensitive
tissues should have been chosen for this function.
Third, neurochemists, endocrinologists and psycho-
logists have not been sufficiently aware of develop-
ments in each others fields. In the future, much

coordinated biochemical, neuroendocrinological and
behavioral work must be done to establish directly
and clearly the relationship between a hormonally-
induced change in genomic activity in the brain,
resulting alterations in key enzymes and other
macromolecules and the final physiological or
behavioral effect of the hormone.

ACKNOWLEDGMENTS

The research described in this paper was supported by Grants NB 07080, MH 13189 and GM 01789
from the United States Public Health Service. The
authors wish to express their appreciation to a
number of people for their excellent technical
assistance throughout these studies: Mrs. Carew
Magnus, Miss Linda Plapinger, Mrs. Leslie Schwartz
and Mrs. Gislaine Wallach.

REFERENCES

ANDERSON, C. H., & GREENWALD, G. S. Autoradio-
    graphic analysis of estradiol uptake in the
    brain and pituitary of the female rat. *Endo-
    crinology*, 1969, *85*, 1160-1165.
ANTON-TAY, F., PELHAM, R. W., & WURTMAN, R. J.
    Increased turnover of ^{3}H-norepinephrine in
    rat brain following castration or treatment
    with ovine follicle-stimulating hormone.
    Endocrinology, 1969, *84*, 1489-1492.
ATTRAMADAL, S. Distribution and site of action of
    oestradiol in the brain and pituitary gland of
    the rat following intramuscular administration.
    In S. Taylor (Ed.), *Proceedings Second Inter-
    national Congress of Endocrinology*, Part 1,
    London: Excerpta Medica Foundation, *Series
    No. 83*, 1965. Pp. 612-616.
AZMITIA, E. C., JR., & MCEWEN, B. S. Corticosterone
    regulation of tryptophan hydroxylase in mid-
    brain of the rat. *Science*, 1969, *166*, 1274-
    1276.
AZMITIA, E. C., JR., ALGERI, S., & COSTA, E. Turn-
    over rate of *in vivo* conversion of tryptophan

into serotonin in brain areas of adrenalectomized rats. *Science*, in press.

BARTON, R. W., & LIAO, S.   A similarity in the
effect of estrogen and androgen on the synthesis of ribonucleic acid in the cell nuclei of
gonadohormone sensitive tissues. *Endocrinology*, 1967, *81*, 409-412.

BELAJEV, D. K., KOROTCHKIN, L. I., BAJEV, A. A.,
GOLUBITSA, A. N., KOROTCHKINA, L. S.,
MAKSIMOVSKY, L. F., & DAVIDOVSKAJA, A. E.
Activity of the genetic apparatus of hypo-
thalamic nerve cells at various stages of the
oestrous cycle in the albino rat. *Nature*
(London), 1967, *214*, 201-202.

BOGOROCH, R.   Studies on the intracellular localiza-
tion of tritiated steroids.   In L. Roth and
W. Stumpf (Eds.), *Autoradiography of Diffusable
Substances*. New York: Academic Press, 1969.
Pp. 99-112.

BRUCHOVSKY, N., & WILSON, J. D.   The conversion of
testosterone to 5α-androstan-17β-ol-3-one by
rat prostate *in vivo* and *in vitro*.   *Journal of
Biological Chemistry*, 1968, *243*, 2012-2021. (a)

BRUCHOVSKY, N., & WILSON, J. D.   The intranuclear
binding of testosterone and 5α-androstan-17β-
ol-3-one by rat prostate.   *Journal of Biological Chemistry*, 1968, *243*, 5953-5960.   (b)

CAMERON, I. L., TOLMAN, E. L., & HARRINGTON, G. W.
Aldosterone receptor sites in tissues and cells
of salamander, chicken, goldfish and mouse.
Texas Reports on Biology and Medicine, 1969,
27, 367-380.

COPPOLA, J. A.   Turnover of hypothalamic
catecholamines during various states of
gonadotrophin secretion. *Neuroendocrinology*,
1969, *5*, 75-80.

CRITCHLOW, V., & BAR-SELA, M. E. Control of the
onset of puberty. In L. Martini and W. F.
Ganong (Eds.), *Neuroendocrinology*. London:
Academic Press, 1967. Pp. 101-162.

DAHLSTRÖM, A., & FUXE, K. Evidence for the existence of monoamine-containing neurons in the
central nervous system. *Acta Physiologica
Scandinavica*, 1964, *62*, Supplement 232, 1-55.

DAVIDSON, J. M.   Feedback control of gonadotrophin
secretion.   In W. F. Ganong and L. Martini

(Eds.) *Frontiers in Neuroendocrinology*.
London: Oxford University Press, 1969.
Pp. 343-388.

DELUCA, H. F.   Recent advances in the metabolism
and function of Vitamin D. *Federation
Proceedings*, 1969, *28*, 1678-1689.

DEVELLIS, J., & INGLISH, D.   Hormonal control of
glycerol phosphate dehydrogenase in the rat
brain. *Journal of Neurochemistry*, 1968, *15*,
1061-1070.

DEVELLIS, J., & INGLISH, D.   Effect of cortisol and
epinephrine on cultured glial cells. *Abstracts, Winter Conference on Brain Research*,
Aspen, Colorado, 1969.

DUPRAW, E. J.   *Cell and Molecular Biology*.   New
York: Academic Press, 1968.

EDSTROM, J. E., & EICHNER, D.   Relation between
nucleolar volume and cell body content of
ribonucleic acid in supraoptic neurons.
Nature (London), 1958, *181*, 619.

EIK-NES, K. B., & BRIZZEE, K. R.   Concentration of
tritium in brain tissue of dogs given (1, 2-^{3}H)
cortisol intravenously. *Biochimica et Biophysica Acta* (Amst.), 1965, *97*, 320-333.

EISENFELD. A. J.   Hypothalamic oestradiol-binding
macromolecules. *Nature* (London), 1969, *224*,
1202-1203.

EISENFELD, A. J., & AXELROD, J.   Selectivity of
estrogen distribution in tissues. *Journal of
Pharmacology and Experimental Therapeutics*,
1965, *150*, 469-475.

ELEFTHERIOU, B. E., & CHURCH, R. L.   Concentrations
of RNA in the brain during oestrus in the
deermouse. *Nature* (London), 1967, *215*, 1195-
1196.

ELEFTHERIOU, B. E., & PATTISON, M. L.   Effect of
amygdaloid lesions on hypothalamic follicle-
stimulating, hormone-releasing factor in the
female deermouse. *Journal of Endocrinology*,
1967, *39*, 613-614.

EVERETT, J. W.   Progesterone and estrogen in the
experimental control of ovulation time and
other features of the estrous cycle of the
rat. *Endocrinology*, 1948, *43*, 389-405.

FANG, S., ANDERSON, K. M., & LIAO, S.   Receptor
proteins for androgens: On the role of

specific proteins in selective retention of
17β-hydroxy-5α-androstan-3-one by rat ventral
prostate *in vivo* and *in vitro*. *Journal of
Biological Chemistry*, 1969, *244*, 6584-6595.

FIMOGNARI, G. M., FANESTIL, D. D., & EDELMAN, I. S.
Induction of RNA and protein synthesis in the
action of aldosterone in the rat. *American
Journal of Physiology*, 1967, *213*, 954-962.

FLERKO, B., MESS, B., & ILLEI-DONHOFFER, A. On the
mechanism of androgen sterilization. *Neuroendocrinology*, 1969, *4*, 164-169.

JORGENSEN, P. L. Regulation of the (Na and K)
activated ATP hydrolyzing enzyme system in rat
kidney. *Biochimica et Biophysica Acta*, 1969,
192, 326-334.

KAMBERI, I. A., & KOBAYASHI, Y. Monoamine oxidase
activity in the hypothalamus and various other
brain areas and in some endocrine glands of
the rat during the estrous cycle. *Journal of
Neurochemistry*, 1970, *17*, 261-268.

KATO, J., & VILLEE, C. A. Preferential uptake of
estradiol by the anterior hypothalamus of the
rat. *Endocrinology*, 1967, *80*, 567-575.

KATO, J., INABA, M., & KOBAYASHI, T. Variable uptake of tritiated oestradiol by anterior
hypothalamus in postpuberal female rats.
Acta Endocrinologica (Kbh), 1969, *61*, 585-591.

KAWAKAMI, M., SETO, K., & YOSHIDA, K. Influence
of corticosterone implantation in limbic
structure upon biosynthesis of adrenocortical
steroid. *Neuroendocrinology*, 1968, *3*, 349-354.

KIDSON, C. Cortisol in the regulation of RNA and
protein synthesis. *Nature* (London), 1967,
213, 779-782.

KING, R. J. B., & GORDON, J. The association of
(6, 7-^{3}H) estradiol with a nuclear protein.
Journal of Endocrinology, 1967, *39*, 533-542.

KNIGGE, K. M. Feedback mechanisms in neural control
of adenohypophyseal function: Effect of
steroids implanted in amygdala and hippocampus.
*Abstracts, 2nd International Congress of
Hormonal Steroids*, Milan, 1966, p. 208.

KOMISARUK, B. R., MCDONALD, P. G., WHITMOYER, D. I.,
& SAWYER, C. H. Effects of Progesterone and
sensory stimulation of EEG and neuronal
activity in the rat. *Experimental Neurology*,

1967, *19*, 494-507.

LAWSON, D. E. M., WILSON, P. W., BARKER, D. C., & KODICEK, E. Isolation of chick intestinal nuclei: Effect of Vitamin D3 on nuclear metabolism. *Biochemical Journal*, 1969, *115*, 263-268.

LIAO, S., LEININGER, K. R., SAGHER, D., & BARTON, R. W. Rapid effect of testosterone on ribonucleic acid polymerase activity of rat ventral prostate. *Endocrinology*, 1965, *77*, 763-765.

LINCOLN, D., & CROSS, B. Effect of oestrogen on the responsiveness of neurones in the hypothalamus, septum and .preoptic area of rats with light-induced persistent oestrus. *Journal of Endocrinology*, 1967, *37*, 191-203.

LISK, R. D. Sexual behavior; hormonal control. In L. Martini and W. F. Ganong (Eds.), *Neuroendocrinology*, Volume II. New York: Academic Press, 1967. Pp. 49-98.

LISK, R. D., & NEWLON, M. Estradiol: Evidence for its direct effect on hypothalamic neurons. *Science*, 1963, *139*, 223-224.

LOVENBERG, W., JEQUIER, E., & SJOERDSMA, A. Tryptophan hydroxylase in mammalian systems. *Advances in Pharmacology*, 1968, *6A*, 21-36.

MAINWAIRING, W. I. P. The binding of (1, 2-^{3}H) testosterone within nuclei of the rat prostate. *Journal of Endocrinology*, 1969, *44*, 323-333.

MANGILI, C., MOTTA, M., & MARTINI, L. Control of adrenocorticotrophic hormone secretion. In L. Martini and W. F. Ganong (Eds.), *Neuroendocrinology*, Volume I. New York: Academic Press, 1966. Pp. 297-370.

MCCANN, S. M., & DHARIWAL, A. P. S. Hypothalamic releasing factors and the neurovascular link between the brain and the anterior pituitary. In L. Martini and W. F. Ganong (Eds.), *Neuroendocrinology*, Volume I. New York: Academic Press, 1966. Pp. 261-297.

MCEWEN, B. S., WEISS, J. M., & SCHWARTZ, L. S. Uptake of corticosterone by rat brain and its concentration by certain limbic structures. *Brain Research*, 1969, *16*, 227-241.

MCEWEN, B. S., WEISS, J. M., & SCHWARTZ, L. S.
   Retention of corticosterone by cell nuclei from
   brain regions of adrenalectomized rats. *Brain
   Research*, 1970, *17*, 471-482. (a)
MCEWEN, B. S., & PFAFF, D. W. Factors influencing
   sex hormone uptake by rat brain regions: I.
   Effects of neonatal treatment, hypophysectomy,
   and competing steroid on estradiol uptake.
   Brain Research, 1970, in press.
MCEWEN, B. S., PFAFF, D. W., & ZIGMOND, R. E.
   Factors influencing sex hormone uptake by
   rat brain regions: II. Effects of neonatal
   treatment and hypophysectomy on testosterone
   uptake. *Brain Research*, 1970, in press. (b)
MCEWEN, B. S., PFAFF, D. W., & ZIGMOND, R. E.
   Factors influencing sex hormone uptake by
   rat brain regions: III. Effects of competing
   steroids on testosterone uptake. *Brain
   Research*, 1970, in press. (c)
MCGUIRE, J. L., & LISK, R. D. Estrogen receptors
   in the intact rat. *Proceedings of the National
   Academy of Sciences*, U.S.A., 1968, *61*,
   497-503.
MCGUIRE, J. L., & LISK, R. D. Localization of
   estrogen receptors in the rat hypothalamus.
   Neuroendocrinology, 1969, *4*, 289-295.
MICHAEL, R. P. Oestrogens in the central nervous
   system. *British Medical Bulletin*, 1965, *21*,
   87-90.
MOSCONA, A. A., & PIDINGTON, R. Stimulation by
   hydrocortisone of premature changes in the
   developmental pattern of glutamic synthetase
   in embryonic retina. *Biochimica et Biophysica
   Acta*, 1966, *121*, 409-411.
MULLINS, R. F., & LEVINE, S. Differential sensi-
   tization of penile tissue by sexual hormones
   in newborn rats. *Communications in Behavioral
   Biology*, Part A, 1969, *3*, 1-4.
MÜHLEN, K., & OCKENFELS, H. Morphologische
   Veränderungen im Diencephalon und Telencephalon
   nach Störungen des Regelkreises Adenohypophyse-
   Nebennierenrinde. III. Ergebnisse beim
   Meerschweinchen nach Verabreichung von Cortison
   und Hydrocortison. *Zeitschrift für
   Zellforschung und Mikroskopische Anatomie*,
   1969, *93*, 126-141.

NADLER, R. D. Masculinization of female rats by
    intracranial implantation of androgen in
    infancy. *Journal of Comparative and Physio-
    logical Psychology*, 1968, *66*, 157-167.
NAUMENKO, E. V. Effect of local injections of
    5-hydroxytryptamine into rhinencephalic and
    mesencephalic structures on pituitary adrenal
    function in guinea pigs. *Neuroendocrinology*,
    1969, 5, 81-88.
NORMAN, A. W., HAUSSLER, M. R., ADAMS, T. H.,
    MYRTLE, J. F., & ROBERTS, P. Basic studies
    on the mechanism of action of Vitamin D.
    American Journal of Clinical Nutrition, 1969,
    22, 396-411.
PFAFF, D. W. Uptake of estradiol-17β-^{3}H in the
    female rat brain. An autoradiographic study.
    Endocrinology, 1968, *82*, 1149-1155. (a)
PFAFF, D. W. Uptake of testosterone-^{3}H and
    estradiol-^{3}H by the male and female rat brain.
    An autoradiographic study. *Science*, 1968,
    161, 1355-1356. (b)
PFAFF, D. W. Behavioral responses of rats to sex
    hormones: Specificity of hormone effects and
    individual patterns of response. *American
    Zoologist*, 1969, 9, 1066.
PFAFF, D. W., & PFAFFMANN, C. Olfactory and hormona
    influences on the basal forebrain of the male
    rat. *Brain Research*, 1969, *15*, 137-156.
PFAFF, D. W., & ZIGMOND, R. E. Neonatal androgen
    effects on sexual and nonsexual behavior of
    adult rats tested under various hormone
    regions. *Neuroendocrinology*, 1970, in press.
RAISINGHANI, K. H., DORFMAN, R. I., FORCHIELLI, E.,
    GYERMEK, L., & GEUTHER, G. Uptake of intra-
    venously administered progesterone, pre-
    gnanedione and pregnanolone by the rat brain.
    Acta Endocrinologica (Kbh.), 1968, 57, 393-404
SAWYER, C. H. Reproductive behavior. In H. W.
    Magoun (Ed.) *Handbook of Physiology, Neuro-
    physiology*, Volume II. Washington, D. C.:
    American Physiological Society, 1960.
    Pp. 1225-1240.
SAWYER, C. H. Some endocrine aspects of forebrain
    inhibition. *Brain Research*, 1967, 6, 48-59.
SCHALLY, A. V., BOWERS, C. Y., CARTER, W. H.,
    ARIMURA, A., REDDING, T. W., & SAITO, M.

Effect of actinomycin D on the inhibitory response of estrogen on LH release. *Endocrinology*, 1969, *85*, 290-299.

SEGAL, S. J., & JOHNSON, D. C.   Inductive influence of steroid hormones on the neural system: Ovulation controlling mechanisms. *Archives d'Anatomie Microscopique et de Morphologie Expérimentale*, 1959, *48*, 261-273.

SEIKI, K., MIYAMATA, M., YAMASHITA, A., & KOTANI, M.   Further studies on the uptake of labelled progesterone by the hypothalamus and pituitary of rats. *Journal of Endocrinology*, 1969, *43*, 129-130.

SHIMADA, H., & GORBMAN, A.   Long lasting changes in RNA synthesis in the forebrains of female rats treated with testosterone soon after birth. *Biochemical and Biophysical Research Communications*, 1970, *38*, 423-430.

SHYAMALA, G., & GORSKI, J.   Estrogen receptors in the rat uterus: Studies on the interaction of cytosol and nuclear binding sites. *Journal of Biological Chemistry*, 1969, *244*, 1097-1103.

SLUSHER, M. A.   Effects of cortisol implants in the brainstem and ventral hippocampus on diurnal corticosterone levels. *Experimental Brain Research*, 1966, *1*, 184-194.

SLUSHER, M. A., & HYDE, J. E.   Influence of limbic system and related structures on the pituitary-adrenal axis.   In E. Bajusz (Ed.) *Physiology and Pathology of Adaptation Mechanisms. Modern Trends in Physiological Sciences,* Volume XXVII, New York: Pergamon Press, 1969. Pp. 146-170.

SMELIK, P. G.   Relation between blood level of corticoids and their inhibition effects on the hypophyseal stress response. *Proceedings of the Society for Experimental Biology and Medicine*, 1963, *113*, 616-619.

STEINER, F. A., RUF, K., & AKERT, E.   Steroid-sensitive neurones in rat brain: Anatomical localization and responses to neurohumors and ACTH. *Brain Research*, 1969, *12*, 74-85.

STERN, J. M., & EISENFELD, A. J.   Androgen accumulation and binding to macromolecules in seminal vesicles: Inhibition by cyproterone. *Science*, 1969, *166*, 233-235.

STUMPF, W. E. Estradiol-concentrating neurons:
    Topography in the hypothalamus by dry mount
    autoradiography. *Science*, 1968, *162*, 1001-
    1003.
SWANECK, G. E., HIGHLAND, E., & EDELMAN, I. S.
    Stereospecific nuclear and cytosol aldosterone-
    binding proteins of various tissues. *Nephron*,
    1969, *6*, 297-316.
SZEGO, C. M., & DAVIS, J. S. Adenosine
    3'5'-monophosphate in rat uterus: Acute
    elevation by estrogen. *Proceedings of the
    National Academy of Sciences*, U.S.A., 1967,
    58, 1711-1718.
TINDAL, J. S., KNAGGS, G. S., & TURVEY, A. Central
    nervous control of prolactin secretion in
    the rabbit: Effect of local oestrogen implants
    in the amygdaloid complex. *Journal of Endo-
    crinology*, 1967, *37*, 279-287.
UNHJEM, O. Binding of androgen to components of
    rat ventral prostate nuclei *in vitro*. *Acta
    Endocrinologica* (Kbh.), 1970, *63*, 69-78.
VELASCO, M. E., & TALEISNIK, S. Release of
    gonadotrophins induced by amygdaloid stimula-
    tion in the rat. *Endocrinology*, 1969, *84*,
    132-139.
VERNIKOS-DANELLIS, J. The regulation of the synthe-
    sis and release of ACTH. *Vitamins and Hor-
    mones*, 1965, *23*, 97-152.
WAGNER, J. W., ERWIN, W., & CRITCHLOW, V. Androgen
    sterilization produced by intracerebral
    implants of testosterone in neonatal female
    rats. *Endocrinology*, 1966, *79*, 1135-1142.
WEISS, J. M., MCEWEN, B. S., SILVA, M. T., &
    KALKUT, M. Pituitary-adrenal alterations and
    fear responding. *American Journal of
    Physiology*, 1970, *218*, 864-868.
WHALEN, R. E. Differentiation of the neural
    mechanisms which control gonadotrophin secre-
    tion and sexual behavior. In M. Diamond (Ed.),
    Reproduction and Sexual Behavior. Bloomington
    Indiana: Indiana University Press, 1968.
    Pp. 303-340.
DE WIED, D., & WEIJNEN, J. (Eds.) *The Pituitary-
    Adrenal Axis and the Nervous System. Progress
    in Brain Research*, 1970, in press.

WILLIAMS-ASHMAN, H. G. New facets of the bio-
    chemistry of steroid hormone action. *Cancer
    Research*, 1965, *25*, 1096-1120.
WOODBURY, D. M. Relation between the adrenal
    cortex and the central nervous system.
    Pharmacological Review, 1958, *10*, 275-357.
ZIGMOND, R. E., & MCEWEN, B. S. Selective retention
    of estradiol by cell nuclei in specific brain
    regions of the ovariectomized rat. *Journal of
    Neurochemistry*, 1970, in press.
ZIMMERMANN, E., & CRITCHLOW, V. Suppression of
    pituitary-adrenal function with physiological
    plasma levels of corticosterone. *Neuroendo-
    crinology*, 1969, *5*, 183-192.

BIOCHEMISTRY OF MENTAL DISORDERS

SOME CURRENT BIOCHEMICAL THEORIES
CONCERNING SCHIZOPHRENIA

Herman C. B. Denber

Manhattan State Hospital

Wards Island, New York

INTRODUCTION

Any rational approach to understanding the
etiology of schizophrenia must take the form of an
integrated overview in the fields of biology,
genetics, biochemistry and psychiatry. The human
being lives in a social field where the major
sensory inputs impinge on the auditory, ocular and
olfactory systems. Their transduction into electrical and biochemical events may well serve as the
substrate for awareness, and one can assume that
the presence of a DNA mediated defect within the
general body economy, particularly the brain with
its neurons related "in series", (Teller & Denber,
1968), can result in distortions of the individual's perception of self, his position in time and
space and his personal relationships. Internally
generated thoughts and memories may precipitate
psychologic phenomena, but their relationship
to this problem is completely unknown. As Fuller
and Thompson (1960, p. 283) point out, "The organic
basis for schizophrenia may be a minor disturbance
in terms of overall metabolism, although of critical importance for behavior". History has already
shown the uselessness of unitary approaches concen-
trating uniquely on the biologic, the psychodynamic
or sociologic aspects. A fuller and complete
comprehension of the schizophrenia problem will

171

only evolve through an integration of the biological substrate with the psychological field.

It would perhaps not be entirely appropriate here to discuss whether schizophrenia is a disease, a diagnosis "that leaves much to be desired" (Grumet, 1969), or even whether mental illness exists at all. The dilemma is best posed by the antithesis between Bellak's definition (1958, pp. 1-63) "Schizophrenia or dementia praecox is a psychiatric syndrome not a single disease. The somewhat variable symptoms generally associated with this diagnostic label must be understood as the final common path of a number of conditions which may lead to and manifest themselves in a severe disturbance of the ego . . ." ("Ego Disintegration", Fenichel, 1945, p. 416), and our own (Teller & Denber, 1968) "Schizophrenia is viewed as a cyclical behavioral disorder due to a defective enzyme in the synaptic membrane based on an abnormal protein structure that is metabolically active and transmitted genetically". Some of these problems have been reviewed by Lehmann (1967, pp. 593-598, 621-648) and Weiner (1967, pp. 603-621). For this paper the biological definition above is coupled with a psychological description, "schizophrenia in its typical form consists in a slow steady deterioration of the entire personality, usually showing itself at the period of adolescence" (Henderson, Gillespie & Batchelor, 1956, p. 300). The disorder probably results from an interaction between the individual as a biological entity and the environment as a psychological substratum. We have no well founded evidence at present to indicate the degree to which each contributes to the final breakdown. Since these interactions theoretically have n possibilities, all possible variations of the classical disease may be seen and may have been the basis for semantic problems presently marking consideration of schizophrenia.

It would seem appropriate in this review on the etiology of schizophrenia briefly to discuss conceptual problems raised by widely discordant ideas concerning etiology. If the truth is a unitary concept, then several different theoretical

possibilities should be susceptible to experimental
verification. This is not the case, and each new
hypothesis goes through the cycle of: 1. report;
2. sceptical review; 3. efforts at confirmation;
4. impossibility to reduplicate the original
findings; and 5. continued work by the original
authors on the supposition that errors were
committed by others (but not by themselves). One
must then wonder if the scientific experiment
demonstrates the truth more by chance than intent.
May it not be frequently an external measure of
internal aspirations which are acted out through
experiments (Denber, 1960, p. 321-334; 1969, 1970)?
Otherwise, why would there be such obsessive support of apparently invalid, and at times untenable
hypotheses? It is in psychiatry primarily that
such extraordinary problems have occurred, for we
deal more with the unknown than with what is known.

The psychologic aspects of schizophrenia will
not be considered here for this would lengthen the
review without really bringing a solution any
closer. Efforts at uniting both approaches are
still somewhat premature, although this will be
necessary in the future.

CONCERNING A GENETIC COMPONENT

One must be able to demonstrate a genetic basis
if schizophrenia is indeed a biochemical disorder.
This has proven to be a formidable obstacle, but
the twin studies method has been useful in elucidating some of the problems. Different interpretations of similar data and different results with
similar techniques but different patient samples
may possibly have resulted from unconscious bias
in designing the experimental protocols.

Ranier (1969, pp. 303-321) reviewed the
problem, discussing the Kallman and Slater studies,
and pointed out that Kallman believed, "the mode
of manifestation depended on the result of the
individual interplay among genetic, constitutional
and environmental factors". Rosenthal (1961) discussed the specific problems of sampling and

diagnosis, and concluded after a critical analysis
that heredity did not account for as much of the
variance "with respect to what is called schizophrenia" as some have previously indicated.
Kringlen (1969, pp. 27-39) on the basis of his
study in Norway, concluded that the more accurate
the sampling, the lower the concordance figures,
but they supported a genetic factor in schizophrenia; its role did not appear as great as had
been assumed (Book, 1960, pp. 23-36; Pollin, Allen,
Hoffer, Stanenau & Harubec, 1969).

Inouye (1961, pp. 524-530) found a highly
significant concordance in monozygotic twins (60%)
as opposed to 12% for dizygotic twins using data
from a Japanese population. Heston (1970) found
that children born of schizophrenic mothers and
permanently separated from them showed a far
greater incidence of schizophrenia when compared
with controls than could be accounted for on other
than a genetic basis. Stabenau and Pollin (1969,
pp. 336-351) were unable to relate a number of
biological variables to the schizophrenic twin in
their study of 16 pairs of monozygotic twins discordant for schizophrenia. Jackson (1960, pp.
37-87) has argued that the twin studies have not
been controlled for non-genetic factors, i.e., the
genetic factor is minimal and the environmental
factor maximal.

Bleuler (1968, pp. 3-12) on the basis of his
study of 208 schizophrenics over a 23 year period
held against the genetic basis of schizophrenia.
His final formulation was psychodynamic and he
denied a biological basis for the disorder. Brief
descriptions of his case material and therapeutic
attempts suggest caution and reserve regarding
interpretation of the data.

The literature is generally in accord that the
biological evidence favors a genetic component in
schizophrenia, but there is a serious dispute
concerning its quantitative and qualitative role.
Methodological, sampling, diagnostic and procedural
differences undoubtedly account for much of the
confusion. It would seem more reasonable to

assume that the *infinite* number of gene combinations possible in man since the original mutation,
can yield an equally *infinite* number of variations
which will produce a relatively *infinite* number of
different clinical patterns of the disease. The
most serious error has been to consider mental
illness as the analog of microbial infections which
follow a fairly similar anatomophysiopathological
process, and even here variability is noted based
on virulence and host resistance. It has also been
apparent that the fit of human genetic data does
not necessarily coincide with the classical Men-
delian crosses. It would be logical to assume as
Slater (1968, pp. 15-25) and Gottesman (1968,
pp. 37-48) that, "the genes resulting in schizophrenia are necessary, but they are not very often
sufficient for the occurrence of the disorder".

ON THE INDOLEAMINE HYPOTHESIS

Serotonin (5-HT), an indoleamine found in
plants and animal tissues, is derived from tryptophane by hydroxylation. It was demonstrated in
brain (Twarog & Page, 1953; Amin, Crawford &
Gaddum, 1954), while Page (1958) who reviewed the
serotonin data to that date found it had a wide
metabolic activity affecting principally the gastro-
intestinal and cardio-vascular systems.

It is uniformly distributed in the brain, but
localized in highest concentration in the hypothalamus and mid-brain (Twarog, 1958, pp. 158-175;
Freedman & Giarman, 1962; Costa, Jessa, Hirsch,
Kuntzman & Brodie, 1962; Eiduson, Geller, Yuwiler &
Eiduson, 1964, pp. 128-147), penetrates the blood-
brain barrier with great difficulty (Udenfriend,
Weissbach & Bogdanski, 1957, pp. 147-154) and only
after large dosages. 5-hydroxytryptophane decarboxylase shows a parallel distribution to 5-hydroxy-
tryptamine, and monamine oxidase which metabolizes
serotonin to 5-hydroxyindoleacetic acid is found
in high concentrations in the hypothalamus. The
exact subcellular locus of this metabolic activity
is uncertain (Sharman, 1965), but appears to be in
the particulate fraction (Freedman & Giarman, 1962).

A defect in brain serotonin metabolism was
first suggested as being possibly related to schizophrenia by Wooley and Shaw (1954), who reasoned
that compounds producing a schizophrenia-like
syndrome in humans (lysergic acid diethylamide,
harmine and yohimbine) were actually serotonin
anti-metabolites (Wooley & Campbell, 1962). Since
they were structural analogues to serotonin, inter-
fered with its function and produced schizophrenic-
like symptoms, it was reasoned that the human
disorder might be due to an enzymatic disturbance
which did not allow normal production and/or usage
of serotonin; a cerebral serotonin deficiency
(Wooley, 1958, pp. 176-189). However, reserpine
produces a sharp fall in central serotonin levels,
and was at one time extensively employed as a major
tranquillizer. The converse, a marked increase in
brain serotonin could be produced by prior administration of tryptophane which gave rise to states
resembling a schizophrenic-like syndrome. Lysergic
acid diethylamide can also increase brain serotonin
(Freedman & Giarman, 1962), even at doses of
130 µg/kg (Aghajanian & Freedman, 1968, pp. 1185-
1193). The same increase in brain serotonin can
be produced by prior administration of iproniazid
followed by serotonin, and similarly, lysergic
acid diethylamide-like effects can be elicited in
rabbits given iproniazid followed by reserpine.
Here serotonin levels are about the same as controls although the behavioral picture is analogous
to that produced by lysergic acid diethylamide
(Shore & Brodie, 1957).

But, since Brom-lysergic acid diethylamide
was a potent serotonin antagonist (Cerletti &
Rothlin, 1955), without marked behavioral effects
(Page, 1957, p. 179), the entire serotonin-mental
illness relationship was questioned (Kety, 1959).
In addition, patients with carcinoid tumors secreting large amounts of circulating serotonin were not
particularly prone to develop psychotic behavior,
although it was claimed that their central serotonin levels were not abnormal (Udenfriend, 1957,
p. 156).

The logical extension of this early work was
a search for related indole compounds known to
produce disorders of thought or feeling. Tryptamine, dimethyltryptamine, 6-hydroxyskatol and
bufotenine would be potentially toxic metabolites
of tryptophane if some defect in enzymatic transformation existed in the schizophrenic brain.
Some of the earlier literature was reviewed by
Denber (1958c, pp. 27-35).

Kemali and Buscaino (1958, pp. 219-222) noted
a qualitatively altered metabolism of indole
substances, finding tryptamines (other than
serotonin), oxyindoles, skatole and other indole
compounds reacting mainly with Ehrlich's Reagent.
Chromatography of schizophrenic urine revealed
five spots not present in normal or neurotic controls. Sohler and Noval (1969, pp. 669-677) were
unable to show any relationship between 6-skatoxyl-
sulfate in schizophrenics, and concluded that 6-
hydroxylation did not appear to be different in
schizophrenic patients from normals. Huszak and
Durko (1961, pp. 674-676) found that 5-hydroxy-
indolacetic acid excretion in schizophrenics
showed a greater fluctuation than normals, but a
significant difference from controls could not be
established (Feldstein, Dibner & Hoagland, 1958,
pp. 204-218; Feldstein, 1962). Szara and Rockland
(1961, pp. 670-673) reported that the dimethyl and
diethyl derivatives of tryptamine were psychotomimetic, with a significant difference existing
between excretion patterns of 6-hydroxydiethyl-
tryptamine in schizophrenic and normal subjects.

Fischer, Poch and Udabe (1964, pp. 408-421)
extensively reviewed the chemistry and metabolism
of indolamine compounds, and Sireix and Marini
(1969) reported an increased urinary excretion of
bufotenine-like substances in acute schizophrenia.
Bonhour, Fischer and Melgar (1967) on the basis of
their clinical and laboratory studies with bufotenine in humans and animals proposed that "the
transformation of serotonin to bufotenine by N-
dimethyltransferase (Axelrod, 1961) could represent
the cause of the principal symptoms of schizophrenia" (Saavedra & Udabe, 1970). Tanimukai,

Ginther, Spaide and Himwich (1967) associated
exacerbation of psychotic behavior with the
presence of free bufotenine. As interesting as
this may be, there is much doubt regarding the
methodology and results (Hollister, 1968, pp. 114-
116), not to mention the validity of equating the
bufotenine-induced state to schizophrenia (Denber,
1958c, pp. 27-35; Faurbye, 1968).

Since methylation was the step which theoretically converted serotonin to bufotenine and Axelrod (1961) provided evidence for a mammalian
N-methyltransferase (rabbit lung), confirmed in
humans by Mandell (1970, personal communication),
it was logical to load schizophrenics with excess
methyl donor substances. Pollin, Cardin and Kety
(1961) observed "marked behavioral changes with
L-methionine loading in 4 of 9 patients receiving
iproniazid", and Berlet, Matsumoto, Pscheidt,
Spaide, Bull and Himwich (1965) made similar observations on chronic schizophrenic patients. However, prolonged administration of tryptophane with
methionine but without an inhibitor of monamine
oxidase did not produce these changes. They suggested that methionine combined with an inhibitor
of monamine oxidase caused a release of tryptophane
and an accumulation of tryptamine which possibly
led to the formation of methylated derivates which
ostensibly were psychotomimetic. Carrying these
observations further, Tanimukai, Ginther, Spaide,
Bueno and Himwich (1968, pp. 6-15) treated 4
schizophrenic patients with L-cysteine and found
bufotenine spots in the urinary chromatograms of
2 patients in both the free and conjugated amine
fractions of a few urine samples after inhibition
of monamine oxidase. Himwich (1970, personal
communication) studied 6 normal and 2 schizophrenic
patients treated with tranylcypromine and cysteine.
The schizophrenic symptoms worsened, and he was
able to identify bufotenine, N,N-dimethyltrypta-
mine and 5-methoxy N,N-dimethyltryptamine.
Himwich (1969, pp. 91-105) and his group have thus
been lead to postulate that "the psychotomimetic
substance related to N,N-dimethyltryptamine was
formed in the body, the methyl groups coming from
methionine and the indole structure from trypto-

phane" (Brune & Himwich, 1962). It is interesting
here to record that methionine sulfoximine, an
anti-metabolite of methionine, retards certain
developmental processes of chick embryo (Sedlacek
& Schade, 1969).

Mandell and Spooner (1969, pp. 496-507) have
concluded that the effects of monamine oxidase-
indoleamine acid loading treatment in man, may be
due to a shunting of the metabolism through relatively minor pathways resulting in the production
of significant amounts of N,N-dimethylated
indoleamines such as bufotenine or dimethyltryptamine.

Tangential support for the indoleamine
hypothesis has come from Frohman, Warner, Barry
and Arthur (1969), who found that alpha-2-globulin
isolated from schizophrenic plasma increases
uptake of tryptophane and 5-hydroxytryptophane by
cells.

ON CATECHOLAMINES AND SCHIZOPHRENIA

Hoffer, Osmond and Smythies (1954) proposed
that adrenochrome and adrenolutin, oxidation
products of epinephrine, had psychotomimetic
properties (Hoffer, 1957, pp. 181-190; 1958,
pp. 127-140). The original idea proposed by
Harley-Mason to Osmond and Smythies (1952) suggested that mescaline-like compounds were formed
from catecholamines by abnormal transmethylation.
Subsequently, Mattok, Wilson and Hoffer (1967)
claimed that dopamine was synthesized normally in
schizophrenia but was metabolized to give "abnor-
mally high concentrations of noradrenaline and
adrenaline". This has not been confirmed (Faurbye,
1968). Hoffer (1967, pp. 435-455) pursuing the
idea further reasoned that feeding large amounts
of methyl acceptors and decreasing transmethylation
would be therapeutic in schizophrenic patients.
This work has never really been confirmed and is
at present under intensive study in Canada (Ban,
1969).

Methylation of dopamine could yield 3, 4-dimethoxyphenylethylamine, closely related to mescaline (2, 3, 4-trimethoxyphenylethylamine), and further research was necessary when Friedhoff and Van Winkle (1962) reported the presence of 3, 4-dimethoxyphenylethylamine in the urine of schizophrenic patients. They were able to show conversion of dopamine to 3, 4-dimethoxyphenyl-acetic acid (Friedhoff & Van Winkle, 1963) using liver biopsy material from schizophrenic patients as an enzyme source. They considered 3, 4-dimethoxyphenylethylamine as having a marked effect on the central nervous system of animals (Friedhoff & Van Winkle, 1966, pp. 277-282). This compound was identified by mass spectrometry (Greveling & Daly, 1967), although the compound was "only a minor constituent of the pink spot and the latter consisted of at least 7 different compounds". Faurbye and Pind (1967, pp. 221-223) could not confirm the dimethoxyphenylethylamine findings and believed it possible that the increased turnover of catecholamines due to phenothiazines may have produced the so-called abnormality. Nishimura and Gjessing (1967, pp. 225-227) could not detect the compound in the urine of a "typical periodic catatonia case".

However, 3, 4-dimethoxyphenylethylamine is ineffective in man (Hollister & Friedhoff, 1966) and Wagner, Cirillo, Meisinger, Ormond, Kuehl and Brink (1966) could not confirm the original findings. The presence of the now famous "pink spot" (Friedhoff & Van Winkle, 1962) was questioned, and its chromatographic demonstration seriously faulted by Boulton and Felton (1966); Perry Hensen, MacDougall and Schwarz (1966); Bell and Somerville (1966); and Perry, Hensen and MacDougall (1967). Kuehl, Ormond and Vandenheuvel (1966) concluded that either the excretion of 3, 4-dimethoxyphenyle-thylamine was "not characteristic of schizophrenia, or the amount of 3, 4-dimethoxyphenylacetic acid present in the urine was not a true reflection of the amount of 3, 4-dimethoxyphenylethylamine present". Friedhoff (1967, pp. 27-34) after reviewing his work has reserved judgment about the "adequacy of the demethylating mechanism in schizophrenia".

ON A SERUM FACTOR

Perhaps some of the most interesting work in the biochemical area has come from the studies of Frohman, Luby, Tourney, Beckett and Gottlieb (1960) and Frohman, Latham, Beckett and Gottlieb (1967, pp. 241-255), who described a "factor" found in the serum of schizophrenic patients which significantly affected metabolism as measured by the lactate/pyruvate ratios in chicken erythrocytes. It was postulated that a protein present in much higher concentrations in schizophrenic patients affected phosphate metabolism and cellular oxidation. This was considered to be an alpha-2-globulin and probably acted on the cell membrane. More recently Frohman, Warner, Barry and Arthur (1969) and Frohman, Warner, Yoon, Arthur and Gottlieb (1969) have shown that the alpha-2-globulin in question increases uptake of amino acids in cells particularly glutamic acid, tryptophane and 5-hydroxytryptophane and would appear to be related to an active transport system. Studies with patient sera using biohpysical techniques indicated that the abnormal protein has a large proportion of alpha helix as opposed to beta conformation in controls (Frohman, Harmison & Gottlieb, 1970).

These studies have been supported by findings of Bergen (1967, pp. 257-267) and Pennell, Pawlus, Saravis and Scrimshaw (1967, pp. 269-282). However, Durell and Ryan (1967, pp. 283-302; 1969, pp. 175-189) have found contrary evidence. Chicken erythrocytes did not exhibit aerobic glycolysis but could be stimulated by damaging the cell membrane or by adding inhibitors of oxidative metabolism. All human sera possess a heterogenetic antibody which in presence of complement can react with plasma membrane antigen leading to its damage, stimulating glycolysis and resulting in secondary hemolysis. Human plasma thus affects chicken erythrocyte metabolism through the action of a complement-linked antibody coupled with a

heterogenetic antigen of chicken erythrocytes
which alters membrane permeability (Ryan, Brown &
Durell, 1966). Mangoni, Balazs and Coppen (1963)
could find no difference in the lactate/pyruvate
ratios between 7 chronic male schizophrenic
patients and 10 controls. Perhaps their use of
chronic patients was responsible, for these
results may be attributed to sample selection
(Frohman *et al.*, 1967, pp. 241-255).

ON THE IMMUNOLOGY OF SCHIZOPHRENIA

Heath and Krupp (1967a, 1967b, pp. 313-342;
1968) have postulated that schizophrenia is an
immunologic disorder. A gamma G immunoglobulin
fraction of sera from schizophrenic patients was
reported to alter brain function by combining with
antigenic sites in the septal region. This
fraction was capable of inducing psychosis and
could be found in acute schizophrenic sera. As
remission took place it was more difficult to
demonstrate. The physiologic and behavioral
changes induced by the gamma G immunoglobulin
were related to taraxein. Heath and Krupp (1967a,
1967b, pp. 313-342) believe that taraxein may be
antibody, and in combining with antigenic sites
in the septal region of schizophrenic patients,
produces symptoms of the disease.

AN OVERVIEW OF CURRENT THEORIES

There is no question that schizophrenia in
the classical sense does not occur if the mutated
gene or genes are lacking. It would also appear
highly probable that unless there is an environmental overload, the biochemical mechanism that
probably subserves "normal behavior" will continue
to function, even if inadequately. Given the
concordance of defective genetic instructions and
abnormal environment, the risk of psychotic breakdown becomes great. What could this "breakdown"
of schizophrenia consist of in a biochemical sense?

The catecholamine and related indoleamine
hypotheses, much of it based on the loading experiments, suggest an abnormal metabolite, something
Buscaino (1953) has studied for years. The
general results indicate that some deviation from
"normal" metabolism takes place under experimental
stress conditions and that the same defect could
conceivably be operating in acute schizophrenia.
Yet, are these studies relevant to the endogenous
physiologic conditions?

Mandell and Spooner (1968, 1969, pp. 496-507)
have indicated that the logic of this general
approach resides in "selectively increasing the
substrate available", resulting in an increase of
end product which in turn exaggerates certain
human behavioral phenomena. Inundating the body
with enzyme inhibitors, amino acid overloads or
precursor substances, or any combination, is a
very long way from reproducing the endogenous
schizophrenic physiology. If a breakdown in
metabolism under abnormal experimental conditions
leads to the appearance of "toxic" metabolites,
whose psychotomimetic properties are not always
assured (i.e., bufotenine) does this indicate a
clear causal relationship to schizophrenia? It
would seem more appropriate to reason that, for
instance, with blockade of the oxidative deamination pathway, the body economy calls in secondary
metabolic systems. These shunt mechanisms may
produce psychotomimetic metabolites (dimethyltryptamine), but are these the cause of schizophrenic symptoms? The evidence, for instance, is
hardly conducive to holding that the appearance of
dimethyltryptamine or other related compounds
makes this etiologic for schizophrenia, even if
their presence has been reported in schizophrenic
urine under experimental conditions and not in
normals. It would seem more likely that we are
dealing with an end result, where the primary
process is still unknown. These studies suggest
that a metabolic defect does exist in schizophrenia,
but then again all of the systems are defective in
this state, including the fingerprints (Mellor,
1967).

ON THE BIOLOGICAL APPROACH

After extensive accumulation of human
clinical, electroencephalographic and biochemical
data (Denber, Merlis & Hunter, 1953, p. 30;
Denber & Merlis, 1954, 1956, pp. 141-144; Denber,
1958a, pp. 120-126, 1958b, 1958c, pp. 27-35;
Denber, Teller Rajotte & Kauffman, 1962) it became
apparent that the mescaline-induced state could
be used as a model for acute schizophrenia. Our
data indicated this analogy was valid and, furthermore, that effective anti-psychotic drugs would
inhibit the behavioral and biochemical changes
produced by mescaline. It would be pointless I
believe, to argue about the purported nosological
or other differences between the drug-induced and
endogenous states, for this hardly advances the
understanding of either condition. Hollister
(1968) holds the concept of a "model psychosis to
be open to much challenge", but another point of
view has been expressed elsewhere (Denber, 1958c,
pp. 27-35). The development of a model is essential
even though imperfect, for otherwise subsequent
research becomes a succession of random choices.

It was possible to show that a close relationship existed between effective anti-psychotic
drugs and their inhibition of the mescaline-induced
fall in total serum amino acid (ninhydrin positive
substances) in human subjects when the anti-
psychotic drugs were given before mescaline
(Denber, 1961; Denber, Teller & Kauffman, 1963).
If given one hour after mescaline, the fall in
ninhydrin positive substances continued without
returning to base-line levels before 48 hours.
We speculated that the anti-psychotic drug was in
some way protecting the cell, perhaps by direct
membranal action and preventing the entrance of
mescaline. Seeman's study (1966) of phenothiazine
effects on red cell membranes seemed to support
this hypothesis. Subsequently David N. Teller and
I began a series of *in vitro* and *in vivo* animal
investigations using the techniques of modern
biology to extend these human observations (Denber
& Teller, 1963; Denber, Teller & Kauffman, 1963;
Teller, Levine, Wackman & Denber, 1967; Teller &

Denber, 1968; Denber & Teller, 1968a, 1968b;
Denber & Teller, 1969; Denber & Teller, 1970).
It was believed essential to determine a subcellular locus of action for psychotomimetic and
psychotropic drugs, and study the drug-site
interaction before reasonable hypotheses could be
drawn regarding human behavioral abnormalities.
If the mescaline-induced model concept was true,
then answers to the following questions would be
necessary (Denber, 1967): 1. What were the
changes in tissue and organ localization of
mescaline-8-^{14}C with time? 2. What was the *in
vivo* rat brain cortical subcellular localization
of mescaline-8-^{14}C at various time periods ranging
between 3.45 minutes to 120 minutes? 3. What
was the subcellular localization of ^{3}H-Chlorproma-
zine? 4. What were the effects of prior administration of various psychotropic drugs on uptake
and localization of mescaline-8-^{14}C?

The materials and methods used in these
studies have been extensively documented (Denber,
1967). Briefly stated, young adult female rats
were injected intravenously with mescaline-8-^{14}C;
intramuscularly with either ^{3}H-Chlorpromazine, or
non-radioactive thioperazine, diethazine, amobarbital sodium or amphetamine. The samples were
homogenized and radioactive determinations done
in a Mark 1 Scintillation Spectrometer (Nuclear
Chicago).

We found that mescaline was maximally concentrated in the kidneys, lungs and liver, fifteen
minutes after injection and decreased slowly so
that less than 1% of the injected dose remained at
120 minutes. The cerebral cortex had the largest
concentration in the brain and this appeared to
be bilaterally symmetrical.

Radioactivity in the right frontal lobe,
thalamus and basal ganglia, mid-brain and pons,
cerebellum, medulla and spinal cord was compared
between animals that had received mescaline-8-^{14}C
alone and were sacrificed at 30 minutes, and to
those animals that received different blocking
agents sacrificed at 30 minutes after mescaline as

well.   Thioperazine decreased mescaline content
of brain sections by one-third.   Amobarbital
sodium decreased the concentration in brain and
blood.   Amphetamine caused an 80% decrease in
brain mescaline-8-^{14}C.   Diethazine increased the
amount of mescaline that remained in the blood
and doubled the amount in the brain.

Thioperazine had no effect on the distribution
of radioactivity between different areas of the
brain.   Amorbarbital increased the radioactivity
in the thalamus, basal .ganglia, cerebellum, medulla
and spinal cord.   Diethazine decreased the activity
in the thalamus, basal ganglia, mid-brain and pons.
Amphetamine markedly reduced the proportion of
mescaline between cortex and sub-cortical areas.

In most cases, 45 minutes after injection,
the mescaline content of the subcellular fraction
was proportional to dosage, although this was not
always the case.   Radioactivity in the myelin-
microsomal-soluble supernatant fraction did not
increase until 15 minutes after injection, reached
a maximum at 30 minutes and declined at 120 minutes.
In contrast, the nerve ending particle fraction
showed a low concentration of the isotope at less
than 6 and 8 minutes and rose steeply at 45 minutes.
This was followed by an equally abrupt fall at 60
minutes with a slow flattened decline to 120
minutes.   Movement of radioactive mescaline to the
mitochondrial fraction was slow, for at less than
5 minutes there was no detectable isotope.   In this
organelle, the maximal concentration was found at
45 minutes.   The purified microsomal pellet showed
the same variations over time, with a very low
total uptake.

However, in comparison to mescaline, there was
at least a ten-fold greater uptake and retention
of ^{3}H-chlorpromazine in the brain sections after
a pharmacologically equivalent dose.   In addition,
the phenothiazine's uptake by the cell particles
was the inverse of mescaline, for the highest
radioactive chlorpromazine counts were found in
the mitochondria, decreasing in the nerve ending

particles, and even less in the myelin-microsomal-soluble supernatant.

Prior administration of diethazine increased by two-fold the amount of radioactive mescaline found in the brain homogenate. The mescaline-8-^{14}C concentration in the myelin-microsomal-soluble supernatant was not influenced by prior drug injection. Chlorpromazine increased the nerve ending particle content of mescaline by a factor of 2.6 when compared to controls; amobarbital sodium by 2; thioperazine by 1.25; while diethazine was without effect. There was a three-fold increase of mescaline in the mitochondrial fraction after prior administration of amobarbital sodium but other drugs were without effect.

A second set of experiments was carried out in an effort to confirm the subcellular localization using groups of three female Wister white rats with an average weight of 255 grams and 75 days old who received mescaline-8-^{14}C HCL (Mallinckrodt Nuclear, specific activity = 21 μc/mg mescaline) intraperitoneally 20, 40 and 60 minutes before sacrifice by cervical dislocation. The average dose injected for animals sacrificed at 20 minutes was 1.59 mg/100g; for the 40 minute group, 1.12 mg/100g; and for the 60 minute interval, 1.01 mg/100g. An additional group of three animals was studied at 60 minutes, making a total of six rats for that time. The experimental procedures were the same as previously used. Material from the subcellular fractions of mescaline-treated animals and a non-treated control were embedded for electron microscope study. Gross and sub-cellular localization of mescaline was determined by scintillation spectrometry in a Mark 1 Nuclear Chicago Spectrometer.

The gross central nervous system uptake of mescaline-8-^{14}C was 0.018%, 0.03% and 0.032% of the injected dose at 20, 40 and 60 minutes, corrected for body weight variations and dosage, with maximum localization in the cerebral cortical fraction.

The percentage of total gradient radioactivity
during the three experimental periods for the
mitochondrial fraction was 3.2%, 7.7% and 11.1%,
with 18.0% of the total gradient protein; for the
nerve ending particle fraction it was 12.4%,
23.4% and 12.2%, with 36.5% of the protein; and
for the myelin supernatant fraction it was 73.5%,
62.1% and 56.5%, with 24.5% of the protein. Total
radioactivity and protein recoveries were 100 ±
2.86, and 100 ± 1.386, respectively, throughout
the separation procedure.

The total mescaline content (nanograms)
showed a low, small steady arithmetic rise for the
mitochondria; a decrease in the myelin fraction
after 20 minutes; and a maximum at 40 minutes in
the nerve ending fraction.

Electron micrographs from the mescaline-
treated animals showed empty synaptic vesicles in
large quantities trapped within myelin figures of
the myelin supernatant. There were occasional
mitochondria in the nerve ending particle layer.
The synaptosomes in the nerve ending particle
fraction showed electron-dense synaptic vesicles
as compared to the pale structure of the control.
Some of the mitochondria appeared abnormal in
structure. The mitochondrial fractions from the
mescaline-treated animals contained poorly pre-
served organelles, resembling those seen after
treatment with thyroxine (Bourne & Tewari, 1964,
pp. 377-421). There were very rare electron-dense
synaptosomes and myelin figures in this layer
(Denber & Teller, 1969).

ON THE BIOLOGICAL APPROACH - A DISCUSSION

The validity of a model depends entirely on
the principal assumptions. We have used the
mescaline-induced state as the experimental model
for the acute schizophrenic psychosis. The drug-
induced abnormal state of feeling and/or thinking
takes place in complete awareness with absolute
recall of the entire period, negating any concept
of a mescaline toxic psychosis.

A great deal of attention has been given to the high concentration of mescaline in the liver (Block, Block & Patzig, 1952), and this has pre-supposed conversion of mescaline to a "toxic metabolite". By analogy a similar mechanism was operative in schizophrenia. It should be noted that the greatest concentration of mescaline was found in those visceral organs with the highest vascular flow. Furthermore, the fact that the liver had 1.14% of the injected dose at 30 minutes and the brain cortex 0.058% did not support the hypothesis of a conversion to an active metabolite (Smythies, 1963, pp. 1-38), or a mescaline protein (Block, 1958, pp. 106-119). The maximal concentration of mescaline is reached at 30 minutes in all organs and begins to fall so that by 45-60 minutes there is only 0.026% of the injected dose in the brain cortex (Denber, 1967). If these hypotheses were correct, one would expect to find the isotope concentration in the brain rising as that in the liver was falling, and this was not the case. In addition, the microsomal concentration was low.

In vitro studies showed that mitochondria probably have a fixed number of binding sites which were rapidly saturated with mescaline and do not change even when additional amounts of the isotope were available in vitro.

The activity of subcellular fractions from brains of animals injected with mescaline-8-^{14}C indicates that mescaline concentration is maximal in the nerve ending particle fraction at 40-45 minutes. The peak human behavioral response is observed with mescaline between 30-60 minutes. At 120 minutes most of the drug has left the rat brain and the acute human behavioral changes usually have begun to recede even though some drug effects are still visible. Mescaline concentration in the nerve ending particle fraction in general was independent of dose and would appear to depend either upon the cell particle's own binding characteristics or on a time-dependent membrane transport system. The findings would suggest that there is an immediate compartmentalization of

mescaline as it penetrates into the neuropil, with
distribution initially in proportion to available
surface area, and secondarily to the relatively
available volume. Further passage of mescaline
at the membrane level in each cell compartment
may be facilitated by active transport. However,
present knowledge suggests only that uptake,
transport, binding and pharmacological effects are
a function of the sterochemistry of the molecule
in passive transport (Denber, 1967).

Certain phenothiazines (i.e. chlorpromazine,
thioperazine) are capable of either preventing or
overcoming the behavioral effects when given before
or after mescaline respectively, and their site of
action is considered to be membranal (Teller, 1964;
Seeman, 1966; Forrest, 1966, personal communication). The phenothiazine activity may strengthen
the membrane against osmotic and physical shock,
and may also incorporate electrostatic and charge
transfer properties into the membrane surface. If
this is the case for a compound that blocks
mescaline activity, then it is reasonable to assume
that the effect of mescaline at the subcellular
site is one of a reversible transitory physical
disruption of the membrane. We reasoned at that
time that under such circumstances synaptic
vesicles would be liberated and norepinephrine
would disappear from the synaptosomal fraction.
This was in fact true.

Several hypotheses were made in the course of
clinical-biochemical studies concerning the effects
of prior administration of psychotropic drugs on
the human behavioral changes induced by mescaline.
It was suggested that "the prior administration of
any effective psychotropic drug either protected
cellular processes against mescaline, inhibiting
the latter's entry or transformation, or else
speeded up its degradation and/or elimination"
(Denber, Teller, Rajotte & Kauffman, 1962). The
present data would support the first of these
suppositions. It was later stated (Denber, Teller
& Kauffman, 1963) that the psychotropic drugs by
altering membrane permeability might prevent both
the entrance of mescaline and its action on

cellular metabolism. The present experiments with
chlorpromazine and thioperazine show that mescaline does enter the cell but apparently does not
affect metabolism.

Chlorpromazine and thioperazine are powerful
phenothiazines that block the mescaline-induced
state, and in clinical treatment produce a gradual
regression of behavioral and ideational symptoms
of schizophrenia. It has been reported elsewhere
that while mescaline enters the brain of chlorpromazine pre-treated rats, the mescaline behavioral
effects do not appear in these animals (Denber &
Teller, 1968a). It was expected that prior
administration of chlorpromazine would inhibit
mescaline uptake into the subcellular fractions
but the amount of mescaline in the nerve ending
particles was almost three times the control. Thus,
the blocking action of chlorpromazine and thioperazine against the symptoms of mescaline cannot be
considered as being solely due to competition for
binding sites.

A possible explanation may be that phenothiazines can stabilize and expand cell membranes
(Seeman, 1966), creating additional binding sites
with retention of more mescaline. No mattter how
the psychotomimetic is held within the cell structures, the phenothiazines by their electronic
characteristics may be able to "reseal" the membrane even if mescaline does penetrate (Teller,
1964). Since, in the presence of chlorpromazine,
no symptoms developed due to mescaline, one can
infer that the membrane was not damaged.

The amount of mescaline that penetrates the
brain is minute, and at the subcellular level there
are probably no more than 200-250 molecules per
cell. The drug is already being excreted at 15
minutes in the rat, and is leaving the brain at a
time when acute behavioral symptoms begin to reach
a maximum. After 60 minutes, the amount of mescaline in the brain is below that capable of inducing
symptoms, and at 2 hours the amount is infinitesi-
mal, yet symptoms still persist. Thus, mescaline
has produced symptoms which were still present

after the drug was exreted, and this would be
consistent with the hypothesis that the symptoms
result from a reversible structural transitory
alteration of membranes through which the drug
has passed (most likely the synaptic membrane).

Observations on silver stained biopsy sections
from the brains of schizophrenic patients undergoing lobotomy are pertinent in this regard, for
they showed argyrophilic granules of the presynaptic endings to be enlarged and distorted.
This material was never reported due to a lack of
suitable control data, but in view of the present
biochemical findings they assume a new meaning
(Denber, 1952).

The evidence from these experiments supports
the hypothesis that the site of action of mescaline
is in the nerve ending. If extrapolated it would
place the schizophrenic disturbance in the synapse.
Whether the actual site is pre-, post-, or inter-
synaptic; whether the effect is upon catecholamine
storage within synaptic vesicles or the synaptic
vesicle membranes; or upon the release of catecholamines awaits further experimental investigations.

Experiments still in progress indicate that
following mescaline, the nerve ending fraction
loses most of its norepinephrine, with the major
portion rising to the upper layers of the gradient
tube above the myelin fraction (Teller, 1970,
personal communication). These results showing a
loss of norepinephrine from the synaptosomes of
the mescaline-treated rats may be relevant to the
finding that L-Dopa exacerbates schizophrenic
symptoms (Merlis, 1970, personal communication).
It would suggest that there is in effect in schizophrenia a neurohumoral transmitter leakage which
is constantly preventing repolarization of the
postsynaptic neuron. It is known, for instance,
that tricyclic antidepressants (i.e., Imipramine)
by preventing reuptake of norepinephrine, probably
exacerbate schizophrenic symptoms.

A genetic abnormality in the synaptic membrane structure rendering it susceptible to breakdown under an increased sensory input ("stress") represents the endogenous analog of our experimental model. Under such environmental conditions, the rate of synthesis of membrane protein would be changed, shifting an already precarious equilibrium into a "state of disorder". It would not be too difficult to conceive of a genetic structurally defective enzyme being incapable of turning over fast enough under an information overload so that even in presence of sufficient substrate, insufficient product was formed. If this be a membranal protein, there would be a continous leakage of transmitter with resultant symptoms (Teller & Denber, 1968), as would appear to be the case from our experimental findings.

The neuroleptic drugs may remedy this defect either by: 1. stabilizing the membrane, thus allowing some semblance of "order" until endogenous non-genetically defective nucleotide precursors could be assembled, or 2. decreasing the afferent sensory input (acoustic, olfactory or auditory) so that membrane resynthesis could keep pace with breakdown, or 3. by allowing both processes to operate simultaneously.

SUMMARY

Evidence from various sources detailed herein indicates that schizophrenia is a genetic disorder which requires an environmental source before the illness becomes acute. The exact role of each component has yet to be determined.

Biochemical studies clearly show that there are metabolic defects in schizophrenia with the formation of abnormal metabolites under stress conditions. Some hold the disease to be immunologic. The exact role of neurohumoral transmitters (i.e., norepinephrine) remains to be demonstrated.

Studies have been briefly described to show that the schizophrenic defect may be in the synapse.

REFERENCES

AGHAJANIAN, G. K., & FREEDMAN, D. X. Biochemical
    and morphological aspects of LSD pharmacology.
    In D. H. Efron (Ed.), *Psychopharmacology.*
    A Review of Progress 1957-1967. Washington,
    D. C.: Public Health Service Publication
    No. 1836, 1968.

AMIN, A. H., CRAWFORD, T. B. B., & GADDUM, H. J.
    The distribution of substance P and 5-hydroxy-
    tryptamine in the central nervous system of
    the dog. *Journal of Physiology,* 1954, *126,*
    596-618.

AXELROD, J. Enzymatic formation of psychotomimetic
    metabolites from normally occurring compounds.
    Science, 1961, *134,* 343.

BAN, T. A. Ongoing national collaborative studies
    in Canada: Niacin in the treatment of schizo-
    phrenia. *Psychopharmacology Bulletin,* 1969,
    5, 5-20.

BELL, C. E., & SOMERVILLE, A. R. Identity of the
    "pink spot". *Nature,* 1966, *211,* 1405-1406.

BELLAK, L. The schizophrenic syndrome. In
    L. Bellak (Ed.), *Schizophrenia: A Review of*
    the Syndrome. New York: Logos Press, 1968.

BERGEN J. R. Possible relationships of plasma
    factors to schizophrenia. In O. Walaas (Ed.),
    Molecular Basis of Some Aspects of Mental
    Activity, Volume II. London: Academic Press,
    1967.

BERLET, H. H., MATSUMOTO, K., PSCHEIDT, G. R.,
    SPAIDE, J., BULL, C., & HIMWICH, H. E.
    Biochemical correlates of behavior in schizo-
    phrenic patients. *Archives of General*
    Psychiatry, 1965, *13,* 521-531.

BLEULER, M. A 23-year longitudinal study of 208
    schizophrenics and impressions in regard to the
    nature of schizophrenia. In D. Rosenthal and
    S. S. Kety (Eds.), *The Transmission of Schizo-*
    phrenia. New York: Pergamon Press, 1968.

BLOCK, W. The mescaline psychosis. In M. Rinkel
    and H. C. B. Denber (Eds.), *Chemical Concepts*
    of Psychosis. New York: McDowell, Obolensky,
    1958.

BLOCK, W., BLOCK, K., & PATZIG, B. Zur physiologie
    des ^{14}C-radioaktiven mescalins im tierversuch.

II. Mitteilung. Verteilung der radioakti-
vitat in den organen in abhangigkeit von der
zeit. Hoppe-Seyler's *Zeitschrift für
Physiologische Chemie*, 1952, *290*, 230-236.

BONHOUR, A., FISCHER, E., & MELGAR, M. C. Estudios
psicofarmacologicos con bufotenina. *Revista
de Psiquiatria y Psicologia Medica*, 1967,
8, 123-143.

BOOK, J. A. Genetical aspects of schizophrenic
psychoses. In D. B. Jackson (Ed.), *The
Etiology of Schizophrenia*. New York: Basic
Books, 1960.

BOULTON, A. A., & FELTON, C. A. The "pink spot"
and schizophrenia. *Nature*, 1966, *211*, 1404-
1405.

BOURNE, G. H., & TEWARI, H. B. Mitochondria and
the Golgi complex. In G. H. Bourne (Ed.),
Cytology and Cell Physiology. (Third ed.)
New York: Academic Press, 1964.

BRUNE, G. E. G., & HIMWICH, H. E. Effects of
methionine loading on the behavior of schizophrenic patients. *Journal of Nervous and
Mental Disease*, 1962, *134*, 447-450.

BUSCAINO, V. M. Extraneural pathology in
schizophrenia. *Acta Neurologica* (Naples),
1953, *8*, 1-60.

CERLETTI, A., & ROTHLIN, E. Role of 5-hydroxy-
tryptamine in mental diseases and its
antagonism to lysergic acid derivatives.
Nature, 1955, *176*, 785-786.

COSTA, E., JESSA, G. L., HIRSCH, C., KUNTZMAN, R.,
& BRODIE, B. B. On current status of serotonin as a brain neurohormone and in action of
reserpine-like drugs. *Annals of the New York
Academy of Sciences*, 1962, *96*, 118-131.

DENBER, H. C. B. Altérations des synapses axo-
somatiques corticales chez l'homme, à la
suite de psychoses et de divers chocs
thérapeutiques. *Comptes Rendus Societe
Biologie*, 1952, *146*, 389.

DENBER, H. C. B., MERLIS, S., & HUNTER, W. The
action of mescaline on the clinical and brain
wave patterns of schizophrenic patients before
and after electroconvulsive treatment.
*Proceedings of the Third International E. E.
G. Congress*, 1953.

DENBER, H. C. B., & MERLIS, S. A note on some
    therapeutic implications of the mescaline-
    induced state. *Psychiatric Quarterly*, 1954,
    28, 635-640.
DENBER, H. C. B., & MERLIS, S. Studies on
    mescaline IV: Antagonism between mescaline
    and chlorpromazine. In N. S. Kline (Ed.),
    Psychopharmacology. Washington: A. A. A.
    S., 1956.
DENBER, H. C. B. Clinical considerations of the
    mescaline-induced state. In M. Rinkel and
    H. C. B. Denber (Eds.), *Chemical Concepts of
    Psychosis*. New York: McDowell, Obolensky,
    1958. (a)
DENBER, H. C. B. Studies on mescaline VIII:
    Psychodynamic observations. *American Journal
    of Psychiatry*, 1958, *115*, 239-244. (b)
DENBER, H. C. B. Drug-induced states resembling
    naturally occurring psychoses. In S.
    Garattini and V. Ghetti (Eds.), *Psychotropic
    Drugs*. Amsterdam: Elsevier, 1958. (c)
DENBER, H. C. B. Some psychodynamic considera-
    tions of the research worker in psychiatry.
    In G. J. Sarwer-Foner (Ed.), *The Dynamics
    of Psychiatric Drug Therapy*. Springfield,
    Illinois: Charles C. Thomas, 1960.
DENBER, H. C. B. Studies on mescaline XI: Bio-
    chemical findings during the mescaline-induced
    state with observations on the blocking
    action of different psychotropic drugs.
    Psychiatric Quarterly, 1961, *135*, 18-48.
DENBER, H. C. B., TELLER, D. N., RAJOTTE, P., &
    KAUFFMAN, D. Studies on mescaline XIII: The
    effect of prior administration of various
    psychotropic drugs on different biochemical
    parameters: A preliminary report. *Annals
    of the New York Academy of Sciences*, 1962, *96*,
    14-36.
DENBER, H. C. B., & TELLER, D. N. A biochemical
    genetic theory concerning the nature of
    schizophrenia. *Diseases of the Nervous
    System*, 1963, *24*, 1-8.
DENBER, H. C. B., TELLER, D. N., & KAUFFMAN, D.
    Studies on mescaline XIV: Comparative bio-
    chemical effects of different drugs. *Diseases
    of the Nervous System*, 1963, *24*, 302-303.

DENBER, H. C. B. Intracellular localization of
    psychotomimetic and psychotropic drugs.
    Doctoral Dissertation. Graduate School of
    Arts and Science, New York University, 1967.
DENBER, H. C. B., & TELLER, D. N. Studies on
    mescaline XVIII: Effect of phenothiazines,
    amphetamine and amobarbital sodium on uptake
    into rat brain and viscera. *Agressologie,*
    1968, *9,* 127-136. (a)
DENBER H. C. B., & TELLER, D. N. Studies on
    mescaline XIX: A new theory concerning the
    nature of schizophrenia. *Psychosomatics,*
    1968, *9,* 145-151. (b)
DENBER, H. C. B. People and Research. Paper pre-
    sented at the annual meeting of the American
    College of Neuropsychopharmacology. San
    Diego, California, 1969.
DENBER, H. C. B., & TELLER, D. N. Mescaline XXI:
    Subcellular localization in adult rats.
    The Pharmacologist, 1969, *2,* 291.
DENBER, H. C. B., & TELLER, D. N. Subcellular
    localization of mescaline at the synapse.
    Arzneimittel-Forsch, 1970, in press.
DENBER, H. C. B. Can psychopharmacology advance.
    Psychosomatics, 1970, *11,* 85-89.
DURELL, J., & RYAN, J. W. The immune lysis of
    chicken erythrocytes and its relationship to
    schizophrenia. In O. Walaas (Ed.), *Molecular
    Basis of Some Aspects of Mental Activity,*
    Volume II. London: Academic Press, 1967.
DURELL, J., & RYAN, J. W. Serum macromolecules
    in schizophrenia. Investigations of a factor
    altering chicken erythrocyte metabolism. In
    A. J. Mandell and M. P. Mandell (Eds.),
    Psychochemical Research in Man. New York:
    Academic Press, 1969.
EIDUSON, S., GELLER, E., YUWILER, A., & EIDUSON,
    B. T. *Biochemistry and Behavior.* Princeton,
    New Jersey: D. Van Nostrand, 1964.
FAURBYE, A., & PIND, K. The catecholamine metabo-
    lism in schizophrenia. In O. Walaas (Ed.),
    *Molecular Basis of Some Aspects of Mental
    Activity,* Volume II. London: Academic Press,
    1967.
FAURBYE, A. The role of amines in the etiology of
    schizophrenia. *Comprehensive Psychiatry,*

1968, 9, 155-177.

FELDSTEIN, A., DIBNER, I. M., & HOAGLAND, H. Two-
dimensional paper chromatography of urinary
indoles in normal subjects and chronic
schizophrenic patients. In M. Rinkel and
H. C. B. Denber (Eds.), *Chemical Concepts of
Psychosis*. New York: McDowell, Obolensky,
1958.

FELDSTEIN, A. Discussion: Exploration of the
central nervous system serotonin in humans.
Annals of the New York Academy of Sciences,
1962, *96*, 117.

FENICHEL, O. *The Psychoanalytic Theory of Neuro-
sis*. New York: W. W. Norton & Co., 1945.

FISCHER, E., POCH, G. F., & UDABE, R. U.
Psicofarmacologia. Buenos Aires: Lopez
Libreros Ed., 1964.

FREEDMAN, D. X., & GIARMAN, N. J. LSD-25 and the
status and level of brain serotonin. *Annals
of the New York Academy of Sciences*, 1962,
96, 98-106.

FRIEDHOFF, A. J., & VAN WINKLE, E. Isolation and
characterization of a compound from the urine
of schizophrenics. *Nature*, 1962, *194*, 897-898.

FRIEDHOFF, A. J., & VAN WINKLE, E. Conversion of
dopamine to 3, 4-dimethoxyphenylacetic acid
in schizophrenic patients. *Nature*, 1963,
199, 1271-1272.

FRIEDHOFF, A. J., & VAN WINKLE, E. A neurotropic
compound identified in urine of schizophrenia
patients. In P. Hoch and J. Zubin (Eds.),
Psychopathology of Schizophrenia. New York:
Grune and Stratton, 1966.

FRIEDHOFF, A. J. Metabolism of dimethoxyphenethyla-
mine and its possible relationship to schizophrenia. In *The Origins of Schizophrenia*. New
York: Excerpta Medica. ICS No. 151, 1967.

FROHMAN, C., LUBY, E. D., TOURNEY, G., BECKETT,
P. G. S., & GOTTLIEB, J. S. Steps toward the
isolation of a serum factor in schizophrenia.
American Journal of Psychiatry, 1960, *117*,
401-408.

FROHMAN, C. E., LATHAM, L. K., BECKETT, P. G. S.,
& GOTTLIEB, J. S. Biochemical studies of a
serum factor in schizophrenia. In O. Walaas
(Ed.), *Molecular Basis of Some Aspects of*

Mental Activity, Volume II.   London:
    Academic Press, 1967.
FROHMAN, C. E., WARNER, K. A., BARRY, C. T., &
    ARTHUR, R. E.   Amino acid transport and the
    plasma factor in schizophrenia. *Biological
    Psychiatry*, 1969, *1*, 201-207.
FROHMAN, C. E., WARNER, K. A., YOON, H. S.,
    ARTHUR, R. E., & GOTTLIEB, J. S.   The plasma
    factor and transport of indoleamino acids.
    Biological Psychiatry, 1969, *1*, 377-385.
FROHMAN, C. E., HARMISON, C. R., & GOTTLIEB, J. S.
    The conformation of a unique plasma protein in
    schizophrenia.   Paper presented at the annual
    meeting of the Society of Biological Psychia-
    try.   San Francisco, California, May 8, 1970.
FULLER, J. L., & THOMPSON, W. R.   *Behavior
    Genetics*.   New York: John Wiley & Sons, 1960.
GOTTESMAN, I. I.   Severity/concordance and diag-
    nostic refinement in the Maudsley/Bethlem
    schizophrenic twin study.   In D. Rosenthal
    and S. S. Kety (Eds.), *The Transmission of
    Schizophrenia*.   New York: Pergamon Press,
    1968.
GREVELING, C. R., & DALY, J. W.   Identification
    of 3, 4-dimethoxyphenethylamine from schizo-
    phrenic urine by mass spectrometry. *Nature*,
    1967, *216*, 190-191.
GRUMET, G. W.   Schizophrenia as a diagnosis and
    disease process.   A theoretical overview.
    Psychiatric Quarterly, 1969, *43*, 456-471.
HEATH, R. G., & KRUPP, I. M.   Schizophrenia as
    an immunologic disorder. *Archives of General
    Psychiatry*, 1967, *16*, 1-9, 10-23, 24-33.   (a)
HEATH, R. G., & KRUPP, I. M.   The biologic basis
    of schizophrenia: An auto-immune concept.
    In O. Walaas (Ed.), *Molecular Basis of Some
    Aspects of Mental Activity*, Volume II.
    London: Academic Press, 1967.   (b)
HEATH, R. G., & KRUPP, I. M.   Schizophrenia as a
    specific biologic disease. *American Journal
    of Psychiatry*, 1968, *124*, 37-42.
HENDERSON, D., GILLESPIE, R. D., & BATCHELOR, I.
    R. C.   *A Textbook of Psychiatry*.   (Eighth ed.)
    New York: Oxford University Press, 1956.
HESTON, L. L.   The genetics of schizophrenic and
    schizoid disease. *Science*, 1970, *167*, 249-256.

HIMWICH, H. E. Biochemistry in the schizophrenias.
    In G. F. D. Heseltine (Ed.), *Psychiatric
    Research in our Changing World*. Amsterdam:
    Excerpta Medica Foundation, 1969.
HOFFER, A., OSMOND, H., & SMYTHIES, J. Schizo-
    phrenia: A new approach. Part II. Result
    of a year's research. *Journal of Mental
    Science*, 1954, *100*, 29-45.
HOFFER, A. Adrenolutin as a psychotomimetic agent.
    In H. Hoagland (Ed.), *Hormones, Brain Function
    and Behavior*. New York: Academic Press, 1957.
HOFFER, A. Relationship of epinephrine metabo-
    lites to schizophrenia. In M. Rinkel and H.
    C. B. Denber (Eds.), *Chemical Concepts of
    Psychosis*. New York: McDowell, Obolensky,
    1958.
HOFFER, A. Treatment of schizophrenia with a
    therapeutic program based upon nicotinic acid
    as the main variable. In O. Walaas (Ed.),
    *Molecular Basis of Some Aspects of Mental
    Activity*, Volume II. London: Academic
    Press, 1967.
HOLLISTER, L. E., & FRIEDHOFF, A. J. Effects of 3,
    4-dimethoxyphenylethylamine in man. *Nature*,
    1966, *210*, 1377-1378.
HOLLISTER, L. E. *Chemical Psychosis*. *LSD and
    Related Drugs*. Springfield, Illinois:
    Charles C. Thomas, 1968.
HUSZAK, I., & DURKO, I. The metabolism of the
    indole compounds in schizophrenia. In the
    *Proceedings of the Third World Congress of
    Psychiatry*, Volume I. Montreal: McGill
    University Press, 1961.
INOUYE, E. Similarity and dissimilarity of schizo-
    phrenia in twins. In the *Proceedings of the
    Third World Congress of Psychiatry*, Volume I.
    Montreal: McGill University Press, 1961.
JACKSON, D. B. A critique of the literature on
    the genetics of schizophrenia. In D. B.
    Jackson (Ed.), *The Etiology of Schizophrenia*.
    New York: Basic Books, Inc., 1960.
KEMALI, D., & BUSCAINO, V. M. Indolic substances
    in schizophrenic patients. In M. Rinkel and
    H. C. B. Denber (Eds.), *Chemical Concepts of
    Psychosis*. New York: McDowell, Obolensky,
    1958.

KETY, S. S. Biochemical theories of schizophrenia.
    Science, 1959, *129*, 1528-1532, 1590-1596.
KRINGLEN, E. Schizophrenia in twins. In the
    Schizophrenia Bulletin N. I. M. H. Bethesda,
    Maryland, 1969.
KUEHL, F. A., ORMOND, R. E., & VANDENHEUVEL, W.
    J. A. Occurrence of 3, 4-dimethoxyphenyl-
    acetic acid in urines of normal and schizo-
    phrenic individuals. *Nature*, 1966, *211*,
    606-608.
LEHMANN, H. E. Schizophrenia. I. Introduction
    and history; IV: Clinical features. In
    A. M. Freedman, H. I. Kaplan and H. S. Kaplan
    (Eds.), *Comprehensive Textbook of Psychiatry*.
    Baltimore, Maryland: Williams and Wilkins
    Co., 1967.
MANDELL, A. J., & SPOONER, C. E. Psychochemical
    research studies in man. *Science*, 1968, *162*,
    1442-1453.
MANDELL, A. J., & SPOONER, C. E. An N,N-indole
    transmethylation theory of the mechanism of
    MAOI-indoleamino acid load behavioral activa-
    tion. In D. V. Siva Sanker (Ed.), *Schizo-
    phrenia Current Concepts and Research*. Hicks-
    ville, New York: PJD Publications Ltd., 1969.
MANGONI, A., BALAZS, R., & COPPEN, A. J. The
    effect of plasma from schizophrenic patients
    on a chicken erythrocyte system. *British
    Journal of Psychiatry*, 1963, *109*, 231-234.
MATTOK, G. L., WILSON, D. L., & HOFFER, A. Cate-
    cholamine metabolism in schizophrenia.
    Nature, 1967, *213*, 1189-1190.
MELLOR, C. S. Fingerprints in schizophrenia.
    Nature, 1967, *213*, 939-940.
NISHIMURA, T., & GJESSING, L. R. Failure to detect
    3, 4-dimethoxyphenylethylamine and bufotenine
    in the urine from a case of periodic catatonia.
    In O. Walaas (Ed.), *Molecular Basis of Some
    Aspects of Mental Activity*, Volume II.
    London: Academic Press, 1967.
OSMOND, H., & SMYTHIES, J. R. Schizophrenia: A
    new approach. *Journal of Mental Science*,
    1952, *98*, 309-315.
PAGE, R. H. Discussion: Biochemical studies on
    serotonin. In H. Hoagland (Ed.), *Hormones,
    Brain Function and Behavior*. New York:

Academic Press, 1957.

PAGE. I. H. Serotonin (5-hydroxytryptamine); The last four years. *Physiological Reviews*, 1958, *38*, 277-355.

PENNELL, R. B., PAWLUS, C., SARAVIS, C. A., & SCRIMSHAW, G. Chemical characteristics of a plasma fraction which influences animal behavior. In O. Walaas (Ed.), *Molecular Basis of Some Aspects of Mental Activity*, Volume II. London: Academic Press, 1967.

PERRY, T. L., HENSEN, S., MACDOUGALL, L., & SCHWARZ, C. J. Urinary amines in chronic schizophrenia. *Nature*, 1966, *212*, 146-148.

PERRY, T. L., HENSEN, S., & MACDOUGALL, L. Identity and significance of some pink spots in schizophrenia and other conditions. *Nature*, 1967, *214*, 484-485.

POLLIN, W., CARDIN, P. V., JR., & KETY, S. Effects of amino acid feedings in schizophrenic patients treated with iproniazid. *Science*, 1961, *133*, 104-105.

POLLIN, W., ALLEN, N. G., HOFFER, A., STABENAU, J. R., & HARUBEC, Z. Psychopathology in 15,909 pairs of veteran twins: Evidence for a genetic factor in the pathogenesis of schizophrenia and its relative absence in psychoneurosis. *American Journal of Psychiatry*, 1969, *126*, 597-609.

RAINER, J. D. A reappraisal of genetic studies in schizophrenia. In D. V. Siva Sanker (Ed.), *Schizophrenia Current Concepts and Research*. Hicksville, New York: PJD Publications Ltd., 1969.

ROSENTHAL, D. Problems of sampling and diagnosis in the major twin study of schizophrenia. *Journal of Psychiatric Research*, 1961, *1*, 116-134.

RYAN, J. W., BROWN, J. D., & DURELL, J. Antibodies affecting metabolism of chicken erythrocytes: Examination of schizophrenia and other subjects. *Science*, 1966, *151*, 1408-1410.

SAAVEDRA, J. M., & UDABE, U. Quantitative assay of bufotenine in psychiatric outpatients. *Psychosomatics*, 1970, *11*, 90-94.

SEDLACEK, J., & SCHADE, J. P. Effect of methionine sulphoximine on some physiological parameters in the developing chick embryo. *Currents in Modern Biology*, 1969, *2*, 320-328.

SEEMAN, P. The erythrocyte as a model for studying membrane stabilization by tranquilizers, anesthetics and steroids. Ph.D. Dissertaion. Rockefeller University of New York, 1966.

SHARMAN, D. F. Metabolism of tryptamine and related compounds in the central nervous system. *British Medical Bulletin*, 1965, *21*, 62-65.

SHORE, P. A., & BRODIE, B. B. LSD-like effects elicited by reserpine in rabbits pretreated with iproniazid. *Proceedings of the Society for Experimental Biology and Medicine*, 1957, *94*, 433-435.

SIREIX, D. W., & MARINI, F. A. Bufotenine in human urine. *Biological Psychiatry*, 1969, *1*, 189-191.

SLATER, E. A review of earlier evidence on genetic factors in schizophrenia. In D. Rosenthal and S. S. Kety (Eds.), *The Transmission of Schizophrenia*. New York: Pergamon Press, 1968.

SMYTHIES, J. R. *Schizophrenia. Chemistry, Metabolism and Treatment*. Springfield, Illinois: Charles C. Thomas, 1963.

SOHLER, A., & NOVAL, J. 6-hydroxylation and schizophrenia. In D. V. Siva Sanker (Ed.), *Schizophrenia Current Concepts and Research*. Hicksville, New York: PJD Publications, Ltd., 1969.

STABENAU, J. R., & POLLIN, W. The pathogenesis of schizophrenia: II. Contributions from the N. I. M. H. study of 16 pairs of monozygotic twins discordant for schizophrenia. In D. V. Siva Sanker (Ed.), *Schizophrenia Current Concepts and Research*. Hicksville, New York: PJD Publications, Ltd., 1969.

SZARA, S., & ROCKLAND, L. H. Psychological effects and metabolism of N,N-diethyltryptamine, an hallucinogenic drug. In *Proceedings of the Third World Congress of Psychiatry*, Volume I. Montreal: McGill University Press, 1961.

TANIMUKAI, H., GINTHER, R., SPAIDE, J., & HIMWICH, H. E. Psychotomimetic indole compound in the

urine of schizophrenics and mentally defective
patients. *Nature*, 1967, *216*, 490-491.

TANIMUKAI, H., GINTHER, R., SPAIDE, J., BUENO, J.
R., & HIMWICH, H. E. Psychotogenic N,N-
dimethylated indoleamines and behavior in
schizophrenic patients. In J. Wortis, (Ed.),
Recent Advances in Biological Psychiatry,
Volume X. New York: Plenum Press, 1968.

TELLER, D. N. Kinetics of binding and inhibition
of enzymatic activity by phenothiazine compounds. Doctoral dissertation. Graduate
School of Arts and Science, New York University, 1964.

TELLER, D. N., LEVINE, R., WACKMAN, N., & DENBER,
H. C. B. Alterations in protein structure
and enzymatic activity: By phenothiazine
tranquillizers. Abstracts, *Seventh International Congress of Biochemistry*, Volume V.
1967.

TELLER, D. N., & DENBER, H. C. B. Defining
schizophrenia with the techniques of molecular
biology. *Diseases of the Nervous System*,
1968, *29*, 93-112.

TWAROG, B. M. The pharmacology of serotonin
(5-HT). In M. Rinkel and H. C. B. Denber
(Eds.), *Chemical Concepts of Phychosis*. New
York: McDowell, Obolensky, 1958.

TWAROG, B. M., & PAGE, I. H. Serotonin contents
of some mammalian tissues and urine, and a
method for its determination. *American
Journal of Physiology*, 1953, *75*, 157-161.

UDENFRIEND, S., WEISSBACH, H., & BOGDANSKI, D. F.
Biochemical studies on serotonin and its
physiological implications. In H. Hoagland
(Ed.), *Hormones, Brain Function and Behavior*.
New York: Academic Press, 1957.

UDENFRIEND, S. Discussion: Biochemical studies
on serotonin. In H. Hoagland (Ed.), *Hormones,
Brain Function and Behavior*. New York:
Academic Press, 1957.

WAGNER, A. F., CIRILLO, V. J., MEISINGER, M. A.
P., ORMOND, R. E., KUEHL, F. A., & BRINK, N.
G. A further study in catecholamine O-
methylation in schizophrenia. *Nature*, 1966,
211, 604-605.

WEINER, H. Schizophrenia III: Etiology. In

A. M. Freedman, H. I. Kaplan and H. S. Kaplan (Eds.), *Comprehensive Textbook of Psychiatry*. Baltimore, Maryland: Williams and Wilkins Co., 1967.

WOOLLEY, D. W., & SHAW, E. A biochemical and pharmacological suggestion about certain mental disorders. *Proceedings of the National Academy of Sciences*, 1954, *40*, 228-231.

WOOLLEY, D. W. Participation of serotonin in mental processes. In M. Rinkel and H. C. B. Denber (Eds.), *Chemical Concepts of Psychosis*, New York: McDowell, Obolensky, 1958.

WOOLLEY, D. W., & CAMPBELL, N. K. Exploration of the central nervous system serotonin in humans. *Annals of the New York Academy of Sciences*, 1962, *96*, 108-117.

COMPARATIVE BEHAVIORAL AND URINARY STUDIES ON SCHIZOPHRENICS AND NORMAL CONTROLS

H. E. Himwich, N. Narasimhachari,
B. Heller, J. Spaide, L. Haškovec,
M. Fujimori and K. Tabushi

Thudichum Psychiatric Research Laboratory
Galesburg State Research Hospital

Galesburg, Illinois

In previous work (Tanimukai *et al.*, 1968, pp. 6-15; 1970), we had made behavioral and bio-chemical observations on four chronic schizophrenic patients before, during and after a chemical stress evoked by the administration of tranylcypromine (Parnate) and later adding L-cysteine to the tranylcypromine. We observed the excretion of N-dimethyltryptamine, bufotenin and 5-methoxy-N-dimethyltryptamine in 24-hour urinary samples. These potentially psychotogenic compounds appeared in the urine in increased concentrations approximately two weeks before behavioral exacerbations and receded only in association with the restoration of the clinical picture observed before the behavioral worsening. In Fig. 1 are presented the naturally occurring amines and their potentially psychotomimetic derivatives. These reactions are facilitated by the enzyme discovered by Axelrod (1961) chiefly in the rabbit lung and more recently by Morgan and Mandell (1969) in the human brain.

RESEARCH DESIGN

In the present investigation, the methods of the previous experiments were largely repeated, using six normal controls and two schizophrenic

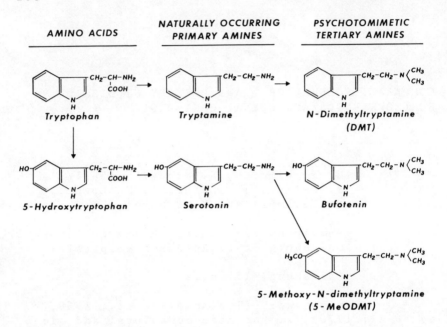

Fig. 1. Chemical structures and metabolic pathways in the conversion of some naturally occurring indoleamines to their psychotomimetic congeners.

patients under as identical conditions as possible, with two principal objectives: 1. Would normals reveal behavioral changes? 2. Would they excrete the three urinary substances reported previously by us? The six normal controls between the ages of 19 to 22 years were selected from a group of 35 college males. Each volunteer was carefully screened according to previous medical history, general health, personality structure and previous experiences. The two chronic schizophrenic patients were 57 and 60 years of age respectively and exhibited active symptoms.

The experiments started on July 1, 1969, for the six normals and two schizophrenics. The clinical observations on the normals were completed on September 1, and for the schizophrenics on September 8, 1969.

METHODS

The two groups were not only studied under similar environmental conditions but also by the same biochemical methods. (see Fig. 2). The study was begun with a control period of 21 days, during which behavioral and biochemical baselines were established. For the experimental period, 10 mg. of tranylcypromine were given to all the subjects three times a day for seven days. On day eight, L-cysteine was added and the combined medication was administered for 20 days. The L-cysteine was administered in 5 gram increments up to a maximum of 20 g per day. Each dose level was given for a five-day period. The experimental period was followed by one of after-loading, two weeks for the normals and three weeks for the schizophrenic patients, and during this time they received neither tranylcypromine nor cysteine.

The subjects were placed on a rigorously controlled, weighed diet and the actual individual food intakes were recorded. All foods known to contain preformed indoleamines were eliminated. The calculated tryptophan, methionine and cysteine contents of the diet offered were 1.27, 2.64 and 1.62 g per day respectively. The entire study was done on a double-blind basis.

The six normal controls were the sole occupants of the same ward which had been used in all previous observations on schizophrenic patients. Two chronic schizophrenic patients with active symptoms were chosen and they occupied a ward across the hall but had their meals in the same ward though in a different room than the normal controls. All psychoactive drugs were withheld from the schizophrenics prior to the study, 17 days for No. 1 and 62 days for No. 2, as well as throughout its duration.

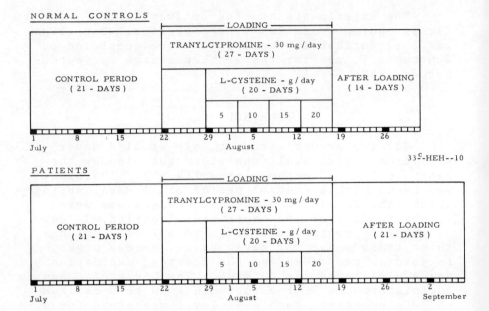

Fig. 2.   Research Design

Rounds were made daily on all eight subjects.
Once each week the psychiatrists specifically
assessed the behavior of the controls as well as
that of the two schizophrenic patients. The evaluations of the subjects were done on a tripartite
basis. Rockland and Pollin's (1965) total rating
score is the sum of three major components, general
appearance and manner, affect and mood, and thought
content and thought process. In addition, a second,
ad hoc, more "loose" type of psychiatric evaluation
was constructed. It consisted of the classic
categories of psychiatric evaluation such as thinking process, mood, clarity of consciousness and
perception of the surroundings, level of energy,
drive and psychomotor activity, sleep, dreams and
physical side effects. The weekly physical check-

ups included the measurement of blood pressure,
heart rate, respiratory rate, weight, temperature
and a standardized neurological examination.

Twenty-four hour collections of urine were
made throughout the study. These were acidified
to pH2 with 6N HCl and stored frozen at -20° C.
before use. Ten percent of the 24-hour urine
collection was used for the analyses of tryptamine
(Sjoerdsma *et al.*, 1959); total 3-indoleacetic
acid (3-IAA) (Weissbach *et al.*, 1959); and creatinine (Hawk *et al.*, 1951).

For the separation of amines from the urine
samples, at least 75% of 24-hour collection (concentrated to 10% of original volume) was used
either for ion exchange chromatography on Dowex
50 (H$^+$ form) or solvent extraction by ethyl acetate
at pH 10-10.4. The basic fractions were then
again fractionated to separate the primary and
secondary amines (Gross and Franzen, 1964) and
final purified concentrates used for thin-layer
(TLC) and gas-liquid (GLC) chromatographic identi-
fications. Recovery experiments were carried out
by adding known quantities of DMT, bufotenin and
5-MeODMT (10 μg each) to urine samples which were
otherwise negative for these compounds and sub-
jecting them to the same methods of separation.
Recoveries of 75% to 80% were obtained in both ion
exchange and solvent extraction methods. Two
spray reagents, p-dimethylaminocinnamaldehyde and
diazotized o-tolidine, were used for identification in TLC method. For gas-liquid chromatography,
the free amines and their trimethylsilyl (TMS)
derivatives were used. The trimethylsilyl derivatives were prepared by a method recently developed
by Narasimhachari *et al.* (1970), using 'Regisil'
[Bis(trimethylsilyl)trifluoroacetamide plus 1%
trimethylchlorosilane] where the trimethylsilyl
group was shown to be on the indolic nitrogen by
mass spectrometry. The trimethylsilyl derivatives
of amine fractions from the urine samples were run
on a 6 ft. 3% SE-30 column on a programmed temperature of 140° with a rate of rise of 5° per minute
and with a standard hydrocarbon mixture ($C_{12}-C_{24}$).
The methylene unit values (MU) of the distinct

peaks in the samples were compared with the values
obtained for standards. In some cases hepta-
fluorobutyryl (HFB) derivatives were used (Vessman
et al., 1969) for GLC. In a few cases, where TLC
and GLC results were positive for DMT or 5-MeODMT
or bufotenin, the samples were run on preparative
TLC or preparative GLC methods and the fractions
corresponding to these three amines were collected
and read on Aminco Bowman Spectrofluorometer and
fluorescence spectra recorded at activation 295
mμ. In this study the results were reported as
positive for any of these three dimethylated
indoleamines only when they were positive by at
least two of the methods used for their identification.

RESULTS

Fig. 3 is a diagrammatic representation of
the behavioral results with the Rockland and
Pollin (1965) scale as well as those obtained with
the chromatographic studies.

Patient Number One

During the control period, Patient No. 1
proved to be a clear-cut paranoid chronic schizophrenic with florid and continuous hallucinations
and paranoid delusions. His delusional ideas were
systematized and centered around the army and its
officers. An analysis of the total scores reveals
that the second and third peaks are obviously
related to increases in thought content and processes because the other two parameters decreased
in intensity at these times in comparison with the
controls. The disturbances of thought processes
included some new delusions in which all of his
five brothers occupied important positions. Chromatographic examination revealed that 24-hour
urinary samples were sporadically positive on
July 4, 5, 8, 12 and 16 and negative for the other
sixteen days of the control period. From July 25
to August 3, while Patient No. 1 received tranylcypromine alone followed by tranylcypromine plus

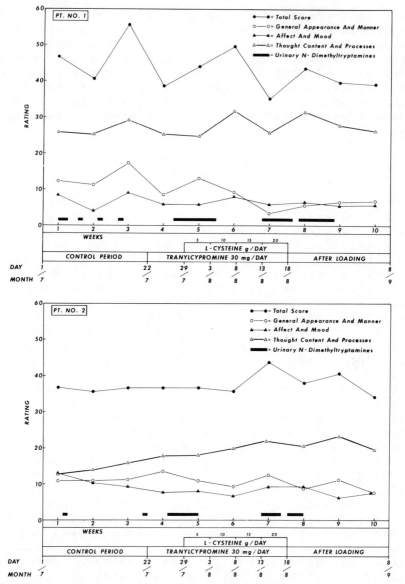

Fig. 3. Patients Nos. 1 and 2 — simultaneous behavioral ratings (Rockland and Pollin, 1965) and chromatographic changes. Reading down, the first three curves are as marked on the figure. The days in which the urinary N-dimethyltryptamines appeared are shown in thick black lines. Next comes the research design and finally the dates.

5 g of L-cysteine, he again showed these three
N-dimethyltryptamines and in greater concentrations
than during the control period. These appeared in
the urine preceding significant behavioral worsening
and were highest in concentration from August 13 to
August 26, with the single exception of August 19,
during and after the combined treatment. These
values were greater than any obtained on Patient
No. 2.

Patient Number Two

During the control period he was found to be
a hebephrenic type of chronic schizophrenic,
socially withdrawn and intellectually regressed.
His thinking was fragmented with obsessional
traits and his thought content was poor. In the
course of the study (Fig. 3), he exhibited only
moderate variations in general appearance and
manner as well as mood and affect. The increased
total scores, during and following the administration of tranylcypromine and L-cysteine, were
largely due to worsening of thought content and
processes, especially obsessional thinking as well
as formation of new delusions. Chromatographic
evaluations during the control period showed mere
traces of DMT and only for two days, July 5 and
21. During the experimental period, from July 26
through July 31, DMT and bufotenin or DMT, bufotenin and 5-MeODMT were detected in his urine and
in larger concentrations than during the control
period. Finally, from August 13 to 20, with the
single exception of August 17, DMT and bufotenin
were observed in the highest concentrations for
this patient. It may be said in general that the
three N-dimethyltryptaminic compounds were detected
in the urine in comparatively large concentrations
immediately before and during behavioral worsening.
It is essential to interpose a remark in regard
to the concentrations of the three urinary
N-dimethyltryptamines--that the differences between
them were semiquantitative and comparative, depending on the heights of the peaks on the gas-liquid
chromatograms.

Normals Number One and Number Two

The peak total scores for Patient No. 1 and
Patient No. 2 were 56 and 44 respectively according to Rockland and Pollin's (1965) scale. In
contrast for the normal controls, No. 1 (Fig. 4)
yielded the highest total score, 8.2, and No. 2
(Fig. 4) the lowest, 2.0, much lower than any of
the scores for the schizophrenic patients. No
psychopathological symptoms such as hallucinations,
illusions, delusions, obsessions or psychotic
behavior were observed, but the normal controls
reacted with nonspecific physical side effects
such as fatigue, dizziness, nausea and insomnia.
At the peak of the combined treatment, occasional
severe gastric cramps and diarrhea as well as
severe insomnia occurred. The mild depressions
which occurred in two normals appeared to be
psychological reactions to the physical side
effects of the combined treatment rather than
results of the biochemical load *per se* and their
symptoms terminated soon after the combined treatment had ceased. Dreams, however, were more numerous, vivid and frequently in technicolor, especially during the first part of the after-loading
period. In regard to the chromatographic results,
in no instance were any of the three N-dimethylated
compounds detected in the urine specimens using our
criterion of identification by two different
methods. Occasionally a bufotenin-like spot was
detected by one method but by no other, i.e.,
spraying with p-dimethylaminocinnamaldehyde might
give a positive result but a negative one was
obtained with diazotized o-tolidine, and in accord-
ance with our criterion of identification by two
methods, these were reported negative. Neither in
the schizophrenics nor in the normals were disturbances of consciousness observed in terms of impairment of the sensorium or in awareness of their
identity and environment. The weekly physical
examinations revealed essentially no neurological
abnormalities except for somewhat elevated tendon
reflexes. There were no significant changes in
blood pressure, pulse rate and respiratory rate
either in the normals or the schizophrenics.

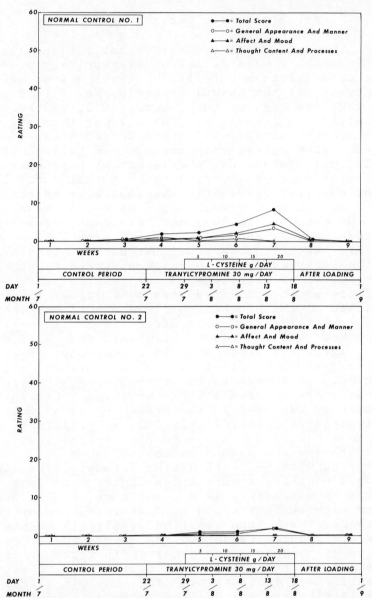

Fig. 4. Normal Controls Nos. 1 and 2 - simultaneous behavioral ratings (Rockland and Pollin, 1965)
and chromatographic changes. The first three
curves are as marked on the figure. Notice failure
of N-dimethyltryptamines to appear in urine. Next
comes the research design and finally the dates.

Tryptamine Results

The starting and peak loading values of urinary tryptamine, µg/day, were for the first normal 200 and the second normal 100 and rose to 3040 and 1750 respectively. Patient No. 1 started at 40 and Patient No. 2 at 130 and increased to 1220 and 2850 respectively (see Fig. 5).

The average tryptamine levels during the period of tranylcypromine and cysteine loading for the two normals were 2333 µg ± 455 (SD) and 1443 µg ± 328 (SD) and for the two patients the levels were lower: 834 µg ± 205 (SD) and 1966 µg ± 537 respectively. It is, therefore, evident that in the production of N-dimethyltryptamines the actual amounts of tryptamine in urine and presumably in the blood are not the limiting factor but rather the ability to methylate tryptamine. Certainly in acute schizophrenics without any medication (Heller *et al.*, 1970; Rosengarten *et al.*, 1970) it was found that they produced N-dimethyltryptamines with normal levels of tryptamine in the urine. In contrast to the enhanced levels of tryptamine, those of 3-indoleacetic acid (3-IAA) did not show significant changes during the loading period. Similarly creatinine levels did not exhibit significant changes throughout the study.

DISCUSSION

Our chief finding in regard to behavior is that normal controls did not exhibit any psychotomimetic effects during the loading period though the chronic schizophrenic patients experienced exacerbations of their symptoms. The changes of thought content and thought processes observed in schizophrenics fitted best with the variations of the three N-dimethyltryptamines in comparison with the alterations of the other two parameters which make up the total score by the method of Rockland and Pollin (1965). Though both schizophrenics and normals exhibited rises of tryptamine during the combined treatment, only the schizophrenics

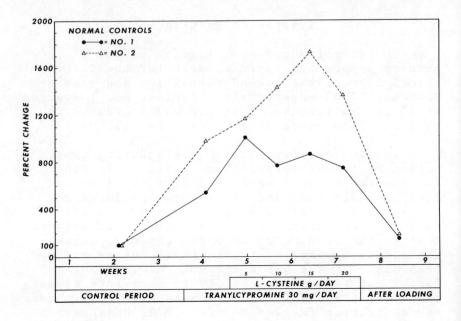

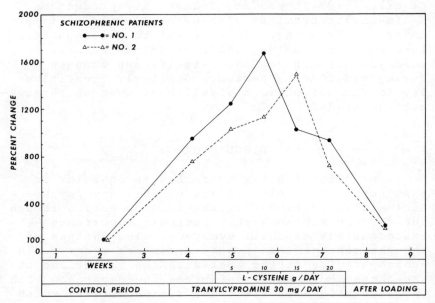

Fig. 5. Normal controls and schizophrenic
patients - changes in urinary tryptamine in course
of the study.

excreted the three N-dimethyltryptamines in the
urine. It is also worthy of note that when behavior improved, the three substances could not be
detected in the patients' urine samples. Our
work suggests that normals cannot produce or cannot accumulate these three N-dimethyltryptamines
despite the presence of an MAO inhibitor which
should prevent the metabolic destruction of these
three compounds. It would thus seem that a biological factor is involved in our results.

It is true that our normals and patients did
not belong to the same age group. But there is
evidence in the literature that N-methylation is
not an age dependent phenomenon. Morgan and Mandell
(1969) have shown the presence of an enzyme which
N-methylates various indole ethylamine substrates
both in infant parietal cortex and in adult frontal
cortex. Furthermore, studies similar to ours made
on chronic patients (Rosengarten *et al.*, 1970) from
21 to 52 years of age have also disclosed N-dimethylated tryptamines in the urine. In our
studies with acute schizophrenics, Heller *et al.*
(1970) demonstrated the presence of N-dimethylated
indoleamines in blood and urine samples in non-
medicated acute schizophrenics 22 to 55 years of
age. Thus, the age differences between our normals
and patients could not have contributed to the
differences in the behavioral alterations and biochemical changes observed in our two groups of
patients.

ACKNOWLEDGEMENTS

We gratefully acknowledge the financial aid
extended for this study by Geigy Pharmaceuticals,
Division of Geigy Chemical Corporation and Roche
Laboratories, Division of Hoffmann-La Roche Inc.;
the gift of tranylcypromine from Smith, Kline and
French Laboratories; Mrs. Rowena Ginther for helping with the management of the diets; Mr. Leroy
Elam, Clinical Psychologist, for helping in the
selection of the normal controls by evaluating the
MMPI results; and various members of our nursing
department for their essential assistance with the
patients.

REFERENCES

AXELROD, J.   Enzymatic formation of psychotomimetic
    metabolites from normally occurring compounds.
    Science, 1961, *134*, 343.
GROSS, H., & FRANZEN, FR.   Zur Bestimmung kör-
    pereigener Amine in biologischen Substraten.
    Biochemische Zeitschrift, 1964, *340*, 403-412.
HAWK, P. B., OSER, B. L., SUMMERSON, W. H.
    Creatinine - 1.   Folin's Method: Principle.
    (determination of creatinine by the Jaffé's
    reaction).   In *Practical Physiological Chem-
    istry*.   Philadelphia: Blakiston Co., 839-842,
    1951.
HELLER, B., NARASIMHACHARI, N., SPAIDE, J.,
    HAŠKOVEC, L., & HIMWICH, H. E.   N-dimethylated
    indoleamines in blood of acute schizophrenics.
    Experientia, 1970, in press.
MORGAN, M., & MANDELL, A. J.   Indole(ethyl)amine
    N-methyltransferase in the brain.   *Science*,
    1969, *165*, 492-493.
NARASIMHACHARI, N., SPAIDE, J., & HELLER, B.   The
    GLC separation of trimethylsilyl derivatives
    of N,N-dimethylindole(ethyl)amines.   1970,
    in preparation.
ROCKLAND, L. H., & POLLIN, W.   Quantification of
    psychiatric mental status.   *Archives of Gen-
    eral Psychiatry*, 1965, *12*, 23-28.
ROSENGARTEN, H., SZEMIS, A., PIOTROWSKI, A., ROMA-
    SZEWSKA, K., MATSUMOTO, H., STENCKA, K., &
    JUS, A.   The occurrence of N,N-dimethyltrypta-
    mine and bufotenine in schizophrenic patients
    without an MAO inhibitor and methionine load-
    ing.   1970, in preparation.
SJOERDSMA, A., OATES, J. A., ZALTZMAN, P., & UDEN-
    FRIEND, S.   Identification and assay of
    urinary tryptamine: Application as an index
    of monoamine oxidase inhibition in man.
    *Journal of Pharmacology and Experimental Thera-
    peutics*, 1959, *126*, 217-222.
TANIMUKAI, H., GINTHER, R., SPAIDE, J., BUENO, J.
    R., & HIMWICH, H. E.   Detection of psychoto-
    mimetic N,N-dimethylated indoleamines in the
    urine of four schizophrenic patients.   *British
    Journal of Psychiatry*, 1970, in press.

TANIMUKAI, H., GINTHER, R., SPAIDE, J., BUENO, J.
    R., HIMWICH, H. E. Psychotogenic N,N-di-
    methylated indole amines and behavior in
    schizophrenic patients. In J. Wortis (Ed.),
    Recent Advances in Biological Psychiatry,
    Volume X, New York: Plenum Press, 1968.
VESSMAN, J., MOSS, A. M., HORNING, M. G. & HORNING,
    E. C. The GLC separation of indole amines
    and indole alcohols as heptafluorobutyryl
    derivatives. *Analytical Letters,* 1969, *2(2),*
    81-91.
WEISSBACH, H., KING, W., SJOERDSMA, A., & UDEN-
    FRIEND, S. Formation of indole-3-acetic acid
    and tryptamine in animals. *Journal of Bio-
    logical Chemistry,* 1959, *234,* 81-86.

DISORDERS OF AMINO ACID METABOLISM
AND MENTAL RETARDATION

Harry A. Waisman

Joseph P. Kennedy, Jr. Memorial
Laboratories
University of Wisconsin Medical Center

Madison, Wisconsin

INTRODUCTION

Early in the twentieth century, the progress
made in organic chemistry and in genetics came at a
propitious time because a number of observations
were made by astute physicians which advanced the
concept that certain diseases occurred in families
and were characterized by excretion of unusual chemicals in the urine. Garrod (1909) deservedly is
credited with recognizing that an "inborn error of
metabolism" was a distinct medical entity. In the
sixty or more years since these cases were first
described, substantial data have been provided that
amino acids, carbohydrates and some lipid components
are all involved in abnormalities seen in humans.
This literature has been reviewed by Hsia, 1966 and
by Stanberry, Wynngarden and Fredrickson, 1970.
Many of these disease states have, as part of their
clinical presentation, some associated brain involvement. A number of disciplines have contributed
valuable knowledge on the scientific approach to
problems of learning, intelligence, behavior and
memory and now, as the 1970's begin, this symposium
brings together biologists and others who have
focused on biochemistry as the most likely discipline which can find valid explanations for abnormalities in behavior, memory and mental retardation.

A number of definitions can be given for mental retardation, but the main sense of the problem is the child's inability to learn properly, to function intelligently and to take his place independently in society. It is not without significance, therefore, that among the inborn errors presently known, mental retardation is frequently an outstanding sign in patients with this type of disease. The amino acids, the fundamental building blocks of protein, are nearly all associated with some inborn error. These patients excrete metabolites of amino acids in urine or show accumulation of the amino acid in tissues and blood.

It is the purpose of this presentation to illustrate those amino acid disorders closely related, directly or indirectly, to mental retardation. The data are the result of experiments both on humans and animals and have just begun to help explain the role of biochemistry in mental retardation, but much remains to be learned about just how each amino acid, individually or in combination, causes specific learning deficits in a particular child. Other than the fact that each amino acid has a characteristic organic structure, individual groups of amino acids have no greater significance in the etiology of mental retardation, nor do they play any role in the incidence than any other group of amino acids. In other words, nearly all amino acids have now been implicated with some cases of mental retardation. Stated still another way, it is characteristic that the amino acid or its metabolite are found in excess in the urine or blood or tissues of some cases of mental retardation and by themselves such data are helpful for classification and identification but have no exact etiological significance.

CLASSIFICATION OF AMINO ACIDS

The three main groupings of amino acids that have metabolic significance for humans are the aliphatic, aromatic and heterocyclic (Table I). Not all of the twenty-five or more amino acids classified under these headings need to be provided in

TABLE I

Classification of Amino Acids and Known Metabolic Disturbances

ALIPHATIC	METABOLIC ERROR
Monoamino Monocarboxylic	
Glycine	Hyperglycinemia With & Without Hypo Oxaluria
Alanine	-
[Isoleucine]	Maple Syrup Urine Disease
[Leucine]	or Leucinosis
[Valine]	or Hypervalinemia
Hydroxy Monoamino Monocarboxylic	
Serine	-
Threonine	-
Monoamino Dicarboxylic	
Aspartic	-
Glutamic	-
Monoamino Decarboxylic ω Amides	
Asparagine	-
Glutamine	-
Diamino Monocarboxylic	
Arginine	Arginino-Succinic Aciduria Excreted in Cystinuria
Lysine	Hyperlysinemia Lysine Intolerance
Sulfur Containing	
Cysteine	-
Cystine	Cystinosis Cystinuria
Homocystine	Homocystinuria
Cystathionine	Cystathionuria
Methionine	Hypermethioninemia
AROMATIC	
Phenylalanine	Classical Phenylketonuria Hyperphenylalaninemia Transient Hyperphenylalaninemia Alkaptonuria
Tyrosine	Transient Tyrosinemia Tyrosinosis Albinism
HETEROCYCLIC	
Tryptophane	Hydroxy Kynureninemia Hartnup Disease
Histidine	Histidinemia
Proline	Hyperprolinemia
Hydroxy Proline	Hydroxy Prolinemia
OTHER AMINO ACIDS	
Sarcosine	Hypersarcosinemia
Citrulline	Citrullinuria
Homocitrulline	Artifactual Homo Citrullinuria →

the diet of humans since some of them are formed
by body processes. These "nonessential" amino
acids constitute a significant percentage of the
body proteins in most tissues and it is curious tha
most of these amino acids are related either
directly or tangentially to patients who have
mental retardation. The cause of the brain damage
cannot be explained at the present time nor is
there any correlation of the chemical structure of
the amino acids to the signs and symptoms demonstrated by the patient.

Aliphatic Amino Acids

Monoamino monocarboxylic acids. Glycine, the
simplest aliphatic amino acid, has been identified
with either ketotic or nonketotic hyperglycinemia
(Gerritsen, Kaveggia & Waisman, 1965). This simply
means that the excess quantity of amino acid can be
accompanied by ketosis or no ketosis in children
who have rather mild symptoms and some degree of
mental retardation.

A disease with the troublesome name of maple
syrup urine disease (troublesome because too few
people are familiar with the odor of maple syrup to
make it commonplace) has been found in less than
seventy-five patients (only twenty of which are
alive early in 1970) since its identification more
than ten years ago. However, the significant point
is that three amino acids are involved in this
disease as originally described by Menkes, 1959,
namely leucine, isoleucine and valine. These amino
acids and their keto acids are in some way related
to the severity of this disease. Children born wit
this disease do not survive unless treatment with a
diet low in these amino acids is begun almost
immediately after birth. Probably the severe acidosis, which results from the respective keto acids
formed from the excess of these amino acids contrib
utes to their early death. The inability to
recognize this disease very early undoubtedly
accounts for the small number of cases found thus
far. As more is known about patients with this
disease, it is becoming clear that perhaps not all

three amino acids need to be related to a specific
case and enough information is already at hand to
indicate that perhaps leucine is the most important
of the three amino acids and the name leucinosis
might be better applied to some of these cases. It
is of interest that these simple amino acids are
involved in such serious and fatal disease and·one
can but speculate, that if the child can be recognized early and his acidosis corrected by any means,
the chances for normal intellectual development
would be good. In other words, any great imbalance
in acid base balance because of the accumulation of
any keto acids can cause death early and the child
can die before any judgement can be made as to
whether brain damage and loss in intelligence would
occur. Nevertheless, disturbance in these amino
acids causes death in a short time in contrast to
the diseases of other amino acids.

Hydroxy monoamino monocarboxylic acids. Serine
is closely identified with one carbon cycle metabolism, i.e., the interconversion of the amino acids,
glycine, sarcosine and serine, although no disease
of serinuria has been uncovered to date. Threonine
is another amino acid which has not had a specific
case of mental retardation associated with it.

Monoamino, di-carboxylic acids. Glutamic acid
has been studied in great detail because of its
high prevalence in brain and its apparent significance in certain metabolic reactions peculiar to
brain which are not yet clearly defined. However,
no disease has been ascribed in any patient specifically with glutamic acid deficiency or excess.
Aspartic acid is another amino acid with no known
inborn error.

One can but wonder about the reason that these
four amino acids are not primarily associated with
disease states. What is so unique about the enzymes
that metabolize these amino carboxylic acids? Does
this group of "non essential" amino acids have some
role in brain biochemistry that is not yet clear?

Diamino monocarboxylic acids. Both arginine
and lysine have been closely identified with some

cases of mental retardation, namely arginino-
succinic aciduria and hyperlysinemia. The occurrence of arginino succinic acid in the urine of some
patients with mental retardation has not been fully
explained, although several cases have been uncovered.

Hyperlysinemia (Ghadimi, Binnington & Pecora,
1965) seems to be due to deficiency of the hepatic
enzyme that metabolizes lysine. The signs and
symptoms of this disease are not specific but more
cases need to be identified and studied before
proper information is available.

The paucity of cases of these two diseases has
prevented adequate study of the mechanism by which
these basic amino acids affect the brain in a
deleterious manner. It is noteworthy that in
arginino-succinic aciduria the levels of this metabolic substance was higher in the cerebrospinal
fluid than in the blood. Here a defect in the urea
cycle has an unexplained harmful effect on the
brain.

Sulfur amino acids. The amino acids, cystine,
methionine and homocystine are represented in
several inborn errors of metabolism. Homocystine
and methionine excess in the plasma are singly each
or together accompanied by a variety of metabolites
in the urine (Gerritsen & Waisman, 1964). Adults
with cystinuria are usually normal and the disease
is really one of renal complications, despite the
lack of an enzyme necessary for proper disposition
of cystine.

Methionine is an essential amino acid for the
proper elaboration of some proteins and only a few
cases have been described in which a methioninemia
or methioninuria are characteristic of some mentally
retarded patients.

Homocystinuria is a more complex disease in
which mental retardation is a most characteristic
finding but a variety of signs can be found in the
patients, such as abnormal bone structure, dislocated lenses of the eye, tendency to thromboembolic

phenomena and variable elevated plasma levels of methionine. A curious circumstance exists in that homocystine is excreted in patients with Marfan's disease, a group of patients who have signs and symptoms similar but not identical with homocystinuria.

Cystathioninuria (Harris, Penrose & Thomas, 1959) is a rare disorder and represents a deficiency in the enzyme system that metabolizes cystathionine into cystine and homo serine. These patients have mental retardation as part of other symptomatology. Hypermethioninemia has also been described in only a rare instance.

Cystinuria is a metabolic disorder, primarily involving the four dibasic amino acids, arginine, cystine, lysine and ornithine. Here is an instance where the defect is not limited to cystine in renal calculi but the stimultaneous excretion of other amino acids is characteristic. Also, no mental retardation is seen in these patients, and the entire amino acid disturbance can be explained as an abnormality in transport.

Cystinosis is a more involved disease in which patients have no mental retardation.

At this point an entire section of this review might be devoted to the variable symptomatology seen in the various amino acidopathies. Some similar signs are found in several diseases but the occurrence of a typical odor in a patient may occur either in maple syrup urine disease or in phenylketonuria. It just happens that the abnormal metabolite of the respective amino acid, the keto acid in each case, is odoriferous. Is it chance or is there a direct influence of homocystine on the anatomy of the developing lens of the eye that causes the lens to be dislocated in these homocystinurics and why are some of these patients mentally retarded? At present, there seem to be no classification of symptomatology with the abnormal metabolite. We really know too little about the role of an amino acid in a particular disease state.

Other Amino Acids

Sarcosine, a compound related to the amino acids, is involved in the pathways of glycine and serine metabolism. Several patients with hypersarcosinemia have now been described (Gerritsen & Waisman, 1966). Not enough patients have been studied to characterize the disease adequately but mental retardation, neurologic involvement and poor developmental milestones were some of the clinical findings in the original patient.

Citrullinuria (McMurray, 1963) is another amino acid disturbance characterized by the occurrence of citrulline in the urine, plasma, erythrocytes and spinal fluid. Progressive developmental regression and poor growth were characteristic in this disease.

Aromatic Amino Acids

Phenylalanine and tyrosine are related to a number of diseases that were part of the concept first described by Garrod (1909) early in the twentieth century. The metabolic pathway of phenylalanine to tyrosine to para-hydroxyphenylpyruvic acid and to homogentisic acid includes four major inborn errors of metabolism reflected in well defined clinical entities, namely phenylketonuria, tyrosinosis, alkaptonuria and albinism. Each of these will be described and special attention will be given to the unfolding of newer clinical and biochemical information which has occurred in the last few years.

Tyrosinosis is a rather rare disease first described by Medes in 1932 and only within the past few years were other cases described which are apparently variants of the same condition. Mental retardation is not part of the syndrome.

Another circumstance which involves tyrosine is a disease best called transient tyrosinemia. It occurs in premature infants whose liver function is not fully matured so that tyrosine is elevated in the plasma until the enzyme tyrosinase is adequately activated. Interestingly, the addition of vitamin C to the diet promptly reduces the tyrosine level to normal.

Phenylalanine must be considered the amino acid which is the keystone of a whole series of diseases of which classical phenylketonuria is the best studied. This disease was first described by Følling in 1934 and is now better understood both clinically and biochemically. It is manifested in a variety of clinical forms best described as a "spectrum" of abnormal phenylalanine metabolism.

Table II lists the various diseases now established as related to phenylalanine, and it will be seen that only classical phenylketonuria is accompanied by mental retardation. The severity of the disease is also related to the excretion of metabolites of phenylalanine as well as to the elevation of phenylalanine in the blood. The method of treatment and the ultimate benefits of treatment must be measured in terms of the exact diagnosis in an individual case. It will be the purpose of the major portion of this discussion to point out and describe some of the newer findings that are now pertinent to children who have this hereditary metabolic defect.

Classical phenylketonuria. This inborn error of human metabolism is characterized by: 1. The excretion of ketoacid metabolites of phenylalanine; 2. Elevated phenylalanine in the blood; and 3. Mental retardation. There is now unanimity among experts in this field that one phenylketonuric child should be found in every 12,000-15,000 live births. This means that between 250 and 350 children with classical phenylketonuria should be identified each year in the U. S. where approximately 5,000,000 children are born annually. In 1970 about forty states have compulsory laws to test the blood of newborns for the possible diagnosis of PKU. Despite the widespread publicity about this disease, the identification of fewer than 100 cases per year are presently made. This unfortunate circumstance prevents proper treatment and achieve-

TABLE II

Diseases of Disordered Phenylalanine and Tyrosine Metabolism

| | Mental Retardation | BLOOD | | Urine Metabolite |
		Phenylalanine mgm%	Tyrosine	
Classical Phenylketonuria	Yes	20 and >	1.0-2.0	Phenyl Pyruvate (OH) Phenyl Pyruvate o. (OH) Phenyl Acetic
Transient Hyperphenylalaninemia	No	6-20	5-10	None
Persistent Hyperphenylalaninemia	No	6 and >	1.0-2.0	None
Transient Tyrosinemia	No	1.0-2.0	4.0-10.0	Variable
Tyrosinemia	No	1.0-2.0	4.0-10.0	p. (OH) Phenyl Pyruvate
Tyrosinosis	No	1.0-2.0	2.0-16.0	p. (OH) Phenyl Pyruvate
Alkaptonuria	No	Homogentisic ↑ 1.0-2.0	1.0-2.0	Homogentisic Acid
Albinism	No	1.0-2.0	1.0-2.0	None

ment of near normal mentality in these unidenti-
fied phenylketonuric children. It is clear from
the data presently available, not only from our
clinic but from a national collaborative study on
the treatment of classical phenylketonuria, that
the unusual irritability, epileptic seizures,
eczema, feeding difficulties and poor developmental
milestones which are characteristic of the untreated
child can all be alleviated by proper administration of a low-phenylalanine diet so as to prevent
the abnormal metabolic disposition of phenylalanine
and yet provide the proper nutrients for optimum
growth.

The hereditary pattern is quite clear since
the parents of the child with classical phenylketonuria are proven heterozygous individuals who
carry the "phenylketonuric gene". The phenylalanine hydroxylase enzyme activity cannot be
quantified except by direct determination of the
enzyme activity in the liver. The exact enzymatic
defect in classical phenylketonurics is due to the
absence of effective phenylalanine hydroxylase
enzyme systems. This enzyme system involves at
least two co-factors-a labile enzyme which requires
NADH and a second stable enzyme which requires
oxygen, NADPH and the co-factor tetrahydrapteridine.
The metabolic block may be of varying severity
which probably accounts for the fact that some
individuals have a reduced defective phenylalanine
hydroxylase activity and therefore show variants of
the disease, some of which will be described below
under hyperphenylalaninemia. The administration of
a "phenylalanine load tolerance test" to suspect
heterozygote individuals is therefore the next
best estimate of enzyme activity (Wang, Morton &
Waisman, 1961). It will establish their inability
to metabolize this amino acid in a normal fashion
within the proper time. Although this test fails
to give definitive information on either the labile
or the stable portion of the enzyme system, for all
practical purposes it is the best available test
for counseling members of the patients' families.

The enzyme is not available in purified form
nor could it be administered without being destroyed

in the intestinal tract. The effective treatment
therefore relies on the elimination of phenylalanine from the diet and reducing the elevated
plasma phenylalanine to moderately low levels
which will prevent the accumulation of phenylalanine metabolites which may have an indirect
effect on the central nervous system causing
mental retardation. The low-phenylalanine diet as
prepared commercially now by a number of firms is
completely acceptable in providing daily requirements of all nutrients and allowing normal growth
to proceed. As the child grows older, low-protein
vegetables and all fruits are permitted but close
monitoring of the phenylalanine level must be done.
Treatment is maintained for at least six to eight
years during the period when the maximum brain
weight is achieved. Now that the dietary management has been carefully done for at least fifteen
years in many clinics, it is manifest that the low-
phenylalanine diet is definitely responsible for
greater intellectual accomplishment. There are,
however, a small group of patients who despite
early treatment and relatively good control do not
achieve normal mentality.

One can summarize the current information on
classical phenylketonuria and say that these cases
comprise the largest number of patients whose
plasma phenylalanine is elevated, and if diagnosed
early enough so adequate treatment is provided,
then near normal intelligence can result. The need
to differentiate classical phenylketonuria carefully from other cases of hyperphenylalaninemia
will determine the optimum treatment.

Hyperphenylalaninemia. It is presently clearly
established that some "atypical phenylketonuric"
patients who have normal or near normal intelligence
are now to be regarded as hyperphenylalaninemics
without phenylketonuria. Presently it is easy to
differentiate these patients since analyses of the
urine fails to give evidence of excretion of phenyl-
pyruvic acid, orthohydroxyphenylacetic acid,
orthohydroxyphenyllactic acid and other ketoacid
metabolites which are characteristic of classical
phenylketonuria. The degree of hyperphenyl-

alaninemia is also variable and the level of
elevated plasma phenylalanine can vary from levels
of six mg% to as high as forty or fifty mg%. The
exact incidence of hyperphenylalaninemia is not
known but probably occurs once for every fifteen
cases of classical phenylketonuria that are identified.

It is still not clear why patients with true
hyperphenylalaninemia fail to excrete ketoacid
metabolites of phenylalanine despite elevated
plasma levels while classical PKU patients with
these levels do show urinary ketoacids. It is
difficult to assign a level of phenylalanine above
which one can expect these excretory products to
appear. Phenylalanine transaminase and the
variable activity of phenylalanine hydroxylase
probably help to explain in part the occurrence of
different excretory patterns. We have seen
patients with hyperphenylalaninemia with levels of
twenty mg% early in infancy who developed normally
without any attempt to lower this level by dietary
treatment. However, not enough information is
presently available about intelligence when these
individuals are eight years or older. The clinical
difference between classical phenylketonuria and
hyperphenylalaninemia now seems clear enough.

The hereditary pattern in hyperphenylalaninemia
is interesting since usually only one parent shows
a pattern of phenylalanine intolerance typical of
a heterozygous state. It is unknown in our experience that both parents will be within the normal
range.

Transient hyperphenylalaninemia. This group
of patients demonstrates variability in the
activation of the enzyme system phenylalanine
hydroxylase. The increase in function with age of
the labile and the stable portion of the enzyme
together with its various cofactors ultimately
influence the effective action of the enzyme concerned with the metabolism of this important amino
acid. Some children show elevated levels of phenylalanine soon after birth but these do not persist
for more than a few weeks or months. The most

typical case of transient hyperphenylalaninemia has
an elevation of both tyrosine and phenylalanine
with the tyrosine level coming to within normal
range much more rapidly than the phenylalanine
level. Any persistently high phenylalanine level
for the first few weeks in a child's life probably
is a reflection of an unusually high protein intake
and very gradual maturation of the phenylalanine
hydroxylase. These children are apparently normal,
do not show any abnormality and there is no evidence that they are heterozygotes.

Maternal phenylketonuria and maternal hyperphenylalaninemia. In all of bio-medical science
there are few circumstances which provide the
opportunity to observe experiments of nature as
seen in pregnant female patients with treated
classical phenylketonuria or hyperphenylalaninemia.
In the past fifteen to eighteen years that patients
with classical phenylketonuria have been treated
it was appreciated that these treated and normal
intelligence individuals would become adults and
have children of their own. The biochemical
defect, the absence of the enzyme and the elevated
plasma level in the blood of treated female patients
would of course persist throughout life. What
effect would these biochemical circumstances have
on the developing fetus? Offspring from females
with classical phenylketonuria or hyperphenylalaninemia would undoubtedly be affected by high
circulating plasma phenylalanine throughout pregnancy. The brain of the fetus is apparently
influenced by both high plasma phenylalanine levels
and its metabolites as shown by work with monkeys.
For most amino acids, including phenylalanine, the
plasma levels of the newborn fetus are twice that
in the mother (Waisman & Kerr, 1965; Kerr &
Waisman, 1966). It is clear from psychological
testing on the behavior and learning ability of
these animals that they show deficits in learning,
behavior and intelligence (Kerr, Chamove, Harlow
& Waisman, 1968; Chamove, Waisman & Harlow, 1970).

In a recent international conference on phenylketonuria, an informal summary of offspring born
to PKU females showed that of the sixty some cases

most of these children were mentally retarded
(Waisman, 1968, pp. 452-4). About three cases
were described where the intelligence was apparently normal. Certainly more information is
necessary to resolve this issue but the potential
for having brain damaged offspring born to treated
phenylketonuric females is a real one and should
command the attention of workers in this field
(Waisman, 1967a).

The offspring born to individuals with hyperphenylalaninemia probably will be similarly
affected since the occurrence of elevated plasma
phenylalanine provided to the fetus is also high.
Several important areas seem worthy of investigation, one of which is the role of the fetal liver
in modifying the phenylalanine provided to it.
Since the liver is functionally immature throughout most of the pregnancy, it is unlikely that the
incompletely developed enzymes in the fetal liver
can modify the elevated phenylalanine. Only late
in pregnancy is it likely that the fetal enzymes
can exert any effect on the phenylalanine provided
to it. By this time, however, the developing brain
will have been influenced by the elevated plasma
level. Additional data are required on the effect
of elevated plasma phenylalanine on myelin formation since most of the myelin is deposited postnatally in the human brain as it is in the rat.

Still another question can be posed as to why
untreated phenylketonuric children, in general,
apparently have lower IQ ultimately than children
born to mothers with phenylketonuria. In other
words, the increased phenylalanine which occurs in
the untreated classical phenylketonuric children
postnatally apparently has a more deleterious
effect on the brain, in contrast to the effect of
increased plasma phenylalanine on the developing
fetus in offspring of phenylketonuric mothers.
These offspring have normal phenylalanine hydroxylase activity in the liver after birth and therefore, have normal plasma phenylalanine levels.
Therefore, if retardation does occur in these latter
patients, any damage must have happened *in utero*.
We can thus contrast the two conditions where in

the one case the damage is primarily postnatal and
in the other case the damage is undoubtedly pre-
natal. The variation expected in individuals and
the variable activity of phenylalanine hydroxylase
in the liver and perhaps a number of factors which
are not yet recognized, all provide opportunity
to clarify the problem of classical phenylketonuria
and hyperphenylalaninemia. Classical phenylketonuria as originally described by Følling in
1934 is probably part of a larger metabolic defect
in which variation in the hereditary pattern, in
the biochemical pattern and in the clinical manifestations needs to be more fully explained.

Heterocyclic Amino Acids

Histidinemia (Ghadimi, Partington & Hunter,
1961) is accompanied by mental retardation and
difficulty with speech in some children. Not all
cases of histidinemia show these signs and of the
more than twenty-five cases reported thus far,
greater variation in symptomatology than previously
supposed is now becoming apparent (Waisman, 1967b).
The diagnosis is usually made following testing of
the urine with ferric chloride. In histidinemia
the ferric chloride test varies from negative or
weakly positive to strongly positive, depending
upon the amount of imidazole pyruvate which is
present. The test is to be differentiated from
the more strongly positive test observed in phenylketonuria since the same reagent is used. Any
patient with a positive ferric chloride test and a
normal phenylalanine level should be further tested
for elevated histidine in the plasma. The cases
of histidinemia are due to a deficiency of histi-
dase.

We have observed an interesting sibship of
four children in whom the clinical manifestations
of encephalopathy were striking throughout the
short lifetimes of these patients. The occurrence
of mildly elevated plasma histidine levels in these
children is not explained at this time.

Hyperprolinemia was described in a family with

electroencephalographic abnormalities, sensitivity
to photic stimulation, mental retardation and
defective renal development. A series of patients
have now been described with variations in symptomatology whose fasting plasma proline levels
varied from 7½ to 10 mg%.

Interestingly, at about the same time, hydroxyprolinemia was also reported in an eleven year
old mentally retarded child who showed excessive
amounts of this amino acid in both plasma and
urine. There were strikingly fewer signs and
symptoms in this patient than in hyperprolinemia.
There is good evidence that hydroxyproline and
proline as well as glycine and perhaps serine
share a common tubular transport system and it is
not unusual that many of these amino acids occur
in excess in the urine. There are too few cases
which provide a clear-cut clinical entity and
additional cases would be valuable to differentiate
between hydroxyprolinemia and hyperprolinemia.

It is most interesting that no case of abnormal mental development has been described for
tryptophan *per se*. It is true that Komrowrer,
Wilson, Clamp and Westall in 1964 described a new
syndrome characterized by an excess of tryptophane
metabolites, 3-hydroxy kynurenine and xanthurenic
acid, in the urine. Since these are metabolic
products of tryptophan, the block must apparently
exist at a point just preceding the formation of
these substances. Apparently kynureninase, together with pyridoxal phosphate as coenzyme, is
decreased or absent. Apparently, the metabolic
conversion of tryptophan to 5-hydroxy indole acetic
acid or to indole pyruvic acid, is undisturbed
and only further down the metabolic pathway of
tryptophan is there one or more defects in this
enzyme system. At the present time one might sup-
pose that other cases of various tryptophan cata-
bolites might be discovered. Since hydroxykyn-
urenine excretion probably represents interference
with the formation of nicotinic acid, the clinic
signs of nicotinic acid deficiency, such as seen
in pellagra, can probably be completely corrected
by the administration of nicotinic acid.

Hartnup's disease should be included in tryptophane related diseases, but mental retardation is not part of the syndrome. Amino aciduria is accompanied by skin lesions and the only central nervous sign is the cerebellar ataxia, which in some cases is self-limiting.

SUMMARY

Any consideration of inborn errors of metabolism must deal with the cause of mental retardation. Whether the excess amino acids in the plasma or their metabolites circulating in the blood have an effect on individual brain cells is not yet fully confirmed. Evidence does exist that protein synthesis is disturbed in animals who have induced hyperaminoacidemia. Whether there is disturbance in neuro-transmitter substances across membrane or nerve endings and synapses has not yet been determined. It is clear, however, that by far the largest number of inborn errors of amino acid metabolism are associated with mental retardation. The challenge for the future is to elicit whether a unitarian principle can be invoked to explain the role of amino acids in brain damage such as some common metabolic substance, or whether more than one metabolite or the amino acid excess itself has a harmful effect on higher brain functions.

REFERENCES

CHAMOVE, A., WAISMAN, H. A., & HARLOW, H. F. Abnormal social behavior in phenylketonuric monkeys. *Journal of Abnormal Psychology*, in Press, 1970.

FØLLING, P. Uber ausscheidung von phenyl-brenz-traubensaüre in den harn als stoffwechsel anomalie in verbindung mit imbezillitat. *Zietschrift für Physiol isches Chemie*, 1934, 227, 169.

GARROD, A. E. *Inborn Errors of Metabolism*. London Henry Frowde, 1909.

GERRITSEN, T., KAVEGGIA, E., & WAISMAN, H. A. A
new type of idiopathic hyperglycinemia with
hypo oxaluria. *Pediatrics*, 1965, *36*, 882-
891.
GERRITSEN, T., & WAISMAN, H. A. Homocystinuria
an error in the metabolism of methionine.
Pediatrics, 1964, *33*, 413-420.
GERRITSEN, T., & WAISMAN, H. A. Hypersarcosinemia,
an inborn error of metabolism. *New England
Journal of Medicine*, 1966, *275*, 66-69.
GHADIMI, H., BINNINGTON, V. I., & PECORA, P.
Hyperlysinemia associated with mental retarda-
tion. *New England Journal of Medicine*, 1965,
273, 723-729.
GHADIMI, H., PARTINGTON, M. W., & HUNTER, A. A
familial disturbance of histidine metabolism.
New England Journal of Medicine, 1961, *265*,
221-224.
HARRIS, H., PENROSE, L. S., & THOMAS, D. H. H.
Cystathionuria. *Annals Human Genetics*, 1959,
23, 442.
HSIA, D. Y-Y. *Inborn Errors of Metabolism*.
(Second ed.) Chicago: Year Book Medical
Publishers, Inc., 1966.
KERR, G. R., CHAMOVE, A. S., HARLOW, H. F., &
WAISMAN, H. A., "Fetal PKU". The effect of
maternal hyperphenylalaninemia during preg-
nancy in the rhesus monkey (*Macaca mulatta*).
Pediatrics, 1968, *42*, 27-35.
KERR, G. R., & WAISMAN, H. A. Phenylalanine:
Transplacental concentrations in rhesus mon-
keys. *Science*, 1966, *151*, 824-825.
KOMROWRER, G. M., WILSON, V., CLAMP, J., & WESTALL,
R. G. Hydroxykynureninuria. *Archives of
Diseases of Children*, 1964, *39*, 250.
MCMURRAY, W. C. Citrullinuria. *Pediatrics*, 1963,
32, 347.
MEDES, G. A new error of tyrosine metabolism:
tyrosinosis. *Biochemical Journal*, 1932, *26*,
917.
MENKES, J. H. Maple syrup disease-investigations
into the metabolic defect. *Neurology*, 1959,
9, 826-835.
STANBURY, J. B., WYNNGARDEN, J. B., & FREDRICKSON,
D. S. *Metabolic Basis of Inherited Disease*.
(Third ed.) New York: McGraw-Hill, 1970.

WAISMAN, H. A.   Role of hyperphenylalaninemia in
     pregnant women as a cause of mental retarda-
     tion in offspring. *American Journal of
     Obstetrics & Gynecology*, 1967a, *99*, 43-45.
WAISMAN, H. A.   Variations in clinical and labora-
     tory findings in histidinemia. *American
     Journal Diseases of Children*, 1967b, *113*,
     93-94.
WAISMAN, H. A.   Hyperphenylalaninemia: clinical
     and experimental considerations. *Proceedings
     of the First Congress of the International
     Association for the Scientific Study of
     Mental Deficiency*, Montpellier, France.
     Michael Jackson Publishing Co., Ltd., 1968.
WAISMAN, H. A., & KERR, G. R.   Amino acid and
     protein metabolism in the developing fetus
     and the newborn infant. *Pediatric Clinics
     of North America*, 1965, *12*, 551-572.
WANG, H. L., MORTON, N. E., & WAISMAN, H. A.
     Increased reliability for the determination
     of the carrier state in phenylketonuria.
     American Journal of Human Genetics, 1961,
     13, 255-261.

BIOCHEMISTRY OF MEMORY

THE ROLE OF CONSOLIDATION IN MEMORY

Anne Geller and Murray E. Jarvik

Departments of Psychiatry
and Pharmacology
Albert Einstein College of Medicine

Bronx, New York

The theory of memory consolidation in its most basic form holds that there is a finite interval between the reception of a learning experience and its permanent storage. During this time the memory trace is held in a short term, impermanent system and is susceptible to disruption. Permanent or long term memory trace formation might occur through the short term system or be initiated independently. The evidence supporting a short term memory system has been obtained largely from studies using ECS in humans and experimental animals, that for a long term system from the effects, in animals, of inhibitors of RNA and protein synthesis. The purpose of this paper is to emphasize the hypothetical nature of these assumptions and to reexamine them in the light of some of the psychological variables involved.

PART I

The evidence for the short term memory system has been frequently and justifiably attacked. Initially derived from the clinical studies of retrograde amnesia following concussion and electroconvulsive shock (ECS) in humans, it has largely been supported by studies using ECS with experimental animals. Earlier objections to these studies

(Coons & Miller, 1960; Adams & Lewis, 1962) have
been answered by the development of one trial
learning techniques. These techniques have yielded
temporal gradients for short term memory which vary
from 10 seconds (Chorover & Schiller, 1966) to
24 hours (Robustelli, Geller & Jarvik, 1969). In
human studies characteristically brief gradients
have been found for ECS (Cronholm & Lagergren,
1959), photosensitive epilepsy (Hutt, Lee & Ounsted,
1963), and petit mal epilepsy (Geller & Geller,
1970). While it is quite possible that short term
memory systems vary widely from species to species,
nonetheless the discrepancy between these results
raises serious questions regarding the procedures
used to obtain them. One trial learning situations,
therefore, have been subject to considerable scru-
tiny and it appears that they present some unique
features which limit and complicate the interpretations of the effects of ECS.

The most widely used one trial learning procedures are those in which the subject is punished
for performing either a previously rewarded or a
spontaneously emitted response. The measure of
retention in these situations is the length of time
for which the animal refrains from performing the
punished response when he is replaced in the training situation. Characteristically, ECS given after
training in such a situation produces a reduction
of the acquired conditioned response tested 24
hours later, the reduction being greater the nearer
in time the ECS administration is to the original
training. This temporally graded retrograde amnesia
has so far constituted the strongest evidence for
a labile short term memory process.

The attack upon this position has come from
two main, independent directions. The first of
these was the contention by Zinkin and Miller
(1967) that the amnesia produced by ECS was not
permanent. Subsequently, other studies (Kohlenberg
& Trabasso, 1965; Miller, 1968) have also shown
recovery from the amnesic effects of ECS. Nevertheless, there is sufficient substantial experimental failure to find recovery from the amnesic
effects of ECS under varied training situations to

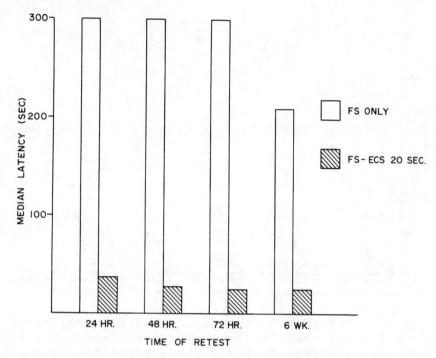

Fig. 1. The permanence of the amnesic effect of
an ECS given 20 seconds after training with retest
intervals up to 6 weeks.

permit the conclusion that at least in some cases
these effects are permanent (Chevalier, 1965;
Luttges & McGaugh, 1967; Geller & Jarvik, 1968).
Fig. 1 and 2 are the results of a series of experiments conducted in our laboratory showing not only
the stability of the amnesic effect of immediate
ECS over a four-week period but also that the
retrograde-gradient is maintained for this time
(Geller, Robustelli & Jarvik, 1970c). These

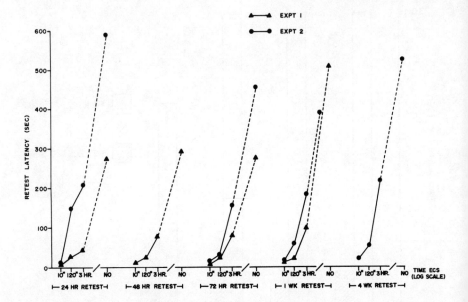

Fig. 2. Permanence of amnesic gradient produced by ECS. Two experiments in which ECS was given 10 seconds, 120 seconds and 3 hours after training with retest intervals up to 4 weeks.

studies fail to demonstrate any recovery from the amnesic effect of an ECS given even three hours after training, a result which is contrasted with clinical studies following head trauma in which, characteristically there is shrinkage over time of the period for which retrograde amnesia is shown (Russell & Nathan, 1946). The fact that in many studies the retrograde amnesia produced by ECS has

been shown to be permanent over long periods of
time, periods far longer than those over which proactive effects have been demonstrated (Aron, Glick
& Jarvik, 1969), is of more theoretical importance
than the fact that there have been some instances
of recovery. These latter instances do not constitute a serious objection to the consolidation
hypothesis of the ECS effect, although a complete
explanation for the occurrence of recovery in some
cases and not in others is still lacking. It has
been suggested by us (Geller *et al.*, 1970c) that,
since those studies in which recovery has been
demonstrated, have used intervals all within the
period in which proactive effects of ECS can be
shown, whereas those showing permanence have used
longer time intervals, the recovery might well be
from the proactive, rather than the retroactive,
effects of the treatment. This would imply that
ECS in these instances had not had any true retrograde amnesic effect. That ECS does not have any
retrograde effects in some situations does not, of
course, contradict a consolidation hypothesis to
account for those situations in which retrograde
amnesia is observed.

A more serious objection has been raised by the
observation that, following one trial learning procedures the conditioned response itself changes
with the training-test interval. This phenomenon
has been termed "incubation," and was first described in one trial learning situations by Mc-
Michael (1966) and Pinel and Cooper (1966a, 1966b).
Fig. 3 demonstrates characteristic incubation
curves obtained in our laboratory (Geller, Robustelli & Jarvik, 1970b) using the step through
apparatus of Jarvik and Kopp (1967). In this study
subjects were not foot shocked immediately upon
stepping into the shock compartment, as is the
usual procedure, but instead, foot shock was
delayed 30 seconds or 240 seconds after the performance of the step through response. This method
has been found to produce conditioned responses
whose strength is in inverse proportion to the
length of the delay of punishment (Robustelli,
Geller & Jarvik, 1968). As can be seen the conditioned response (measured by latency to step into

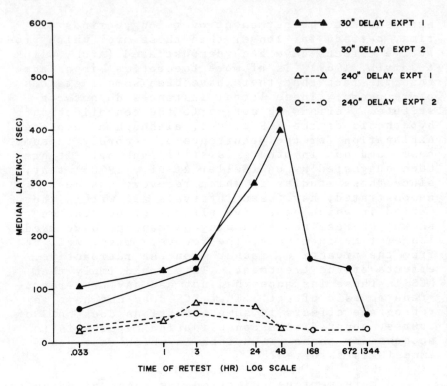

Fig. 3. Retest latencies over an 8-week period of passive avoidance conditioned responses obtained by delaying punishment 30 seconds or 240 seconds after the step through response in training.

the compartment in which foot shock had been delivered) undergoes a progressive increase with the passage of time after training in both delay of punishment conditions. This reaches a maximum at 48 hours and then declines over the weeks following training in the shorter (30 seconds) delay of punishment condition. In the longer (240 seconds) delay of punishment condition, incubation can also be seen but in this situation the response strength

is weaker, the maximum is reached at a shorter
time after training, and the decay is more rapid.

The ascending or incubation portion of Fig. 3
has been found in a number of studies in which
aversive conditioning has been used (McMichael,
1966; Pinel & Cooper, 1966a, 1966b; McGaugh, 1966;
Irwin, Banuazizi, Kalsner & Curtis, 1968; Tarpy,
1966; Black, 1969).

The finding of incubation in those learning
situations in which ECS produces a temporal gradient of amnesia is considered by some authors
(Pinel & Cooper, 1966a, 1966b; Irwin et al., 1968;
Spevak & Suboski, 1969) to make an interpretation
of the ECS effect on the basis of a consolidation
hypothesis unnecessary. The ECS effect is explained as a consequence of disruption of the
incubation process. However, for this to constitute
a serious criticism of the consolidation-disruption
hypothesis of ECS action, it has to be shown on
the one hand that the temporal gradients of ECS
and incubation correspond to each other in a variety
of tasks, and on the other hand, that incubation
is not itself a direct reflection of consolidation
(McGaugh, 1966). If, however, it could be shown
that the gradients for incubation and retrograde
amnesia were quite different in the same task, or
that the time response curve of incubation was
itself a curve of retention, then the ECS effect
could be accounted for within the consolidation
framework. It should be noted at this point that
the validity of consolidation theory is independent
of hypotheses concerning the mode of action of ECS.
Nevertheless, since the bulk of the evidence for
the existence of a short term memory trace existing
for more than 10 seconds has been derived precisely
from the presumed retrograde amnesic effect of ECS
in one trial learning situations the finding of a
plausible alternative explanation of this effect
would remove some of the strongest support for this
theory.

To deal first with the similarity between the
incubation and ECS curves, Black (1969) has presented evidence that in two learning situations in

which incubation occurred, ECS gradients were
obtained which were quite similar to the incubation
gradients in each case. McGaugh, on the other
hand, has cited his 1966 paper as evidence of the
separability of the two curves. We have conducted
a series of experiments designed to separate the
two curves and have failed to do so. A prediction
derived from a consideration of Fig. 3 would be
that in our conditioning situation, where the time
course of incubation is at least two days, long
temporal gradients would be obtained with ECS,
were the incubation and ECS gradients related in
some way. And indeed, as can be seen in Fig. 4,

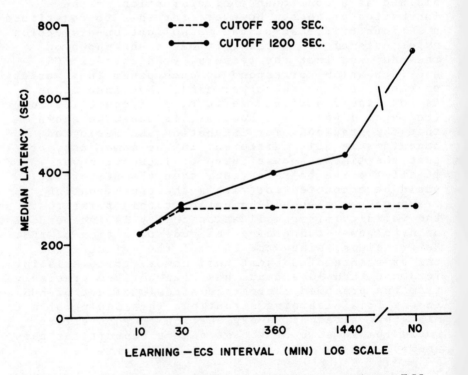

Fig. 4. Retest latencies for subjects given ECS
10 minutes, 30 minutes, 6 hours and 24 hours after
training. Retest 1 week after training.

a gradient of up to 24 hours (the experiment was
not carried beyond this point) can be obtained if
the cut-off latency is set at a high enough level
for it to be demonstrated.

A further prediction from Fig. 3 which could
be made on this basis would be that, since in our
conditioning situation, the slope of the incubation gradient varies with the delay of punishment
used during training, the slope of the ECS gradient should vary in a corresponding fashion. Fig. 5
shows the result of an experiment designed to test

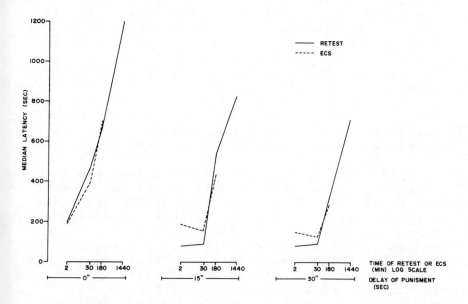

Fig. 5. Incubation and ECS gradients in three different training conditions obtained by delay of
punishment 0 seconds, 15 seconds or 30 seconds
after the step through response.

this prediction. Foot shock was delayed either
0 seconds, 15 seconds or 30 seconds after the step
through response on the training trial, resulting,
as can be seen in Fig. 5, in different levels of
the acquired conditioned response, when the subjects were retested 2 minutes, 30 minutes, 3 hours
or 24 hours after training. Subjects given ECS
at the same time intervals, but retested 24 hours
after training, showed latencies which, for each
delay of punishment condition, corresponded with
the appropriate retest latency. Even though the
first two points on the incubation curve are flat
in this experiment for the 15 seconds and 30 seconds delay of punishment conditions, this is faith-
fully reflected in the ECS gradient.

In the above experiment since the selected
time intervals were rather widely separated, it
was decided to investigate the early portion of the
incubation curve more closely in an attempt to
separate the incubation and ECS gradients. Fig. 6
shows the result of such an experiment. As can
be seen, the incubation curve is not a simple
monotonic function, but instead shows a peak at
around 5 minutes after training in our situation
(Robustelli, Geller & Jarvik, 1970b). Biphasic
incubation curves have also been obtained by Irwin
et al. (1968) and Zerbolio (1969). However, the
most remarkable finding is that the curve for the
subjects given ECS at the same time intervals, but
tested 24 hours later, shows the same biphasicity.

That the incubation and ECS curves are so
similar even in their nuances suggests, but does
not prove, of course, that they are related to a
similar underlying process. It is, however, too
premature to reject the ECS gradient as being unrelated to a memory consolidation process on the
basis of this evidence. It has first to be shown
that incubation is itself not a reflection of consolidation and secondly that incubation and ECS
gradients are both related to a common process
unconnected with memory. So far this has not been
done, nonetheless a strong case can be made for
the contention that the incubation curve does not
reflect progressively improving retention and

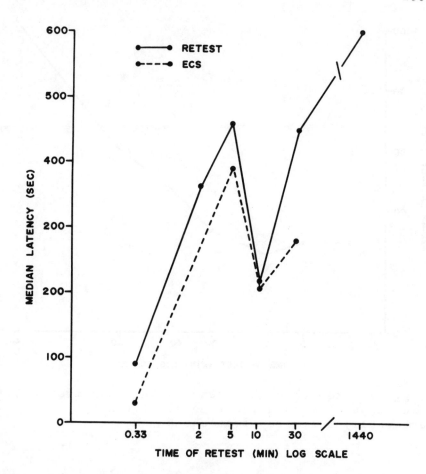

Fig. 6. Incubation and ECS gradients at short intervals after training.

plausible hypotheses can be advanced which account for incubation on the basis of performance changes following training and which connect the incubation and ECS curves on the same basis.

   If subjects are foot-shocked on a grid, out-side the step through apparatus and dissimilar from it, they show a characteristic incubation curve when their step through latencies are meas-

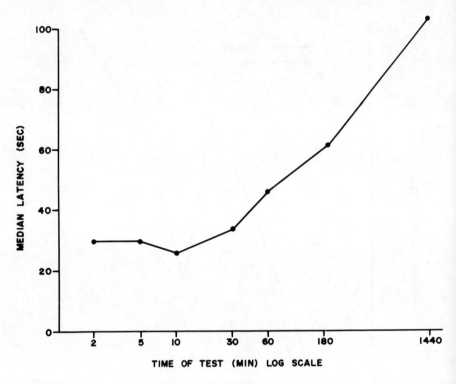

Fig. 7. Step through latencies in a passive avoidance apparatus as a function of time after an
externally delivered foot shock.

ured within the step through apparatus (Fig. 7),
indicating that incubation occurs even when the
training and retest conditions are not the same.

    In Fig. 8 are shown the incubation curves
corresponding to three different training retest
situations. The subjects of one group were given
a foot shock in the normally safe outer compartment of the step through apparatus, from which they

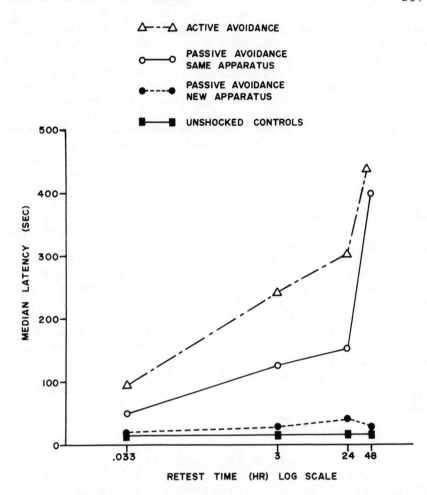

Fig. 8. Retest latencies for subjects to step out of a compartment in which they had been shocked (active avoidance), to step into a compartment in which they had been shocked (passive avoidance – same apparatus), or to step through in a different apparatus (passive avoidance – new apparatus).

were permitted to escape into the inner compartment. They were placed at retest in the compartment in which they had been shocked. The subjects of the other two groups were trained in the usual manner, but whereas one of these groups was

retested in the outer compartment of the same
apparatus in which it had been trained, the other
group was retested in an apparatus having the same
dimensions as the training apparatus, but quite
different in other respects. Incubation occurred
in all three conditions. Although the curve is
lower in the last mentioned situation, the incubation trend is still significant. As can be seen
from Figs. 7 and 8 (making allowances for the
different latency scales), there is considerable
generalization following a single foot shock
experience to a naive animal, but latencies are
much lower when the conditions at the time of foot
shock differ markedly from those at the time of
testing. However, when training and testing take
place in the same apparatus, latencies are similar
no matter whether the subjects are placed in the
safe compartment or in the shock compartment at
the retest trial. Latencies increasing with time
after foot shock are demonstrated in all these
situations. Incubation then, does not reflect an
increased discrimination of the training situation,
but occurs as a response to foot shock independently of the place in which the foot shock took
place. Giving subjects a 10 minute activity test
in activity boxes quite different from the place in
which foot shock took place, also produces an incubation curve, that is, the activity progressively
declines with time after foot shock.

As has been seen the incubation curve is an
inverted U shaped function, the time relations of
which vary with the training-test parameters
(Fig. 3), and it appears that the peak of the
inverted U is higher and is reached later the
stronger the original training and the more similar
the training and test situations. However, from
Fig. 7 it is apparent that within the same apparatus the incubation curves for animals replaced at
testing in the safe compartment, and those replaced
in the compartment in which they had been shocked
are similar in time course and in the height of
the incubation curve. It might be suggested then,
that following a foot shock there develops a progressive tendency to inhibit movement when the
animal is placed in an environment in any way simi-

lar to the one in which foot shock took place. In
the case of a naive animal with prior experience
only of the home cage almost any new environment
would suffice to produce this response (Zammit-
Montebello, Black, Marquis & Suboski, 1969). This
progressive inhibition of movement reaches a lower,
and earlier peak, and dissipates more rapidly the
more dissimilar the training and test situations.
This may well explain the frequent failure to find
any effect on latencies of externally delivered
foot shock in several experiments in which the
subjects have been tested 24 hours later. It is
clear therefore, that while incubation may reflect
increasing retention of a generalized inhibitory
response it certainly does not reflect an increasing retention of the specific features of the
training environment. Why, however, does this
generalized inhibition of movement take time to
develop? The two most convincing explanations of
this both lack experimental data.

The first is that proposed by Brush and Levine
(1966) to explain the Kamin effect in active avoidance conditioning. They proposed that following a
foot shock experience there is a progressive
release of some substance (corticosteroids were
suggested). This substance produces an increased
tendency to freeze when the animal is confronted
with fear-eliciting stimuli. The diminished ability of hypophysectomized animals to form a passive
avoidance response (Weiss, McEwen, Silva & Kalkut,
1969) and their improvement following ACTH administration can be cited in support of this. Note
that memory in the conventional sense, is not implicated here, merely a hormonally induced increase
of reactivity to fear provoking stimuli. Interesting as this hypothesis is, the failure of Marquis
and Suboski (1969) to obliterate incubation by
hypophosectomy or adrenalectomy raises a serious
objection.

A second explanation advanced by us is not
that fear incubates but that the aftereffects of
foot shock dissipate. Following a shock there is
an excitation which produces disinhibition of movement. This shock-induced disinhibition competes

with the passive avoidance conditioned response, which requires inhibition of movement. With the passage of time after training this shock-induced disinhibition diminishes and the "true" passive avoidance conditioned response progressively emerges. There is evidence (Hudson, 1960; Adams & Calhoun, 1970) for the disinhibitive aftereffects of shock. The similarity between the incubation and ECS curves might be explained in the following manner: ECS by an unknown mechanism, but one not necessarily related to memory, produces reduction of a generalized inhibitory response. The extent of this reduction is dependent upon the strength of the ECS. A foot shock alters the physiological background on which a subsequent ECS acts and effectively increases its strength. This enhancement of the ECS progressively diminishes as the time between foot shock and ECS increases. If the disinhibitive aftereffects of foot shock and its ECS enhancing effects were related to the same underlying mechanism, which is not implausible, both might be expected to decline along the same time course. In support of this hypothesis, the studies of Schneider and Sherman (1968) and Chorover and DeLuca (1969) have shown an interaction between ECS and foot shock both behaviorally and on the EEG. While this explanation is merely speculative and lacks direct experimental support, nonetheless it is a plausible alternative to the consolidation-disruption hypothesis of the ECS gradient and one which takes into account the striking similarities between ECS and incubation gradients.

Although an alternative and more plausible hypothesis can be proposed to account for the long temporal gradients for ECS-produced amnesia in passive avoidance conditioning situations, the possibility that ECS may disrupt consolidation over much shorter periods in other tasks (appetitive-Herz, 1967; Pinel, 1969) and discriminated avoidance (Suboski, Black, Litner, Grenner & Spevak, 1969) still remains. Furthermore, it is important to recognize that consolidation theory itself is independent of theories concerning the mechanism of action of ECS and is not invalidated by alternative explanations of the ECS effect.

PART II

The second part of this paper is not concerned with the hypothetical short term memory trace, but with permanent, long term memory formation. Whether a short term memory trace is formed at all and whether if it is, it is independent of or initiates the formation of a long term trace, remains speculation. Nevertheless, that memories are stored in some way is a fact, and in a variety of animal species and a number of behavioral tasks, inhibition of protein synthesis at or shortly after learning appears to interfere with retention of the learned response. This has been interpreted by most investigators to be due to an interruption of long term storage processes. However, the time course for this effect varies widely in different experimental situations (Flexner, Flexner & Stellar, 1963; Agranoff, Davis, Casola & Lim, 1967; Barondes & Cohen, 1968) and with psychological manipulations within the same training situation (Davis & Agranoff, 1966; Davis & Klinger, 1969). In a series of experiments with the antibiotic, cycloheximide, in our laboratory, we have investigated the role of some of these psychological variables in determining the duration and extent of amnesia produced by this inhibitor of protein synthesis.

Using post-trial injections of cycloheximide (150 mg/kg) in the one trial passive avoidance task of Jarvik and Kopp (1967), and testing the animals one week after training, we obtained a temporally graded retention deficit by injections of the drug up to 30 minutes after training (Geller, Robustelli, Barondes, Cohen & Jarvik, 1969) (see Fig. 9). This is a longer gradient than that obtained in some other studies with mice in which glutarimide derivatives have been used. Cohen and Barondes (1968a) injected cycloheximide following training in an appetitive task and found a slight impairment with immediate post-trial injections, but none at all if the injections were delayed for 30 minutes after training. A similar short gradient has been obtained with acetoxycycloheximide in a light dark discrimination task (Barondes & Cohen, 1968).

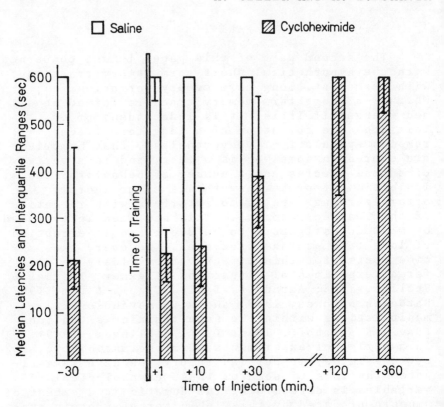

Fig. 9. Median retest latencies as a function of time of injection of 150 mg/kg of cycloheximide subcutaneously.

However, with goldfish as the experimental subjects, impaired retention has been demonstrated
with intracranial injections of acetoxycycloheximide up to one hour after training in a shuttle
box task (Agranoff *et al.*, 1967). It would seem
then, that in some situations, sufficient protein
synthesis to subserve long term memory has taken
place within minutes after the completion of
training, whereas in other situations synthesis has

not progressed sufficiently even after one hour.
That there are differences between species in this
respect is not too surprising, but that within the
same species differences are found on the basis
of the particular training situation presents
another aspect in the consolidation of the long
term storage processes.

Cohen and Barondes (1968b) have demonstrated
the importance of task and level of conditioning
within the same task in determining the amnesic
effect of inhibition of protein synthesis. They
found that pretrial injections of acetoxycycloheximide produced a decrease in retention when a
left-right discrimination was carried out to a
criterion of 3 out of 4 correct, but not when
training was extended to a 9 out of 10 criterion.
In a visual discrimination, thought on the basis
of trials to criterion to be a more difficult
task, injections of acetoxycycloheximide were still
effective when the subjects were trained to 9 out
of 10 correct, but were not at a 15 out of 16
training criterion. These results show that not
only does sensitivity to inhibition of protein
synthesis differ across tasks, but within the same
task it depends upon the criterion reached during
training. Cohen and Barondes suggested that a
left-right discrimination might be a more "natural"
task for the mouse than a light-dark discrimination and that, therefore, more neuronal pathways
would be available for storage, increasing the
probability that one of them escapes the inhibition
of protein synthesis.

In a study (Geller *et al.*, 1970a) with passive avoidance conditioning, we examined the relationship between delay of punishment during training and the amnesic effect of protein synthesis
inhibition obtained with immediate post-trial
injections of cycloheximide. This is of interest
in the light of the hypothesis suggested by Cohen
and Barondes since the same response (passive avoidance) is tested, yet for each delay of punishment
condition the training itself is different. It
might be considered that varying the delay of punishment during training is more analogous to using

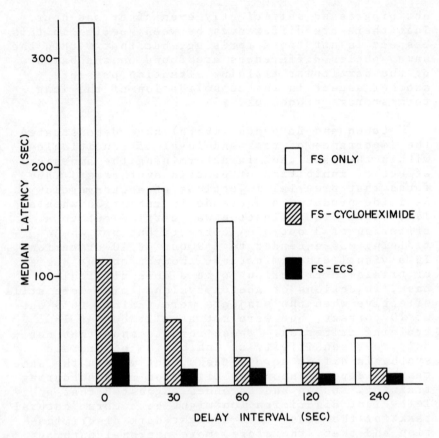

Fig. 10. Median retest latencies for subjects
trained with 0, 30, 60, 120 or 250 seconds delay
of punishment and given either no treatment or
cycloheximide or ECS immediately after training.

different tasks than to using different criteria.
As can be seen in Fig. 10, the latency on the
retest trial to enter the chamber in which shock
had been delivered is an inverse function of the
length of the delay of punishment during training.
The highest latencies obtained with the shortest
delays of punishment were merely reduced by the

cycloheximide, whereas in the longest delay of
punishment the conditioned response was completely
abolished by the drug. Since the response which
is learned is the same in each training condition,
it might be assumed that the same pathways are
potentially available for storing the information.
The variable in this case would appear to be the
difficulty of the association between the conditioned and the unconditioned stimulus. It might
be then, that the more difficult the association,
the longer it might take to process the information and, therefore, the more sensitive the task
might be to interruption of protein synthesis
during this time. It would follow from this, that
the length of the temporal gradient of amnesia
produced by inhibition of protein synthesis would
be a function of the difficulty of the task. As
has been mentioned above, we have obtained a gradient extending to 30 minutes, but not to 1 hour
with the shortest (0 delay) punishment condition.
Accordingly, we examined the gradient obtained by
cycloheximide with three delay of punishment conditions (0, 30 and 120 seconds), with cycloheximide
given immediately, 10 minutes, 60 minutes and 180
minutes after training. Contrary to prediction,
for all delay of punishment conditions cycloheximide was effective in reducing the acquired conditioned response when given immediately or 10
minutes after training, but was without any effect
when given 60 minutes or 180 minutes after training. If a difference in gradient does exist, it
has to be within a rather small time period (some-
where between 30 and 60 minutes after training).
This is currently under investigation.

In Fig. 3 of Part I of the present paper, it
can be seen that the weaker the conditioned
response, the more rapid the decay (forgetting).
It might be predicted that a task in which forgetting is rapid might be more sensitive to the effect
of inhibition of protein synthesis following training. Habituation of exploratory activity is subject to a fairly rapid decay, and thus might be
expected to be sensitive to protein synthesis inhibition. Under the experimental conditions in our
laboratory, mice given a 10 minute exploratory

session in an activity box, 12 x 12 inches wide
and 6 inches high, show a reduction in activity
when replaced in the same box 1 day, 2 days, but
not 4 days after the initial exploratory session.
We, therefore, investigated the effect of post-
trial injections of cycloheximide upon habituation in this situation.

Cycloheximide, itself, produces a reduction
of activity which is marked 3 hours after injection and very slight 24 hours after. There is no
detectable effect upon activity 48 hours after
injection of cycloheximide. Accordingly, cycloheximide was injected immediately, 10 minutes
and 30 minutes after a 10 minute exploratory session and the animals were retested 2 days later.
As can be seen in Fig. 11, which shows the first
5 minutes of each session, immediate post-trial
injection of cycloheximide was without any effect
upon the habituation of activity. The reduction
in activity on the second trial was significant for
both the saline and cycloheximide treated subjects,
but they did not differ from each other. The
period of exploration of the first session was then
shortened to the minimum which would result in a
reduction of activity 2 days later. Even when
given immediately after this brief, 5 minute
exploratory session, cycloheximide was without
effect on the habituation.

Since some time is required to achieve maximum inhibition of protein synthesis following a
subcutaneous injection of cycloheximide (Cohen &
Barondes, 1968a), we investigated the effect upon
habituation of pretrial injections of the drug.
An unexpected finding resulted which made it impossible to interpret habituation data from this study.
Given subcutaneously immediately, 10 minutes or 30
minutes before an activity session, cycloheximide
produced a marked increase in activity as can be
seen in Fig. 12. The reason for this activity
increase is as yet unknown, but the time course of
the activity changes produced by subcutaneous
injection of cycloheximide has been documented by
us. The drug-induced increase in activity is
greatest when the injection is given 2 minutes

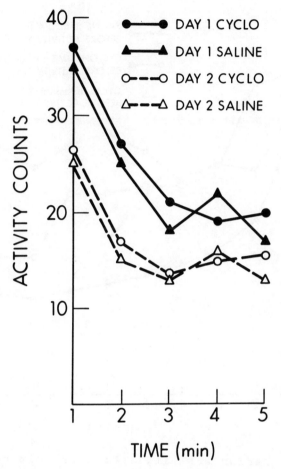

Fig. 11. Median activity scores per minute for
first 5 minutes of a 10 minute session. Subjects
were given either saline or cycloheximide subcutaneously immediately after activity on Day 1. Day
2 was 48 hours later.

before the activity test. When given 30 minutes
before, the increase is still marked. It is slight
at 45 minutes and absent at 1 hour. If given more
than 1 hour before the activity test, activity of
the cycloheximide treated animals is lower than
controls and this decrease of activity is profound
when injections are given 3 hours before testing,

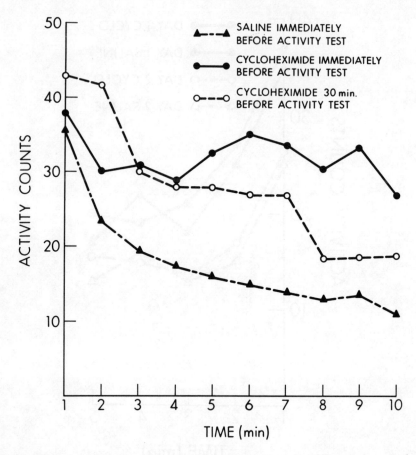

Fig. 12. Median activity scores per minute. Subjects were given cycloheximide subcutaneously
either immediately or 30 minutes prior to activity.
Saline injections immediately or 30 minutes
before did not differ and pooled data are plotted.

at which time the treated animals hardly move at
all. The depression of activity persists up to
24 hours as has been mentioned earlier. These
marked fluctuations in activity, an initial brief
(30 minutes) increase followed by a long-lasting
depression have to be taken into consideration in

those experimental situations in which either
training or testing of the animals takes place
during this period. This observation, however, is
pertinent neither to the passive avoidance nor to
the habituation studies where injections were
given after training and testing took place more
than 24 hours later. In view of the rapidity with
which habituation decays, and, by inference the
rather tenuous conditioning established, it is
remarkable that it is completely insensitive to
inhibition of protein synthesis. It is not, however, contradictory to suggest that habituation
may involve very simple and rapid association pathways, even though the conditioning itself is weak.

Another possibility is suggested by the results
of Davis and Agranoff (1966), Misanin, Miller and
Lewis (1968), Davis and Klinger (1969), and
Schneider and Sherman (1969). Davis and Agranoff
(1966) found that the length of time after training during which puromycin produced an amnesic
effect in goldfish could be prolonged by maintain-
ing the animals in the training environment during
the training injection interval instead of returning them to their home tanks. Davis and Klinger
(1969) further found that an amnesic effect of
acetoxycycloheximide could be produced by injection
24 hours after training if the subjects were
returned to their training environment for a brief
period before injection. Their hypothesis to
explain these results is that during the exposure
to the training situation, the specific memory
trace is either kept activated or reactivated and
thus rendered more susceptible to the amnesic agent.
An alternative explanation not involving a specifically reactivated trace might be that the subjects' level of arousal is increased by returning
it to the training environment and that this increased level of arousal alters metabolic rate,
increases protein turnover and increases the possibility that inhibition of protein synthesis will
affect whatever portion of the information is not
yet stored in fully permanent form. This implies
that the permanent stable storage of memory covers
a longer period of time than has been usually proposed, but it is known from clinical studies that

there is a diminishing susceptibility to amnesia
producing events with increasing age of the memory
and that the effects of these events can extend
over periods involving weeks and sometimes months.
It might be proposed that the passive avoidance
training procedure produces in its wake an increase
in arousal level which persists for some time. An
exploratory session involving no aversive experience is associated with less intense and briefer
periods of arousal. The greater susceptibility of
the former task to amnesic agents might thus be
explained. Similarly, it has been suggested
(Kamin, 1957) that an animal who has only partly
or incompletely learned a given task is more
aroused than one who has mastered the situation.

It, therefore, seemed of interest to examine
the interaction between detaining the animal in the
training environment after passive avoidance training and injection of cycloheximide. If the animal
is already highly aroused after the passive avoidance training, detention might not produce any
additional increment of arousal and would not prolong the cycloheximide susceptible period of
memory formation. If, on the other hand, activation or reactivation of a memory trace is involved,
one would predict results similar to those obtained
by Davis and Agranoff (1966). Fig. 13 shows the
results of such an experiment in which 35 subjects
per group were used. Not all the groups are shown
in the figure to avoid unnecessary complexity.
However, the basic control groups were given subcutaneous injections of saline or cycloheximide,
10 minutes or 60 minutes after training. The
experimental groups were detained in the safe compartment of the conditioning apparatus for 10
minutes, immediately after training, for 10 minutes
beginning 50 minutes after training or for 60
minutes beginning immediately after training.
Injections of saline or cycloheximide were given
at the end of the detention period in each case.
In agreement with our previous results, cycloheximide given alone, 10 minutes after training, had
an amnesic effect but had no effect given 60
minutes after training. Detention for 10 minutes,
immediately after training, produced a decrement

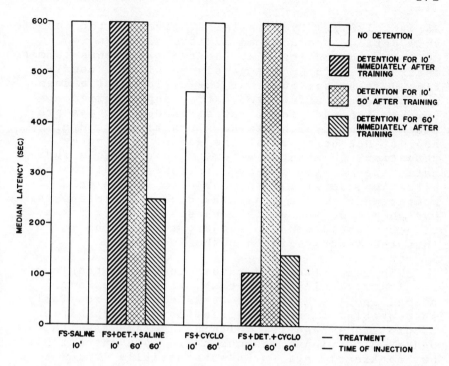

Fig. 13. Median latency scores for subjects given
subcutaneous injections of cycloheximide or saline
either alone or immediately following detention
in the safe compartment of the conditioning apparatus. Detention was for 10 minutes or 60 minutes
beginning immediately after the training trial or
for 10 minutes, beginning 50 minutes after the
training trial.

in retention on the retest trial, an effect which
we have hypothesized to be the consequence of a
generalized extinction (Robustelli, Geller &

Jarvik, 1969). Cycloheximide, given at the end of this period, produced an additional retention deficit, suggesting that the two treatments summate their effects upon the passive avoidance conditioned response, but that the cycloheximide does not appear to affect the extinction experience. However, no additional retention deficit was· produced by the cycloheximide given at the end of 1 hour of detention or at the end of 10 minutes detention, 50 minutes after training. This indicates that in the passive avoidance conditioning situation, detaining the subjects in the safe compartment of the apparatus does not prolong the cycloheximide-susceptible phase of memory formation and would tend to support the arousal rather than the reactivation hypothesis.

To summarize this rather confusing tangle of results it would appear that, within the same animal species different tasks are differentially susceptible to the amnesic effects of inhibition of protein synthesis. Within the same task the weaker conditioned responses are more susceptible, but apparently not for a substantially longer period of time. Re-exposure, or continued exposure after training to the training environment does not prolong the susceptible phase of memory storage in a task presumed to be associated with high levels of arousal.

In conclusion, this paper has attempted to demonstrate the importance of psychological variables in determining the extent and duration of amnestic effects and in the interpretation of these effects when they occur. For any theory of consolidation to be acceptable it has to account in some way for the influence of these variables upon the mnemonic processes.

ACKNOWLEDGEMENTS

This research was supported by USPHS grant MH 05319 and a Special Fellowship from the National Institute of Neurological Diseases and Stroke 1F10 NSO223201.

These experiments were conducted in our laboratory with the collaboration of Dr. Francesco Robustelli now at the Instituto di Psicologia del Consiglio Nazionale delle Ricerche, Roma, Italia.

The activity experiments were conducted in collaboration with Dr. Larry Squire.

REFERENCES

ADAMS, R. M., & CALHOUN, W. H. Time dependent memory storage: An alternative interpretation of some data. *Psychonomic Science*, 1970, *18*, 42-43.

ADAMS, H. E., & LEWIS, D. J. Retrograde amnesia and competing responses. *Journal of Comparative and Physiological Psychology*, 1962, *55*, 302-305.

AGRANOFF, B. W., DAVIS, R. E., CASOLA, L., & LIM, R. Actinomycin D blocks formation of memory of shock avoidance in goldfish. *Science*, 1967, *158*, 1600-1601.

ARON, C., GLICK, S. D., & JARVIK, M. E. Long lasting proactive effects of a single ECS. *Physiology & Behavior*, 1969, *4*, 785-790.

BARONDES, S. H., & COHEN, H. D. Memory impairment after subcutaneous injection of acetoxycycloheximide. *Science*, 1968, *160*, 556-557.

BLACK, M. Incubation of discriminated avoidance responses: ECS does not interrupt long term memory consolidation. Paper presented at the meeting of the Eastern Psychological Association, Philadelphia, April, 1969.

BRUSH, F. R., & LEVINE, S. Adrenocortical activity and avoidance learning as a function of time after fear conditioning. *Physiology & Behavior*, 1966, *1*, 309-311.

CHEVALIER, J. A. Permanence of amnesia after a single post-trial electroconvulsive seizure. *Journal of Comparative & Physiological Psychology*, 1965, 59, 125-127.

CHOROVER, S. L., & DELUCA, A. M. Transient change in electrocorticographic reaction to ECS in the rat following foot shock. *Journal of Comparative & Physiological Psychology*, 1969,

69, 141-149.

CHOROVER, S. L., & SCHILLER, P. H.   Re-examination
of prolonged retrograde amnesia in one trial
learning. *Journal of Comparative & Physiological Psychology*, 1966, *61*, 34-41.

COHEN, H. D., & BARONDES, S. H.   Cycloheximide
impairs memory of an appetitive task. *Communications in Behavioral Biology*, 1968, *1*,
337-339. (a)

COHEN, H. D., & BARONDES, S. H.   Effects of
acetoxycycloheximide on learning and memory of
a light-dark discrimination. *Nature*, 1968,
216, 271-273. (b)

COONS, E. E., & MILLER, N. E. Conflict versus
consolidation of memory traces to explain the
retrograde amnesia produced by ECS. *Journal
of Comparative & Physiological Psychology*,
1960, *53*, 524-531.

CRONHOLM, B., & LAGERGREN, A.   Memory disturbance
after electroconvulsive therapy. *Acta Psy-
chiatrica et Neurologica Scandinavica*, 1959,
34, 283-310.

DAVIS, R. E., & AGRANOFF, B. W.   Stages of memory
formation in goldfish: Evidence for an
environmental trigger. *Proceedings of the
National Academy of Science*, 1966, 55, 555-559.

DAVIS, R. E., & KLINGER, P. D.   Environmental
control of amnesic effects of various agents
in goldfish. *Physiology & Behavior*, 1969, *4*,
269-271.

FLEXNER, J. B., FLEXNER, L. B., & STELLAR, E.
Memory in mice as affected by intracerebral
puromycin. *Science*, 1963, *141*, 57-59.

GELLER, A., & JARVIK, M. E.   Electroconvulsive
shock induced amnesia and recovery. *Psychonomic Science*, 1968, *10*, 15-16.

GELLER, A., ROBUSTELLI, F., BARONDES, S. H., COHEN,
H. D., & JARVIK, M. E.   Impaired performance
by post-trial injections of cycloheximide in
a passive avoidance task. *Psychopharmacologia*,
1969, *14*, 371-376.

GELLER, A., ROBUSTELLI, F., & JARVIK, M. E.   A
parallel study of the amnesic effects of cycloheximide and ECS under different strengths of
conditioning. *Psychopharmacologia*, 1970, *16*,
281-289. (a)

GELLER, A., ROBUSTELLI, F., & JARVIK, M. E. In-
    cubation and the Kamin effect. *Journal of
    Experimental Psychology*, 1970, in press. (b)
GELLER, A., ROBUSTELLI, F., & JARVIK, M. E. Per-
    manence of a long temporal gradient of retro-
    grade amnesia induced by electroconvulsive
    shock. *Psychonomic Science*, 1970, in press.
    (c)
GELLER, M., & GELLER, A. Brief amnestic effects
    of spike wave discharges. *Neurology*, 1970,
    in press.
HERZ, M. J. Interference with one trial appetitive
    and aversive learning by ether and ECS.
    *Proceedings of the 75th Annual Convention
    of the American Psychological Association*,
    1967, pp. 83-84.
HUDSON, B. B. One trial learning in the domestic
    rat. *Genetic Psychology Monographs*, 1950,
    41, 99-147.
HUTT, S. J., LEE, D., & OUNSTED, C. Digit memory
    and evoked discharges in four light sensitive
    epileptic children. *Developmental Medicine
    in Child Neurology*, 1963, 5, 559-571.
IRWIN, S., BANUAZIZI, A., KALSNER, S., & CURTIS, A.
    One trial learning in the mouse. I. Its
    characteristics and modification by experi-
    mental-seasonal variables. *Psychopharma-
    cologia* (Berl.), 1968, *12*, 286-302.
JARVIK, M. E., & KOPP, R. An improved one trial
    passive avoidance learning situation.
    Psychological Reports, 1967, *21*, 221-224.
KAMIN, L. J. The retention of an incompletely
    learned avoidance response. *Journal of Com-
    parative & Pysiological Psychology*, 1957,
    50, 457-459.
KOHLENBERG, R., & TRABASSO, T. Recovery of a
    conditioned emotional response after one or
    two electroconvulsive shocks. *Journal of
    Comparative & Physiological Psychology*, 1968,
    65, 270-273.
LUTTGES, M. W., & MCGAUGH, J. L. Permanence of
    retrograde amnesia produced by electroconvul-
    sive shock. *Science*, 1967, *156*, 408-410.
MARQUIS, H. A., & SUBOSKI, M. D. Hypophysectomy
    and ACTH replacement in the incubation of
    passive and shuttle box avoidance functions.

Proceedings of the 77th Annual Convention of the American Psychological Association, 1969, pp. 207-208.

MCGAUGH, J. L. Time dependent processes in memory storage. *Science*, 1966, *153*, 1351-1358.

MCMICHAEL, J. S. Incubation of anxiety and instrumental behavior. *Journal of Comparative & Physiological Psychology*, 1966, *61*, 208-211.

MILLER, A. J. Variations in retrograde amnesia with parameters of electroconvulsive shock and time of testing. *Journal of Comparative & Physiological Psychology*, 1968, *66*, 40-47.

MISANIN, J. R., MILLER, R. R., & LEWIS, D. J. Retrograde amnesia produced by electroconvulsive shock after reactivation of a consolidated memory trace. *Science*, 1968, *160*, 554-555.

PINEL, J. P. J. A short gradient of ECS produced amnesia in a one trial appetitive learning situation. *Journal of Comparative & Physiological Psychology*, 1969, *68*, 650-655.

PINEL, J. P. J., & COOPER, R. M. Incubation and its implications for the interpretation of the ECS gradient effect. *Psychonomic Science*, 1966, *6*, 123-124. (a)

PINEL, J. P. J., & COOPER, R. M. The relationship between incubation and ECS gradient effects. *Psychonomic Science*, 1966, *6*, 125-126. (b)

ROBUSTELLI, F., GELLER, A., & JARVIK, M. E. Delay of punishment in passive avoidance conditioning. *Perceptual and Motor Skills*, 1968, *27*, 553-554.

ROBUSTELLI, F., GELLER, A., & JARVIK, M. E. Temporal gradient of 23 hours with electroconvulsive shock and its implications. *Communications in Behavioral Biology*, 1969, *4*, 79-84.

ROBUSTELLI, F., GELLER, A., & JARVIK, M. E. Combined action of two amnesic treatments. *Communications in Behavioral Biology*, 1970, in press. (a)

ROBUSTELLI, F., GELLER, A., & JARVIK, M. E. Biphasicity of the incubation curve. *Psychonomic Science*, 1970, in press. (b)

RUSSELL, W. R., & NATHAN, P. W. Traumatic amnesia. *Brain*, 1946, *69*, 280-300.

SCHNEIDER, A. M., & SHERMAN, W.   Amnesia: A
     function of the temporal relation of foot
     shock to electroconvulsive shock. *Science*,
     1968, *159*, 219-221.
SPEVAK, A. A., & SUBOSKI, M. D.   Retrograde effects
     of electroconvulsive shock on learned
     responses. *Psychological Bulletin*, 1969, *72*,
     66-76.
SUBOSKI, M. D., BLACK, M., LITNER, J., GRENNER,
     R. T., & SPEVAK, A. A.   Long and short term
     effects of ECS following one trial discrim-
     inated avoidance. *Neuropsychologia*, 1969, *7*,
     349-356.
TARPY, R. M.   Incubation of anxiety as measured by
     response suppression. *Psychonomic Science*,
     1966, *4*, 189-190.
WEISS, J. M., MCEWEN, B. S., SILVA, M. T., & KALKUT,
     M. F.   Pituitary adrenal influences in fear
     responding. *Science*, 1969, *163*, 197-198.
ZAMMIT-MONTEBELLO, A., BLACK, M., MARQUIS, H. A.,
     & SUBOSKI, M. D.   Incubation of passive
     avoidance in rats. *Journal of Comparative
     & Physiological Psychology*, 1969, *69*, 579-582.
ZERBOLIO, D. J.   Memory storage: The first post-
     trial hour. *Psychonomic Science*, 1969, *15*,
     57-58.
ZINKIN, S., & MILLER, A. J.   Recovery of memory
     after amnesia induced by ECS. *Science*, 1967,
     155, 102-104.

THE EFFECT OF SHORT EXPERIENCES
ON MACROMOLECULES IN THE BRAIN

E. Glassman and J. E. Wilson

Department of Biochemistry
and the Neurobiology Program
The University of North Carolina

Chapel Hill, North Carolina

There is much research that suggests that
the storage of memory involves successive stages.
Initially, memory is presumed to be retrievable
from a short-lived form, short term memory, but
as this declines, memory is then retrievable from
a more permanent form, long term memory (see John,
1967, and others for a discussion of the evidence
for this). These steps in the learning process
and memory storage are shown in Fig. 1.

In this scheme, chemical changes produce
intraneuronal modifications that allow the formation of interneuronal pathways in which experiential information is stored.

It is now becoming accepted that it is the
early stages of the formation of long term memory
that are sensitive to agents that interfere with
memory consolidation. The role of chemicals in
this process is not known, but certain guesses
can be made. While it is not likely that chemicals
encode experiential information within their own
structure, they probably do play a role in encoding
information in the nervous system, possibly by
producing intraneuronal changes that enable the
neurons to form the interneuronal pathways which

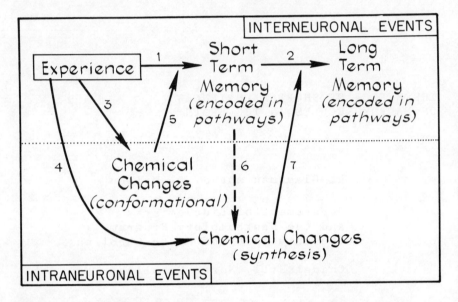

Fig. 1. Possible involvement of macromolecules
in the formation of short and long term memory.

encode information. Because short term memory
formation is not sensitive to inhibitors of RNA or
protein synthesis, it may be that this process is
not directly dependent on the synthesis of these
macromolecules (Agranoff, Davis & Brink, 1965,
1966; Agranoff, Davis, Casola & Lim, 1968; Appel,
1965; Barondes & Jarvik, 1964; Barondes & Cohen,
1966, 1967; Flexner & Flexner, 1967; Shashoua,
1968). There is no knowledge of whether pre-
existing chemicals are utilized, but it is difficult to imagine the formation of new pathways
without the involvement of chemical changes of
some type, presumably conformational, at the
synapse or in the cell (Fig. 1). The formation
of long term memory, however, *is* prevented when
protein or RNA synthesis is inhibited during and
immediately after training (Flexner & Flexner,

1968; Agranoff *et al.*, 1968; Barondes & Cohen, 1968), and it is likely that this process depends on the synthesis of these macromolecules. The sensitivity to these inhibitors is short lived, however, and thus the perpetuation of long term memory is not specifically dependent on the continuous synthesis of RNA and protein (Fig. 1). There are data that suggest that other agents that affect consolidation processes, such as ECS (MacInnes, McConkey & Schlesinger, 1970) and KCL-induced spreading depression (Bennett & Edelman, 1969) may also affect protein synthesis, and it is therefore possible that many, if not all, agents that affect consolidation do so by affecting the synthesis of RNA or protein. It is tempting to speculate that inducing localized increases in protein synthesis with drugs in brain may have the effect of increasing memory consolidation in mammals, a result that may have great significance for improving mental processes in humans.

The model shown in Fig. 1 suggests that neuronal electrical activity by itself will not produce these chemical changes (see Edstrom & Grampp, 1965, and Bondeson, Edstrom & Beviz, 1967). Some form of excitement (arousal) also may be necessary, as shown by McGaugh (1968) and Barondes and Cohen (1968). Indeed it is possible that certain types of novel or intense sensory stimulation and experience can produce this excitement and the subsequent chemical events without the formation of short term memory, and would account for many of the chemical changes caused by novel sensory stimulation (see Glassman, 1969).

Clearly an extensive coordinated research project involving many neurobiological disciplines is necessary to study the role of macromolecules in nervous system function, particularly during memory consolidation. Such a project has been initiated within the Neurobiology Program of the University of North Carolina. A behavioral task that is rapidly learned by a mouse was used because the goal was to measure the incorporation of precursors into RNA, proteins, lipids and other substances while the mouse was learning in the

hope that we could detect the synthesis of macromolecules associated with memory consolidation.
Thus far only RNA has been studied. The mouse was
chosen because it has been used extensively in
behavioral, biochemical and genetical studies,
but recent studies with the rat have produced
comparable data (Coleman, Pfingst & Glassman,
1970a). To minimize genetic variation, only 6 to
8 week old males of strain C57B1/6J supplied by
the Jackson Laboratories were used, but female
mice show the same chemical changes when conditions
are right (Coleman *et al.*, 1970a). The methods
and the data have been published in detail elsewhere (Zemp, Wilson, Schlesinger, Boggan &
Glassman, 1966; Zemp, Wilson & Glassman, 1967;
Adair, Wilson & Glassman, 1968a; Adair, Wilson,
Zemp & Glassman, 1968b; Coleman *et al.*, 1970a;
Coleman, Wilson & Glassman, 1970b; Kahan, Krigman,
Wilson & Glassman, 1970).

THE TRAINING APPARATUS

The "jump box" consists of a box divided into
two sections with a common electric grid floor
(Zemp *et al.*, 1966; Schlesinger & Wimer, 1967).
One mouse is placed in each section. A light and
a buzzer are attached to the outside of the box so
that each mouse receives equal stimulation. The
sections are identical except that one side has a
shelf onto which the mouse in that section can
jump. The light and buzzer are presented for three
seconds after which the electric foot shock is
applied. Initially, both mice jump in response to
the shock and the animal that has the shelf uses
it as a haven. The shock is terminated as soon as
it does so. After 15 seconds the mouse is then
removed from the shelf, placed on the grid floor
and another trial commences. The training lasts
for 15 minutes and between 25 and 35 trials are
carried out in this interval. The mouse that has
the shelf will usually start to avoid the shock in
response to light and buzzer by the fifth trial
and is performing to a criterion of 9 out of 10 by
10 minutes. The mice are thus over-trained. The
untrained mouse also receives equivalent handling

at random during the training. Thus with respect
to lights, buzzers, shocks, handling and injection,
the untrained mouse is *yoked* to the *trained* mouse.

BIOCHEMICAL METHODOLOGY

The experiments utilize a double isotope
labeling method. One mouse of a pair is injected
intracranially with ^{14}C-uridine, the other with
^{3}H-uridine. Intraperitoneal injections are
equally effective, but more isotope must be used
(Entingh, unpublished). Thirty minutes later, one
of the mice is trained for 15 minutes in the jump
box, while the other serves as the yoked animal.
After the training period, the brains of both mice
are homogenized simultaneously in the same homo-
genizer. The homogenate is then fractionated into
nuclei, ribosomes or polyribosomes and a supernatant fraction (Zemp *et al.*, 1966; Adair *et al.*,
1968b). UMP is isolated from the supernatant
fraction while RNA is extracted from each of the
subcellular components, and the amount of ^{14}C and
^{3}H in each is determined (Zemp *et al.*, 1966). The
purpose of using two isotopes is to avoid the
problem of differential losses of RNA that easily
occur during the prolonged manipulations used to
isolate the RNA and to enable a direct comparison
of the radioactivity profiles of the RNA or polysomes from trained and untrained mice after sucrose
gradient centrifugation or other procedures. The
ratio of ^{3}H to ^{14}C in the isolated UMP is a useful
indicator of the relative amount of uridine that
entered brain cells, and it is used to correct the
observed ratio of ^{3}H to ^{14}C in the RNA. The use
of crude homogenates or supernatants to obtain
this correction factor is not as reliable as using
the isolated UMP; the reason for this has not been
investigated.

THE INCORPORATION INTO RNA

Preliminary experiments indicated that more
radioactive uridine was incorporated into the RNA
extracted from brain nuclei or from brain ribosomes

of the trained mouse, and coded blind experiments
were carried out thereafter. Only after the biochemical analysis was completed and all the data
were computed was it revealed which isotope (^{3}H
or ^{14}C) the trained mouse received. Almost every
trained mouse incorporated more radioactivity into
brain RNA than did its untrained control
(Zemp *et al.*, 1966). The average increase in RNA
isolated from nuclei was 31%; the range was 6.5 to
69%. The average increase in RNA isolated from
the ribosomal pellet was 41%; the range was 7 to
73%. These differences cannot be unequivocally
ascribed to increased synthesis of RNA in the
trained animal. It could, for example, be due to
decreased destruction of RNA, to increases in permeability of the cells or their nuclei to uridine,
to a decrease in the synthesis of endogenous
uridine, to changes in blood flow (see Sokoloff,
1961), or to other alternatives. It is difficult
to pursue this problem directly because of technical difficulties. To avoid specifying a mechanism
we refer only to a change in incorporation. A
similar uncertainty exists for most experiments
involving the incorporation of a radioactive precursor in any tissue, but usually this problem is
not discussed.

THE RESPONSE OF OTHER TISSUES

By giving intraperitoneal and intracranial
injections of radioactive uridine, it was possible
to show that trained and untrained animals had no
significant differences in the incorporation of
radioactive uridine into RNA or polysomes of liver
or kidney, while these same animals showed pronounced differences in the brain (Zemp *et al.*,
1966; Adair *et al.*, 1968b). It is therefore concluded that while tissues other than the liver and
kidney might be responding to the experience, the
effect seems to be specific to brain.

LOCALIZATION IN THE BRAIN

It is of paramount importance for a deeper

insight into this phenomenon to ascertain those
cells in which the chemical response takes place.
Chemical analyses of brains after gross dissection
have indicated that the changes in RNA occur
primarily in the diencephalon and associated areas
(Zemp *et al.*, 1967). These studies also showed a
small significant decrease in the cortex. Autoradiography has confirmed this (Kahan *et al.*,
1970). Most areas and cells of the brain seem to
incorporate similar amounts of radioactivity in
trained and untrained animals. This is an important point since we have no independent measure of
the amount of radioactivity that gets into each
brain, and it indicates that injections were
equally effective and similarly distributed in
both sets of animals. Neurons were the only cells
to be consistently labeled, whereas the only glial
elements that showed any consistent labeling were
the ependyma. The silver grains were concentrated
over the neuronal nuclei.

There are, however, areas and cells in parts
of the limbic system of trained mice that produce
many silver grains, while what appear to be the
corresponding areas in the brains of untrained
mice produce very few grains in the autoradiogram.
Although our analysis has not proceeded to the
point where we can catalog all of the areas that
show a difference between trained and untrained
animals (especially where these differences are
not so striking), there are nuclei throughout the
olfactory and entorhinal cortices, hippocampus,
amygdala, thalamus, hypothalamus and mammillary
body in which there is incorporation in all trained
mice with little incorporation into their untrained
yoked controls.

In contrast to the structures discussed above,
the outer layers of the neocortex showed the
reverse situation, i.e., there is less radioactivity incorporated in the cells of this region
of trained mice than in their untrained yoked
controls. This is in agreement with the previous
report (Zemp *et al.*, 1966), based on gross dissection, that there is a significantly lower

incorporation in this part of the brain of a
trained mouse than in that of its yoked control.

This work indicates how important it is to
know the full extent of the involvement of the
brain in chemical responses to behavioral stimuli
in order to gain proper perspective. The significance of the changes in macromolecules associated
with experience and behavior will not be fully
understood until the functional relationships
between the cells where the chemical changes take
place are known. Autoradiography, and perhaps
histochemistry, seem well suited for elucidating
the cellular relationships (see also Beach, Emmens
& Kimble, 1969). There are, however, two major
technical problems that must be solved before the
results of autoradiographic studies can be interpreted definitively. First, there is the problem
of establishing that equal amounts of radioactive
precursors are similarly distributed in the brains
of the trained and the untrained mice. This is
done by determining the radioactivity in UMP in
biochemical experiments (Zemp *et al.*, 1966), and
appropriate modification of this technique might
be applicable to autoradiographic studies. A
second problem is the difficulty of reliably
establishing that the same neurons of trained and
untrained mice are being compared. Only careful
attention to these possible sources of error will
prevent investigators from drawing unwarranted or
erroneous conclusions.

THE NATURE AND FUNCTION OF THE RNA

To study the nature of the RNA, over 20 of the
^{14}C and ^{3}H labeled RNA mixtures from yoked and
trained animals were sedimented in sucrose
gradients to see if the increased radioactivity
was located in a single species of RNA that might
have a unique function (Zemp *et al.*, 1966). In
all cases, the increased radioactivity associated
with the RNA of the trained mouse was quite hetero-
genous with respect to sedimentation rate. The
patterns of radioactivity were of the same general
shape for RNA from the brain, livers or kidneys

from both trained and untrained mice. Thus the
increased incorporation into brain RNA resembled
that found after RNA synthesis had been stimulated
in liver by hydrocortisone or in uterus by estrogen.
This suggested that the increased radioactivity
was not confined to a single species of RNA and
that a general increase had occurred in the synthesis of rapidly-labeled RNA owing to a *metabolic
stimulation* of brain cells. In addition, the
increased incorporation into polysomes of the brain
during the training experience suggested that the
increased radioactivity is either in messenger RNA
or in preribosomal RNA (Adair *et al.*, 1968b; Coleman, 1970a). The radioactivity can be dissociated
from the polysomes with lithium dodecyl sulphate
(Coleman, 1969). Thus we find no evidence for an
RNA with a function that does not involve protein
synthesis; indeed the RNA we do find is similar to
RNA extracted from other tissues. Further work is
needed to determine whether this brain RNA is
involved in the synthesis of new proteins or in
the replenishment of, or an increase in, the
proteins already present.

THE BEHAVIORAL TRIGGER

There are many differences between the trained
and yoked mice in addition to learning. For
example, the trained mouse has a change in cue
and his attention is now directed toward a stimulus
that the untrained mouse probably views as benign.
Also, the stresses on the trained mouse are different, as are his responses to them. Finally,
the trained mouse jumps more often than the yoked
mouse, and quickly learns to organize his locomotion to reach the shelf, while the untrained
mouse jumps randomly. To facilitate this analysis,
the training experience will be arbitrarily divided
into three stages.

The first stage is one of confusion. Random
activity and nonspecific stimulation by the light,
buzzer, shock and handling are probably occurring,
and the responses of the animal are random with
respect to locomotion, emotions, stress, etc.

The second stage is one in which insight into
the situation develops. The length of this stage
cannot be defined exactly, but it is probably
characterized by less random locomotor responses
and by more specific adaptive responses. Emotional
responses and stress that occur in this stage may
be more specifically related to the learning
process than in stage one.

The third stage is a post-learning phase.
The animal has already developed insight and is
performing the task with a high degree of regu-
larity. His locomotion is organized with respect
to the shelf and new stresses and emotional
responses (motivation, attention, etc.) may be
present owing to the fact that the light and buzzer
are now known to signal a painful shock if a jump
is not made.

The problem is to ascertain in which stage
the behavioral trigger operates and then to try to
identify the relevant variable(s). The first stage
can be easily eliminated. The fact that yoked
mice and randomly shocked mice do not show the
increased incorporation of uridine into brain RNA
or polysomes when compared with quiet mice clearly
demonstrates that the non-specific stimuli of the
first phase are not responsible for this chemical
response (Zemp *et al.*, 1966; Adair *et al.*, 1968b).

We can test the involvement of the last phase,
the post-learning phase, where the animal is merely
performing the task, by using a previously trained
mouse and requiring it to perform the task after
the injection of radioactive uridine. The results
demonstrated that a mouse performing the previously
learned response does *not* show increased incorporation into brain polysomes (Adair *et al.*, 1968a).
This lack of chemical response in the performing
mouse could mean that the relevant behavioral
trigger is not present in the third phase. It may
be, however, that the behavioral trigger occurs
in this phase during training, but that conditions
were not right when the mouse was only performing
the task. For example, the previously trained
mouse might have experienced reduced stress or

arousal because it habituated to the training
experience or because it received far fewer shocks
when performing than a naive mouse receives when
it undergoes training. Although shocks by themselves have been ruled out as a causative stimulus
(Zemp *et al*., 1966; Adair *et al*., 1968a, b), shocks
may be needed in combination with other stimuli to
produce the chemical responses.

In order to distinguish between these alternative explanations for the lack of chemical response
in the performing mouse, we used a behavioral
experience in which the animal was also habituated
and in which there also were no shocks. These
occurred when the performance of the previously
trained mouse was extinguished by repeated presentation of the conditioned stimuli (light and
buzzer) without the unconditioned stimulus (the
foot shock). Under such conditions, the previously
trained mouse stopped jumping to the shelf when the
light and buzzer were presented (Schlesinger &
Wimer, 1967). This experience was accompanied by
an increased incorporation of uridine into brain
polysomes at levels comparable to those observed
in naive mice undergoing training (Coleman *et al*.,
1970b). Since we do not know whether the cells
that respond under these two different conditions
are the same, however, we cannot be sure that the
chemical response observed during the extinction
of avoidance behavior is the same as that observed
during acquisition. But it is clear that a
previously trained mouse can show increased incorporation during an experience to which the mouse
has habituated and in which no electric shock had
been given. This rules out the possibility that
habituation or the absence of electric shock were
responsible for the lack of chemical response by
the performing animal and eliminates the third
(performing) stage of the training experience as
the one containing the behavioral trigger for the
chemical response.

The extinction process can also be divided
into three arbitrary phases. During the first
phase, the mouse performs the task as he previously
learned it. Our previous data suggest that mere

performance does not trigger the increased incorporation of uridine into polysomes, and this phase
of extinction can be excluded as the source of the
behavioral trigger. The second phase is insight
development, and seems again to be the phase containing the behavioral trigger, since the third
phase is one in which the mouse no longer performs
the task, and it would be hard to ascribe the
behavioral trigger to this non-performing stage.

We are thus left with the insight development
phase of the training or extinction experience as
the one which contains the stimulus for the
chemical response. This does not mean that the
encoding of the experience in the nervous system
is the trigger for the chemical reactions since
the insight development phase also contains special
stresses, levels of excitement, emotional responses
and other phenomena that may be related to the
learning process or to other processes, such as
those responsible for restoring chemicals used
during this phase of nervous system activity. It
is not clear which of these processes are causing
or are related to the chemical response.

The insight development phase of jump box
training can itself be broken up into several
arbitrary phases. Such avoidance conditioning can
be considered to consist of an initial association
of the conditioned stimulus (light and buzzer) with
the unconditioned stimulus (the shock) similar to
classical conditioning as well as the development
of the awareness that the shock can be escaped by
jumping to the shelf. A final phase is the coupl-
ing of these processes into the realization that
the shock can be avoided entirely by jumping to
the shelf when the light and buzzer are presented
(John, 1967). Experiments have been initiated to
determine whether the behavioral trigger can be
associated with any of these steps. Mice have been
exposed to classical conditioning for 15 or 30
minutes by pairing light-buzzer and shock in the
yoke side of the jump box; such mice do not show
increased incorporation of radioactive uridine into
brain polysomes (Adair *et al.*, 1968a; Coleman,
1969). Thus this phase of insight development

probably lacks the behavioral trigger. Further
experiments along these lines are contemplated.

In addition to the behavioral trigger, it is
important to understand the intermediate chemical
and physiological steps that lead to increased
incorporation into RNA and polysomes. In mammals
this usually involves an hormonal intermediate,
and animals with various glands removed have been
tested for: a.   trainability, and b.   uridine
incorporation into polysomes. The experiments
sought to ascertain whether the biochemical
response that occurs during 15 minutes of avoidance
training is dependent on the release of hormone
from a functioning gland during this time. We
were not concerned here with long term debilitating
effects. Our data indicate that the adrenal, the
pituitary, the testes and the ovary are not necessary for a mouse to learn the avoidance task, or
for the increased incorporation of uridine into RNA
that accompanied it (Adair *et al.*, 1968a; Coleman
et al., 1970a). The possible effects of other
glands are being investigated. Other processes
have been related to increased incorporation into
RNA in other mammalian tissues. We are in the
process of studying changes in histones, norepinephrine, cyclic AMP and adenyl cyclase. These are
substances believed to be intermediates between a
stimulus and a change in RNA in many tissues of
mammals, and they may be important in this brain
response as well.

THE SIGNIFICANCE OF THESE RESULTS

During the past decade, much research has
suggested that macromolecules, particularly RNA,
undergo changes when experiential information is
coded in the nervous system (Adair *et al.*, 1968a,
b; Bateson, Horn & Rose, 1969; Beach *et al.*, 1969;
Bogoch, 1968; Bowman & Strobel, 1969; Coleman *et
al.*, 1970a, b; Delweg, Gerner & Wacker, 1968;
Hydén & Egyhazi, 1962, 1963, 1964; Hydén & Lange,
1963; Kahan *et al.*, 1970; Machlus & Gaito, 1968a,
b; Rose, Bateson, Horn & Horn, 1970; Shashoua,
1968, 1970; Zemp *et al.*, 1966, 1967; and articles

by Hydén, Bowman and others in this volume; also
see Glassman, 1969, for a review of this field).
The behavioral trigger for such chemical changes
has not been elucidated. It may be that the
learning, *per se*, or the special stresses and
emotional and motivational effects of learning are
responsible for triggering such chemical responses
but it is also possible that the changes in RNA
are due to non-specific stimuli or to the activity
associated with the training experience. The
effects of visual (Appel, Davis & Scott, 1967;
Talwar, Chopra, Goel & D'Monte, 1966; White &
Sundeen, 1967), auditory (Hamberger & Hydén, 1945),
rotary (Hamberger & Hydén, 1949a, b; Watson, 1965;
Attardi, 1957; Jarlstadt, 1966a, b), olfactory
(Rappoport & Daginawala, 1968) and stress stimulation (Altman & Das, 1966; Bryan, Bliss & Beck,
1967) have been reported to cause changes in RNA
or polysomes in the nervous system, and it is not
unexpected that such stimuli would be effective
during training. In the work described in this
paper, such non-specific stimuli have been eliminated and the behavioral trigger has been narrowed
down to the insight development phase, but the
exact mechanism has not been delineated.

Another consideration is the function of these
macromolecules in the brain. Their role may be to
replenish chemicals used in nerve activity, similar
to the restorative role macromolecules play in all
cells, and thus they are responsible for the
maintenance of function and the health of cells.
Another possibility is that such chemical changes
are related more specifically to altering the
probability that a post-synaptic neuron will fire
when impulses arrive from presynaptic nerves so
that new pathways are formed. This can be accomplished through processes that change the effectiveness of the neurotransmitter, by increasing
its concentration, by decreasing the activity of
enzymes that inactivate it or by increasing the
number or effectiveness of the receptor sites on
the post-synaptic neuron. Thus, macromolecules
may play the important role of regulating connectivity between neurons even though they do not
encode the experiential information themselves.

There is still not enough information to reach
an unequivocal conclusion concerning our results.
The training experience obviously causes both a
change in behavior (learning) and a chemical
change in the brain, but there are many pitfalls
in trying to correlate chemical changes in the
nervous system with a behavioral trigger. In
particular, there are no data that establish
whether either of these changes is the cause of
the other, or whether they might be unrelated
responses to two different stimuli. This uncertainty affects all research where an experience
exerts one or more behavioral, biological and
chemical responses. Thus it is not known whether
the chemical response has anything to do with the
learning process *per se*, or with a process inci-
dental to it. It is therefore extremely difficult
to correlate our results with the consolidation
of memory (Fig. 1), although it is extremely
tempting to do so. The RNA might code for proteins
that may be involved in the consolidation of long
term memory (Fig. 1, step 6), possibly by rendering
permanent the synaptic associations that developed
during short term learning (Fig. 1, step 2). The
protein may be related to the peptide(s) postulated
to be involved in the maintenance and retrieval of
memory by Flexner and Flexner (1968) and Bohus and
de Wied (1966). We are continuing to analyze this
process in the hope that future experiments will
cast light on these phenomena.

ACKNOWLEDGEMENTS

This research was supported in part by
research grants from the U. S. Public Health
Service (GM-08202; NB-07457), the National Science
Foundation (GB-18551) and by a Research Career
Development Award (GM-K3-14,911) to E. Glassman
from the Division of General Medical Sciences,
National Institutes of Health.

REFERENCES

ADAIR, L. B., WILSON, J. E., & GLASSMAN, E.   Brain

function and macromolecules. IV. Uridine
incorporation into polysomes of mouse brain
during different behavioral experiences.
*Proceedings of the National Academy of
Sciences*, 1968, *61*, 917-922. (a)

ADAIR, L. B., WILSON, J. E., ZEMP, J. W., & GLASS-
MAN, E. Brain function and macromolecules.
III. Uridine incorporation into polysomes
of mouse brain during short-term avoidance
conditioning. *Proceedings of the National
Academy of Sciences*, 1968, *61*, 606-613. (b)

AGRANOFF, B. W., DAVIS,.R. E., & BRINK, J. J.
Memory fixation in the goldfish. *Proceedings
of the National Academy of Sciences*, 1965, *54*,
788-793.

AGRANOFF, B. W., DAVIS, R. E., & BRINK, J. J.
Chemical studies on memory fixation in
goldfish. *Brain Research*, 1966, *1*, 303-309.

AGRANOFF, B. W., DAVIS, R. E., CASOLA, L., & LIM,
R. Actinomycin-D blocks formation of memory
of shock-avoidance in goldfish. *Science*,
1968, *158*, 1600-1601.

ALTMAN, J., & DAS, G. D. Behavioral manipulations
and protein metabolism of the brain: Effects
of motor exercise on the utilization of
leucine-^{3}H. *Physiology and Behavior*, 1966,
1, 105-108.

APPEL, S. H. Effect of inhibition of RNA synthesis
on neural information storage. *Nature*, 1965,
207, 1163-1166.

APPEL, S. H., DAVIS, W., & SCOTT, S. Brain polysomes: Response to environmental stimulation.
Science, 1967, *157*, 836-838.

ATTARDI, G. Quantitative behavior of cytoplasmic
RNA in rat Purkinje cells following prolonged
physiological stimulation. *Experimental Cell
Research*, 1957, Supplement 4, 25-53.

BARONDES, S. H., & JARVIK, M. E. The influence of
actinomycin-D on brain RNA synthesis and on
memory. *Journal of Neurochemistry*, 1964, *11*,
187-195.

BARONDES, S. H., & COHEN, H. D. Puromycin effect
on successive phases of memory storage.
Science, 1966, *151*, 594-595.

BARONDES, S. H., & COHEN, H. D. Delayed and sus-
tained effect of acetoxycycloheximide on

memory in mice. *Proceedings of the National Academy of Sciences*, 1967, *58*, 157-164.

BARONDES, S. H., & COHEN, H. D. Arousal and the conversion of "short-term" to "long-term" memory. *Proceedings of the National Academy of Sciences*, 1968, *61*, 923-929.

BATESON, P. P. G., HORN, G. & ROSE, S. P. R. Effects of an imprinting procedure on regional incorporation of tritiated lysine into protein of chick brain. *Nature*, 1969, *223*, 534-535.

BEACH, G., EMMENS, M., KIMBLE, D. P., & LICKEY, M. Autoradiographic demonstration of biochemical changes in the limbic system during avoidance training. *Proceedings of the National Academy of Sciences*, 1969, *62*, 692-696.

BENNETT, G. S., & EDELMAN, G. M. Amino acid incorporation into brain proteins during spreading cortical depression. *Science*, 1969, *163*, 393-395.

BOGOCH, S. *The Biochemistry of Memory*. London: Oxford University Press, 1968.

BOHUS, B., & DEWIED, D. Inhibitory and facilitatory effect of two related peptides on extinction of avoidance behavior. *Science*, 1966, *153*, 318-320.

BONDESON, C., EDSTROM, A., & BEVIZ, A. Effects of different inhibitors of protein synthesis on electrical activity in the spinal cord of fish. *Journal of Neurochemistry*, 1967, *14*, 1032-1034.

BOWMAN, R. E., & STROBEL, D. A. Brain metabolism in the rat during learning. *Journal of Comparative and Physiological Psychology*, 1969, *67*, 448-456.

BRYAN, R. N., BLISS, E. L., & BECK, E. C. Incorporation of uridine-^{3}H into mouse brain RNA during stress. *Federation Proceedings*, 1967, *26*, 709.

COLEMAN, M. S. Incorporation of radioactive precursors into polysomes and RNA of mammalian brain during short term behavioral experiences. Ph.D. Dissertation, University of North Carolina at Chapel Hill, 1969.

COLEMAN, M. S., PFINGST, B., WILSON, J. E., & GLASSMAN, E. Brain function and macromolecules. VIII. Uridine incorporation into polysomes of hypophysectomized rats and ovariectomized mice during avoidance conditioning. *Report*, 1970, in preparation. (a)

COLEMAN, M. S., WILSON, J. E., & GLASSMAN, E. Brain function and macromolecules. VII. Uridine incorporation into polysomes of mouse brain during extinction. *Report*, 1970, in preparation. (b)

DELWEG, G., GERNER, R., & WACKER, A. Quantitative and qualitative changes in ribonucleic acid of rat brain dependent on age and training experiments. *Journal of Neurochemistry*, 1968, *15*, 1109-1119.

EDSTROM, J. E., & GRAMPP, W. Nervous activity and metabolism of ribonucleic acids in the crustacean stretch receptor neuron. *Journal of Neurochemistry*, 1965, *12*, 735-741.

FLEXNER, L. B., FLEXNER, J. B., & ROBERTS, R. B. Memory in mice analysed with antibiotics. *Science*, 1967, *155*, 1377-1383.

FLEXNER, L. B., & FLEXNER, J. B. Intracerebral saline: Effect on memory of trained mice treated with puromycin. *Science*, 1968, *159*, 330-331.

GLASSMAN, E. The biochemistry of learning: An evaluation of the role of RNA and protein. *Annual Review of Biochemistry*, 1969, *38*, 605-646.

HAMBERGER, C. A., & HYDÉN, H. Cytochemical changes in the cochlear ganglion caused by acoustic stimulation and trauma. *Acta Oto-Laryngologica* (Stockholm), 1945, Supplement 61, 1-29.

HAMBERGER, C. A., & HYDÉN, H. Production of nucleoproteins in the vestibular ganglion. *Acta Oto-Laryngologica* (Stockholm), 1949, Supplement 75, 53-81. (a)

HAMBERGER, C. A., & HYDÉN, H. Transneuronal chemical changes in Deiters' (sic) nucleus. *Acta Oto-Laryngologica* (Stockholm), 1949, Supplement 75, 82-113. (b)

HYDÉN, H., & EGYHAZI, E. Nuclear RNA changes of nerve cells during a learning experiment in rats. *Proceedings of the National Academy of Sciences*, 1962, *48*, 1366-1373.

HYDÉN, H., & EGYHAZI, E. Glial RNA changes during

a learning experiment in rats. *Proceedings of the National Academy of Sciences*, 1963, 49, 618-624.

HYDÉN, H., & EGYHAZI, E. Changes in RNA content and base composition in cortical neurons of rats in a learning experiment involving transfer of handedness. *Proceedings of the National Academy of Sciences*, 1964, 52, 1030-1035.

HYDÉN, H., & LANGE, P. W. A differentiation in RNA response in neurons early and late during learning. *Proceedings of the National Academy of Sciences*, 1965, 53, 946-952.

JARLSTEDT, J. Functional localization in the cerebellar cortex studied by quantitative determinations of Purkinje cell RNA. I. RNA changes in rat cerebellar Purkinje cells after proprio- and exteroreceptive and vestibular stimulation. *Acta Physiologica Scandinavica*, 1966, 67, 243-252. (a)

JARLSTEDT, J. Functional localization in the cerebellar cortex studied by quantitative determinations of Purkinje cell RNA. II. RNA changes in rabbit cerebellar Purkinje cells after caloric stimulation and vestibular neurotomy. *Acta Physiologica Scandinavica*, 1966, Supplement 271, 1-24. (b)

JOHN, E. R. *Mechanisms of Memory*. New York: Academic Press, 1967.

KAHAN, B., KRIGMAN, M. R., WILSON, J. E., & GLASSMAN, E. Brain function and macromolecules. VI. Autoradiographic anaylsis of the effects of a brief training experience on the incorporation of uridine into mouse brain. *Proceedings of the National Academy of Sciences*, 1970, 65, 300-303.

MACINNES, J. W., MCCONKEY, E. H., & SCHLESINGER, K. Changes in brain polyribosomes following an electro-convulsive seizure. *Journal of Neurochemistry*, 1970, 17, 457-460.

MACHLUS, B., & GAITO, J. Detection of RNA species unique to a behavioral task. *Psychonomic Science*, 1968, 10, 253-254. (a)

MACHLUS, B., & GAITO, J. Unique RNA species developed during a shock avoidance task. *Psychonomic Science*, 1968, 12, 111-112. (b)

MCGAUGH, J. L.   A multi-trace view of memory
    storage processes.   In D. Bovet, F. Bovet-
    Nitti and A. Oliverio (Eds.), *Attuali
    Orientamenti della Ricerda Sull Apprendimento
    e la Memoria*, Volume CIX.   Rome: Accademia
    Nazionale de Lincei, 1968.
RAPPOPORT, D. A., & DAGINAWALA, H. F.   Changes
    in nuclear RNA of brain induced by olfaction
    in catfish.   *Journal of Neurochemistry*,
    1968, *15*, 991-1006.
ROSE, S. P. R., BATESON, P. P. G., HORN, A. L. D.,
    & HORN, G.   Effects of an imprinting pro-
    cedure on the regional incorporation of
    tritiated uracil into chick brain RNA.
    Nature, 1970, *225*, 650-651.
SCHLESINGER, K., & WIMER, R.   Genotype and con-
    ditioned avoidance learning in the mouse.
    *Journal of Comparative and Physiological
    Psychology*, 1967, *63*, 139-141.
SHASHOUA, V. E.   RNA changes in goldfish brain
    during learning.   *Nature*, 1968, *217*, 238-240.
SHASHOUA, V. E.   RNA metabolism in goldfish brain
    during acquisition of new behavioral patterns.
    *Proceedings of the National Academy of
    Sciences*, 1970, *65*, 160-167.
SOKOLOFF, L.   Local cerebral circulation at rest
    and during altered cerebral activity induced
    by anesthesia or visual stimulation.   In
    S. S. Kety and J. Elkes (Eds.), *Regional
    Neurochemistry*.   London: Pergamon Press,
    1961.
TALWAR, G. P., CHOPRA, S. P., GOEL, B. K., &
    D'MONTE, B.   Correlation of the functional
    activity of the brain with metabolic para-
    meters.   III.   Protein metabolism of the
    occipital cortex in relation to light
    stimulus.   *Journal of Neurochemistry*, 1966,
    13, 109-116.
WATSON, W. E.   An autoradiographic study of the
    incorporation of nucleic-acid precursors by
    neurones and glia during nerve stimulation.
    Journal of Physiology, 1965, *180*, 754-765.
WHITE, R. H., & SUNDEEN, C. D.   The effect of
    light and light deprivation upon the ultra-
    structure of the larval mosquito eye.   I.
    Polyribosomes and endoplasmic reticulum.

  Journal of Experimental Zoology, 1967, *164*,
  461-478.
ZEMP, J. W., WILSON, J. E., SCHLESINGER, K.,
  BOGGAN, W. O., & GLASSMAN, E.   Brain function
  and macromolecules. I. Incorporation of
  uridine into RNA of mouse brain during short-
  term training experience. *Proceedings of the
  National Academy of Sciences*, 1966, *55*,
  1423-1431.
ZEMP, J. W., WILSON, J. E., & GLASSMAN, E.   Brain
  function and macromolecules. II. Site of
  increased labeling of RNA in brains of mice
  during a short-term training experience.
  *Proceedings of the National Academy of
  Sciences*, 1967, *58*, 1120-1125.

REGIONAL BRAIN RNA METABOLISM AS A FUNCTION OF DIFFERENT EXPERIENCES

Robert E. Bowman and Paul D. Kottler

University of Wisconsin Psychology
Department and Wisconsin Regional
Primate Research Center

Madison, Wisconsin

In the last decade, studies of brain metabolism during simple behavioral experiences of short duration have provided evidence of measurable phenomena, particularly as regards changes in RNA metabolism. This area of investigation bears a logical resemblance to the study of electrical responses of brain during behavior, and can therefore be christened as chemoencephalography. The animal is subjected to a behavioral experience, sacrificed and the metabolic pattern of the brain at that point in time is analyzed. The intent is to discover metabolic events which may be specific to the experience and localized regionally in brain. These metabolic events may not necessarily be correlated in any simple way with the electrophysiology also occurring at the same time and may thus reflect neural processes different from those detectable by electrical signals.

As an example, which initially motivated our own research, the processes involved in the consolidation of long-term memory almost certainly include metabolic events, which may or may not be accompanied by electrical events. However, even if electroencephalographic events do accompany consolidation, we know of no current theories which predict

301

characteristics for the unique identification of
these events. On the other hand, there are several
theoretical positions by which one might expect
that brain RNA changes would be correlated with
memory consolidation. To illustrate, many theories
of consolidation are based on the concept of synaptic alterations which modify the probability of
the firing of the affected neurons (John, 1967).
Synaptic alterations which have been suggested
include changes in available neurotransmitter or
neurotransmitter enzymes, changes in pre- or post-
synaptic membrane structures, the growth of neural
processes or changes in glial cells. Each of these
mechanisms would require the synthesis of structural proteins or enzymatic proteins or both.
Since protein can only be synthesized via RNA, any
of the above consolidation theories would therefore
predict that some alteration in RNA metabolism
would accompany consolidation. Of course, consolidation theories based on the formation of "memory
specific" RNA or protein molecules would also predict the same thing. The major question for all
of these theories would be whether or not such
changes were of measurable magnitude.

This is not meant to imply that measurable
RNA changes which might be found accompanying
learning would necessarily reflect processes of
memory consolidation. It is, for example, very
plausible that increased RNA and protein metabolism
would be required, in a more or less proportional
amount, for cellular activity associated with increased neuronal firing, e.g., for the replenishment of neurotransmitter expended during firing.
Increased neuronal firing might accompany learning
in association with any number of physiological and
psychological processes, such as attentional processes, emotional reactions, motor activity, processing of sensory information, stress reactions,
associational learning, memory consolidation, etc.
It is also possible that altered RNA metabolism
could accompany any of the above processes through
mechanisms other than altered rates of neuronal
firing. As one theoretical example, stress reactio
might be accompanied by saturation of corticostero
binding sites in the hippocampus (see McEwen,

Zigmond, Azmitia, & Weiss, this Symposium) and
could possibly alter RNA or protein synthesis in
the course of enzyme induction, without altering
the electrical activity of the hippocampus. These
latter possibilities are the most exciting for the
future of this area of behavioral-biochemical
research, since to the extent that RNA metabolism
is independent of neuronal firing, the measurement
of that metabolism will explore brain-behavioral
relationships which could not be detected by electroencephalographic measurements.

In our present state of knowledge, none of the
above possibilities can be ruled out, and we can
only look forward to research directed towards
establishing which biochemical-electrophysiological-
behavioral relationships hold in brain. Because
of the variety of possible relationships, such
research may often prove difficult to interpret.
This difficulty, while it may perplex the individual
investigater, is no worse than that encountered in
electroencephalographic research, and therefore in
no way deprecates the worth of such studies. This
difficulty does mean that considerable research
will need to be done, with many behavioral conditions, before the meanings of various chemoencephalographic results will be established. However, such
research promises to present the neurosciences with
new phenomena which may help us to understand such
problems of current interest as that dealing with
the processes involved in memory consolidation.

Nucleic acid chemoencephalograms during learning or training experiences were first investigated
by Hydén and Egyhazi (1962, 1963, 1964), who reported that training situations involving the climbing
of a wire or the developing of a forced change in
handedness produced both an increased RNA content
and a change in base ratios of RNA in selected
brain tissue of the rat. At that time, Hydén postulated that the formation of specific RNA molecules
might encode the storage of specific memories. This
theory generated both excitement and controversy,
in the course of which Hydén has modified his
position (Kandel & Spencer, 1968, p. 116). In
addition, Hydén interpreted his experiments as proof

for his theory, whereas serious questions can and
have been raised that the conditions and controls
in these studies were not adequate to determine
which of the possible behavioral components presumably operating in Hydén's training situations
were responsible for the observed RNA changes
(e.g., consolidation, acquisition, motor activity,
frustration, etc.). Despite these questions as
to whether Hydén had discovered the explanation
for his results, the results themselves represented
a major contribution by indicating that certain
empirically defined, brief training situations
were sufficient to produce measurable metabolic
alterations in the RNA of brain tissue.

These results encouraged other investigators
in similar studies. Using a one-way shock avoidance task, Glassman and colleagues found an increased uptake of radioactively labelled uridine
into RNA of subcortical portions of brain of the
instrumentally conditioned mouse (reviewed by
Glassman, 1969; and by Glassman & Wilson in this
Symposium). In another approach, Shashoua (1968,
1970) reported alterations in uridine/cytidine
ratios in RNA of goldfish learning to swim with
a float attached to their underside. These alterations were not seen in control groups given various
treatments such as puromycin injection, swimming
in a "whirlpool," swimming with a float too large
to manage, KCl-induced convulsions, etc. Turning
to behavioral factors other than those presumed
to reflect learning, Bryan, Bliss and Beck (1967)
found increased incorporation of precursor into
RNA in the brains of mice tied for 1 to 24 hours to
a wooden dowel whereas liver and other peripheral
organs exhibited decreased incorporation into RNA.
Similarly, Appel (1967) reported increased polysome
aggregation in the cortex of rats given 15 minutes
of exposure to light following three days of con-
finement in the dark.

These studies, and our own to be described,
have now established in several laboratories that
various kinds of relatively simple and brief
behavioral experiences are reliably accompanied by
altered RNA metabolism in various regions of the

brain. The meanings of these phenomena still remain
to be clearly delineated, although a beginning has
been made. These and other studies have been well
reviewed by Booth (1967) and most recently by
Glassman (1969).

Our work began with the finding that 60
minutes of training on repeated spatial reversals
for water reinforcement in a Y-maze produced an
increased synthesis of RNA in the cell nuclei of
the hippocampus (more properly, Ammon's horn) of
the rat (Bowman & Strobel, 1969). In this study
all rats were originally trained following 23 hours
of daily water deprivation for four daily sessions
of 100 trials each to go to one spatial position
(left goal box or right goal box) in an automated
Y-maze (Fig. 1) to obtain about .02 ml of water
per trial. After a response of entering a goal
box and either receiving a water reinforcement or
not, the rats had to return to the start box in
order to trigger the goal boxes so that water would
be delivered upon a subsequent correct goal box
entry (a noncorrection procedure). On the last
two sessions of original training, water was delivered on 75% of the correct goal box entries. This
training provided all rats with a well-learned
response and considerable adaptation to the apparatus. It also gave them experience with non-rewarded
trials. On the day following the last session of
original training, the rats were all injected
through a chronic jugular catheter with tritiated
cytidine (cytidine-5-T, Nuclear Chicago). The
chronic catheter avoided the stress of injury,
surgery or anesthesia just prior to testing, and
minimized handling stress; it also provided highly
reliable delivery of the precursor into the vascular system. Half the rats were then trained for
60 minutes exactly as they had been trained on the
last two sessions on original training (control
rats), on the supposition that they would simply
be performing an already learned task. The remaining (experimental) rats were also similarly trained
on the identical task, except that they were
initially required to go to the opposite arm to
which they had been previously trained in order to
find water (spatial discrimination reversal). As

Fig. 1. Automated Y-maze used in reversal learning experiments.

soon as they had mastered this spatial reversal
to a criterion of 9 correct responses out of 10
consecutive trials, they were reversed to the
original side. As soon as the second reversal was
mastered, they were reversed again, etc. They
averaged between 5 and 6 reversals in 60 minutes.
All rats were trained in yoked pairs (in each
pair, one rat was trained immediately after the
other in the maze) throughout the 400 original
training trials and the final 60 minute session.
One rat of each pair served as an experimental
rat and one as a control rat, determined randomly
just prior to the final session. In addition
during this final session, if water delivery did
not occur during a goal box entry, following either
a correct or an incorrect response, water was
delivered in the start box as soon as the rat
returned there. Thus, the experimental rats
received one reinforcement per trial, even though
making many goal box errors during their reversal
training. The control rats similarly received one
reinforcement per trial, thereby equating the reinforcement ratio for both groups. As an interesting
aside, rats on this kind of reversal schedule obtain
one reinforcement per trial no matter what their
response and thus receive no differential reinforcement for learning. Nevertheless, most rats do
exhibit reversal learning.

Immediately after the final 60 minute training
session, all rats were decapitated, the fresh brain
was quickly dissected into the following five gross
regions (discarding olfactory bulbs, cerebellum,
and lower brainstem up through the pons and inferior
colliculus): hippocampus, remaining subcortex,
pyriform cortex, anterior cortex and posterior cortex. The tissue was homogenized and a crude nuclear
pellet was spun down. Cytoplasmic and nuclear
fractions were then subjected to extraction with 5%
TCA (Schneider, 1945). Total RNA and DNA were
determined by orcinol and diphenylamine color tests,
and the disintegrations per minute (DPM) of tritium
incorporated into RNA, as well as that present in
the cold TCA extracts, which contained cytidine and
cytidylic acid, were determined by scintillation
counting. The radioactivity incorporated into RNA

was corrected for brain pools of precursor radioactivity by dividing the incorporated DPM by the
DPM present in the cold TCA extracts, on the basis
of an observed direct proportionality between the
incorporated and pool radioactivity (the rationale
for this was discussed by Bowman & Strobel, 1969).

Statistically significant changes in RNA were
noted only in the hippocampus (Ammon's horn). Total
RNA (orcinol color test) increased by 15% and pool
corrected ^{3}H-RNA increased by 26% (Table I) in the
hippocampal nuclei of reversal trained rats compared to control rats. These results suggested
increased RNA synthesis. Alternatively, the above
results could have been brought about by decreased
RNA catabolism or by decreased passage of RNA from
the nucleus to the cytoplasm. However, the specific
radioactivity of the nuclear RNA was increased in
the reversal rats, whereas decreased catabolism
should have produced a decreased specific radioactivity. Furthermore, the ratio of ^{3}H-RNA in the
nucleus to that in the nucleus and cytoplasm together was the same for both reversal and control
rats, indicating no difference in retention of RNA
by the nucleus. These observations strengthened the
conclusion that the reversal learning situation had
produced increased RNA synthesis in the hippocampus.

The next series of experiments was done in collaboration with Paul Kottler. We first asked
whether one reversal in a 20 minute training session
was sufficient to produce the altered RNA metabolism.
The behavioral training was basically the same as
before. For purposes discussed below, we now injected the labelled cytidine via a chronically implanted needle guide (Kottler & Bowman, 1968) into
the right lateral ventricle, employing a small amount
of dissolved dye (Coumassie Brilliant Blue,) in order
to confirm visually that each injection had spread
throughout the ventricles. The final training was
begun 10 minutes after the intracranial injection.
The brain dissections were also changed somewhat;
i.e., the "remaining subcortex" was divided into
"basal ganglia" and "midbrain and diencephalon" and
the neocortex was divided into right and left halves
instead of anterior and posterior portions. In

TABLE I

Pool corrected radioactivity incorporated into RNA (in DPM per 10³ DPM of pool) and total RNA (in μg/gm wet weight brain) in cell nuclei of different brain regions. Data are expressed as the experimental mean minus the control mean.

	Hippo-campus	Sub-cortex	Pyriform Cortex	Ant. Neo-cortex	Post. Neo-cortex	S. E. & Error df
Tritium in RNA	+52** +26%	+ 9 + 5%	+10 + 6%	- 2 - 1%	-16 - 9%	±18 128 df
Total RNA	+54* +15%	-26 - 7%	+15 + 4%	-12 - 4%	+12 + 4%	±24 91 df

* p < .05; ** p < .01.

addition, the biochemistry was simplified by omit-
ting the separation of cell nuclei and the RNA and
DNA color tests, and by using the filter paper
method of Bollum (1966, p. 296-300) to extract
tissue RNA. Samples of 10 mg each of homogenized
whole brain tissue was applied to 2.5 cm. filter
paper discs (Whatman #1), subjected to extractions
with 5% cold TCA, and the counts per minute (CPM)
were determined from the paper discs placed directly
in a dioxane cocktail in a liquid scintillation
spectrometer (Packard Tri Carb). Although this
technique was subject to count losses due to absorption, quench and/or efficiency losses, its validity
for purposes of comparison between experimental and
control groups appeared excellent on the following
grounds. First, the brain tissue samples from each
yoked pair of rats were treated identically and
analyzed blind side by side by the technicians.
Second, the CPM incorporated into RNA were graphed
versus the CPM in the cold TCA pools, and were
almost perfectly linear through the origin over the
complete range of pool values, with Pearson product-
moment correlation coefficients averaging .95 and
higher. The rationale for the validity of these
criteria has been discussed elsewhere (Bowman &
Strobel, 1969).

The results of a 20 minute single reversal
indicated no change in the uptake of pool corrected,
labelled cytidine into hippocampal RNA, but did
demonstrate a significant increase in precursor
incorporation into RNA of the basal ganglia (Table
II). To resolve the differences between these
results and those of Bowman and Strobel (1969) in
which rats were trained on multiple reversals for
60 minutes, two further experiments were performed.
The first, employing intracranial injection of the
labelled cytidine, and training on a single reversal
for 60 minutes, demonstrated no significant differences in precursor incorporation into RNA of any
brain region (Table II). The next experiment then
examined multiple reversal training for 60 minutes,
with intracranial injections of precursor. To our
surprise, this replication of the Bowman and Strobel
(1969) training produced no significant alterations
in uptake of precursor into RNA of any brain region

TABLE II

Pool corrected radioactivity incorporated into RNA in various experiments. The data refer to the mean difference (and in parentheses the mean difference expressed as the percent of the control mean) by which the experimental rats were above (+) or below (−) the control rats. The key to the experimental conditions is: duration of training (20 min. or 60 min.), single reversal (S.R.) or multiple reversals (M.R.), the mean number of multiple reversals (in parentheses), and whether the route of injection was intracranial (I.C.) or intravenous (I.V.).

Exp. Condition	No. of Pairs	Hippo-campus	Basal Ganglia	Midbrain + Dien-cephalon	Pyriform Cortex	Left Neo-cortex	Right Neo-cortex	S.E. + df
20 min. S.R. I.C.	15	.009 (+ 7)	.027[2] (+15)	.012 (+ 8)	.000 (0.0)	.015 (+13)	.006 (+ 5)	.010 / 154
60 min. S.R. I.C.	10	.007 (+ 4)	-.018 (- 8)	.006 (+ 3)	-.003 (- 2)	-.002 (- 1)	.000 (0.0)	.013 / 99
60 min. M.R. (4.4) I.C.	7	-.040 (- 7)	-.007 (- 1)	-.030 (- 6)	.010 (+ 2)	-.116 (-22)	-.053 (-11)	.077 / 77
60 min. M.R. (5.9) I.V.	14	.042[3] (+55)	.023[1] (+30)	.012 (+16)	.021[1] (+27)	.020[1] (+30)	.015 (+21)	.009 / 143
60 min. M.R. (4.0) I.C.	21	.017 (+ 7)	-.024 (- 6)	-.014 (- 5)	.001 (+ 6)	.023 (+12)	.046 (+21)	.027 / 220
60 min. M.R. (2.8) I.V.	5	.052[2] (+51)	-.013 (-14)	-.018 (-19)	.006 (+ 7)	.015 (+20)	.003 (+ 4)	.018 / 44

[1]p < .05; [2]p < .01; [3]p < .001.

(Table II). This led us then to repeat the same
behavioral situation (multiple reversals for 60
minutes) using the original intravenous injection
of cytidine-5-T, as well as the original Schneider
method for the extraction of nucleic acids (Bowman
& Strobel, 1969), applied in this experiment however to whole tissue homogenates. The results of
this experiment were basically the same as initially
noted by Bowman and Strobel (1969), namely, a large
significant increase in precursor incorporation
into hippocampal RNA (Table II); this increase
occurred in 11 of the 14 yoked pairs (in two of the
three negative pairs, the differences were virtually
zero). There were marginally significant increases
in other brain regions also, although these were
not consistent across subjects, nor have they proven
generally replicable.

    It appeared from the above studies that the
route of injection of the precursor was a critical
variable. This raised the possibility that injection trauma might be altering brain function following the intracranial injections, and in fact,
histological examination of the site of the intracranial injections in pilot rats indicated damage to
the hippocampal commissure and the right fornix following the injection. Consequently, another experiment with multiple reversals for 60 minutes was
done using 21 yoked pairs of experimental and control
rats, in which intracranial injections of 10 μL of
cytidine-5-T were made into the right lateral ventricle well anterior to the downward curve of the
fornix. In these studies, brain homogenates were
again placed on filter paper discs for TCA extraction; however the cold TCA pools eluted from each
disc were dissolved in the dioxane cocktail for
liquid scintillation counting. The nucleic acids
were then eluted from each disc with .05N KOH and
were similarly dissolved in the dioxane cocktail for
counting. In brain tissue samples extracted by this
technique and also by the Schneider method used in
the intravenous injection studies above, the CPM
determined by both methods were identical. As with
the previous intracranial injection studies, abso-
lutely no significant changes in precursor incorporation into RNA were noted in any brain region (Table

II). Another experiment with identical training as
above was then done with 5 yoked pairs of rats,
using intravenous injections and Schneider extractions; reversal rats again incorporated significantly more precursor into hippocampal RNA (Table II),
and 4 of the 5 pairs demonstrated the experimental
effect. Finally, a recent experiment by William
Haasch in our laboratory repeated the above training conditions and employed intracranial injections
of cytidine-5-T with 10 yoked pairs of rats and
intravenous injections with another 12, concurrently run, yoked pairs. The Brilliant Blue dye was
omitted from these intracranial injections to avoid
any possible metabolic interference from its presence. In addition, the Schneider method for nucleic
acid extractions previously used for all intravenous
studies was used here for all rats from both the
intravenous and intracranial injection groups. As
with all the studies above, the reversal rats with
intravenous injections exhibited significantly
increased incorporation of precursor into hippocampal RNA, whereas the reversal rats with intracranial injections failed to differ significantly
from the controls (Table III); 10 of the 12 intravenous pairs exhibited the experimental effect,
whereas only 6 of the 10 intracranial pairs did so,
compared to 5 out of 10 on chance expectations.

These repeated studies have convinced us that
the increased incorporation of cytidine into RNA of
rats learning spatial reversals is a highly reliable
phenomenon when employing intravenous injections
of precursor, but not when employing intracranial
injections. The failure with intracranial injections could be a result of injection trauma, although
concurrent electrophysiological measurement in a few
pilot animals showed none of the seizure activity
(to which the hippocampus is so prone) accompanying
injections into the ventricle. Alternatively, the
failure could result from a steep, declining gradient of penetration of the cytidine-5-T from the
ventricle into interior regions of the hippocampus,
assuming that these interior regions contained the
cells critical for the effect we observe. Altman
and Chorover (1963) in fact have reported steep
penetration gradients for nucleosides passing from

TABLE III

Mean results of concurrent intravenous and intraventricular experiments. Means were calculated from pool corrected data (i.e., DPM-RNA ÷ DPM-pool). Because of the heterogeneity of variance, F tests were done separately on each of the six comparisons, with DF = 1 & 9 for each F. Although hippo-campal data were available for 12 pairs of intravenous rats, two of these pairs were not included in the analysis of variance because data from one or another of their other brain regions were lost during assay. One of these pairs had an experimental-control difference of +.0185 (+57%) and the other, of +.0425 (+133%).

| | | Group Means | | Difference & Difference | |
Injection Route	Brain Part	Experi-mental	Control	As % of Control	F
Intravenous	Hippocampus	.0926	.0660	+.0266 (+ 40%)	9.75*
Intravenous	Basal Ganglia	.0637	.0313	+.0324 (+104%)	3.49
Intravenous	Midbrain and Diencephalon	.0755	.0697	+.0058 (+ 8%)	0.08
Intraventricular	Hippocampus	.3508	.2892	+.0610 (+ 21%)	2.73
Intraventricular	Basal Ganglia	.4799	.4192	+.0607 (+ 14%)	1.48
Intraventricular	Midbrain and Diencephalon	.4067	.3702	+.0365 (+ 10%)	0.70

* p < .025.

the ventricles into the hypothalmus. We have also
observed that the uptake of precursor from the
brain ventricles is much greater into subcortical
regions than into the cortex, whereas the uptake
from the blood following an intravenous injection
is equal (on a per gm brain weight basis) in all
brain regions examined, with the exception of the
basal ganglia which may be lower because of fewer
cells per gram of tissue due to the large content
of mylinated fibers of the corona radiata (Table
IV).

        This failure of the intracranial injections
has general methodological implications. The distribution of small doses of drugs to the brain via
the brain ventricles has been frequently used by
many investigators to "bypass" the blood-brain
barrier and thereby to determine the effects of
these drugs on brain and on behavior. Our above
studies illustrate the subtle and serious danges inherent in this procedure. In initial intracranial
pilot studies, and in all of our intracranial studies reported above, the uptake of label into both
RNA and its precursor pools was at least fifty-fold
greater into hippocampus than was obtained by intravenous injection. In no brain region did these data
suggest any adverse effect of the intracranial route
on RNA synthesis or on the adequacy of incorporation
of the label. Only in terms of the relative distribution of the label across brain regions was there
a suggestion of any possible difficulty, and this
difficulty appeared only marginal for all brain
regions except the basal ganglia in terms of pool
corrected incorporation into RNA (Table IV). We
were only able to detect the inadequacy of the
intracranial route of administration for this drug
in this task by virtue of comparison with our
initial and later work using intravenous injections.
It is an interesting question as to how many studies
employing intracranial injections of drugs may have
drawn false negative conclusions about brain-drug-
behavioral interactions by reason of unrecognized
difficulties similar to ours. Even in the presence
of positive effects such as those obtained by Glassman and Wilson (in this Symposium), one must wonder
whether the magnitude of the effect might be influ-

TABLE IV

Distribution of incorporation by brain regions. Values were calculated as either CPM or DPM per gram wet weight for each brain region and were then converted to percent of these values totaled for all six regions. Values expressed below are the means of these percents taken over the control animals from all the reversal training experiments reported in this paper (except for the Strobel and Haasch studies). Standard errors of the means are in parentheses. For perfectly even distribution of the label across all brain regions, all values would be 16.7%. Routes of injection were intravenous (IV) anterior intracranial (A-IC) and posterior intracranial (P-IC).

Route	Hippo-campus	Basal Ganglia	Midbrain + Dien-cephalon	Pyriform Cortex	Left Cortex	Right Cortex
			^{3}H in RNA			
IV	17.1 (1.4)	14.7 (1.5)	17.4 (1.2)	17.3 (0.5)	16.6 (0.6)	16.8 (0.6)
A-IC	20.2 (2.2)	33.9 (2.7)	22.1 (2.0)	6.3 (0.6)	4.8 (0.8)	12.7 (2.1)
P-IC	27.7 (2.7)	28.2 (3.3)	25.6 (1.5)	6.6 (0.5)	3.1 (0.3)	8.8 (1.2)
			^{3}H in Pools			
IV	16.9 (0.3)	14.7 (0.3)	16.7 (0.3)	17.2 (0.1)	17.2 (0.1)	17.2 (0.1)
A-IC	22.0 (1.5)	24.2 (1.4)	23.2 (1.4)	8.3 (0.4)	6.0 (0.6)	16.7 (1.2)
P-IC	30.7 (2.0)	20.8 (2.3)	26.4 (1.7)	7.4 (0.5)	3.7 (0.3)	11.0 (1.5)
			Pool Corrected Incorporation			
IV	17.7 (1.2)	16.5 (1.4)	17.4 (1.0)	16.9 (0.5)	15.3 (0.8)	16.2 (0.5)
A-IC	16.7 (1.1)	26.5 (1.7)	17.6 (1.2)	13.3 (0.9)	13.3 (0.8)	12.7 (1.3)
P-IC	15.6 (0.7)	22.8 (1.1)	17.1 (0.6)	15.6 (0.5)	14.4 (1.0)	14.5 (0.8)

enced artifactually by the use of intracranial
injections, and whether any regional pattern of
these differences might include a lack or alteration of effects in some regions due to the use of
intracranial injections. The answers to these
questions would seem to require comparison with
alternate modes of injection, particularly intravenous routes. The intravenous route would appear
to be less subject to artifact, reasoning from the
distribution data described above, and from the
fact that the vascular system is in more intimate
contact with all areas of the brain, and from a
concern for minimizing physiological insult to the
animal.

Whatever the reasons for intracranial injections to fail in our reversal learning task, there
is certainly no question that intracranial injections are efficacious in demonstrating increased
incorporation of precursor into RNA in the one-way
shock avoidance task of Glassman and Wilson (this
Symposium). This suggests the possibility that the
cell populations, and perhaps brain regions, involved in these two different rodent species trained
in two different tasks may not be the same. In
line with this possibility, the autoradiographic
data described by Glassman and Wilson in fact indicate that their task involves a number of limbic
structures aside from the hippocampus. However,
this possible difference in brain regional profiles
of RNA metabolism with different species or behavioral tasks clearly remains to be explored explicit-
ly before definitive conclusions can be reached.

We turn now to a series of studies employing
a much simpler task than spatial reversal learning.
In these studies, we were interested in the possible
influence of behavioral components of the maze task
on brain RNA metabolism. Accordingly, an experiment
was devised to test the effect of learning to drink
water from a goal box fountain whenever the fountain
was activated by the solenoid (magazine training -
with drinking). As one control group for this task,
rats were also trained in the goal box with the
water tube disconnected from the fountain (magazine
training - with no drinking). As a control condi-

tion for the effects of drinking water, rats were
given water in a bottle attached to their home
cage (Home cage - with drinking), or were simply
given an empty water bottle on their home cage
(Home cage - with no drinking). None of the animals had food available during this test session.
This constituted a 2 x 2 factorial experiment and
consequently four rats were run daily as a yoked
set, one rat assigned to each of the four factorial
conditions in each yoked set. In this experiment,
rats were obtained from the supplier (Holtzman),
and placed immediately on water deprivation. The
next day, a jugular cannula was implanted and the
water deprivation was continued for another day.
The rats were then injected intravenously with 100
uCi cytidine-5-T and were trained in the above
conditions for 60 minutes. Rats so used within
about two days of receipt were termed "non-adapted"
rats. The rats were decapitated immediately after
the 60 minute training session and the brains were
dissected and analyzed as described above for the
later intravenous studies.

As with the reversal learning task, the only
significant effects were noted in the hippocampus,
in which there was a significant increase in incorporation of precursor into RNA in drinking rats or
magazine trained rats compared to home cage, nondrinking rats, but no differences between the three,
increased groups (Fig. 2). This suggested that
water drinking or a novel environment (the goal box)
might be adequate stimuli for the hippocampal RNA
effect.

Since all of our reversal learning experiments
had been done with "adapted" rats (i.e., rats
present in the laboratory for 7 or more days), the
experiment immediately above was repeated with
rats placed on 23 hour daily water deprivation for
9 days after receipt from the supplier before being
subjected to the final two-day regimen of water
deprivation, cannulation and training. There were
no statistically significant RNA effects in these
adapted rats, although an elevation of precursor
incorporation into hippocampal RNA of rats in the
two conditions of magazine training approached

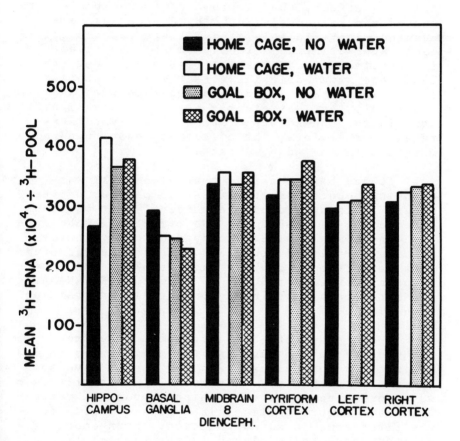

Fig. 2.   Pool corrected radioactivity incorporated into RNA in various brain regions of rats subjected to magazine training and water drinking.

significance (Table V). However, the effect of
drinking water in the home cage had clearly disappeared.

To test the reliability of the home cage, water
drinking effect, the two home cage conditions were
tested simultaneously in both adapted and non-
adapted rats. In this study, there was a significant water drinking effect, and no significant
interaction with adaptation (Table V). Nevertheless, the water drinking effect was not statistically significant in the adapted rats when analyzed
separately, but was clearly statistically significant in the non-adapted rats when analyzed separately. Therefore, the effect at least appeared
marginal in the adapted rats.

It had been observed that almost all water
drinking occurred in the first 15 minutes of the 60
minute training period. Accordingly, it was considered possible that any RNA effect might be more
pronounced at 30 minutes compared to 60 minutes,
particularly in adapted rats. Therefore, adapted
rats were trained on home cage drinking and nondrinking for either 30 or 60 minutes. No RNA effect
was noted in any brain region for either training
time (Table V).

There have not been sufficient experiments in
the water drinking-magazine training series to draw
definitive conclusions. However, we do have some
speculations that may be plausible. The effects of
water drinking observed on hippocampal RNA metabolism have occurred always in groups drinking for
the first time in a new location. Even among
adapted rats, being placed in the new location of
the magazine appeared perhaps to have some marginal
effect on hippocampal RNA metabolism. It may be
then that novel situations are those which give
rise to the hippocampal RNA effect.

If this is so, then one further speculation
suggests itself. The hippocampus has a well-known
theta rhythm which has been correlated with attentional or observing responses. These theta
responses arise in early learning experiences or in

TABLE V

Mean pool corrected DPM ($\times 10^3$) in the hippocampus of all animals from Drinking Studies. Each experiment included only those groups for which table entries are shown. In Experiment I there was a significant difference between drinking (D) and nondrinking (ND) animals ($F = 6.2$, $p < .05$). This effect was present only in the home cage animals as shown by the significant drinking magazine interaction ($F = 4.1$, $p < .05$). In Experiment III there was also a significant effect of drinking ($F = 16.2$, $p < .001$) but it should be noted that the difference was 67% greater in the nonadapted animals (25 vs. 15 units) and was not significant in the adapted animals when analyzed separately (see text).

	60 Min.								30 Min.	
	Home Cage				Magazine				Home Cage	
	Adapt		Nonadapt		Adapt		Nonadapt		Adapt	
Exp.	D	ND	D	ND	D	ND	D	ND	D	ND
I			41	27			38	36		
II	145	151			167	158				
III	110	96	107	82						
IV	116	103							102	102

novel situations (Radulovacki & Adey, 1965; Karmos, Grastyan, Lonsonczy, Vereczkey & Grosz, 1965; Bennet, 1970). It is accordingly tempting to wonder whether the increased precursor incorporation into hippocampal RNA which has been observed in these various experiments is a correlate of the cellular activity associated with the hippocampal theta rhythm. This same explanation could be suggested also to account for the results observed with Y-maze spatial reversals, and appears to be an interesting hypothesis to test.

As a final comment, it is possible that the above observed RNA changes are a result of differential stresses affecting the groups undergoing the various treatments (Bryan *et al.*, 1967). The demonstration by McEwen *et al.*, (in this Symposium) that corticosterone is bound in high concentration by the rat hippocampus provides further reason to consider this possibility. However, we have measured serum corticosterone concentrations in many of the above conditions, and found no relationship between those measures and the observed RNA change. Samples of blood were collected at the moment of decapitation from the animals used in most of the reversal training studies and in all of the drinking studies. The serum fraction of each sample was separated within 5 minutes and stored frozen until analyzed for corticosterone by a protein binding method (Bowman & DeLuna, 1969). The results showed that the reversal training conditions which produced measurable changes in the hippocampal RNA metabolism did not produce any differential corticosterone levels, which suggested no differential stress (Table VI). The steroid data from the drinking studies (Table VII) showed that for all experiments the drinking treatment decreased stress and for the unadapted rats, the magazine training increased stress. The steroid changes did not generally correlate with the RNA changes (the latter are summarized in Fig. 2 and in Table V). As one example, the unadapted animals showed RNA increases with both magazine training and drinking (Fig. 2) while their corticosterone level decreased with drinking and increased with magazine training (Table VII). These results tend to decrease the attrac-

TABLE VI

Reversal Training Experiments. Mean μg Corticosterone per 100 ml of Serum. The Experimental Conditions Were as Follows: Single Reversal (S.R.), Multiple Reversal (M.R.), Intraventricular (I.C..) and Intraveneous (I.V.).

Experimental Conditions	Number of Pairs	Exp.	Cont.	Diff.	S.E.	t
20 min. S.R. I.C.	12	4.8	5.4	- .6	4.8	.13
60 min. S.R. I.C.	10	11.8	17.2	-5.4	21.4	.25
60 min. M.R. I.C.	7	5.2	3.0	+2.2	4.7	.47
60 min. M.R. I.V.	14	18.9	22.2	-3.3	17.4	.19

TABLE VII

Drinking Experiments. Mean μg Corticosterone per 100 ml of Serum and Summary Tables of the Analyses of Variance. The Experimental Conditions Were as Follows: Home Cage Drinking (HD), Home Cage Nondrinking (HND), Magazine Drinking (MD) and Magazine Nondrinking (MND).

Unadapted Animals

HD	HND	MD	MND
23.9	34.6	34.2	42.3

S.V.	MS	F	p
Drinking	884	6.9	< .05
Magazine	814	6.4	< .05
Drink x Mag.	17	< 1	---

MS error = 128; df error = 39

Adapted

HD	HND
24.2	41.6

S.V.	MS	F	p
Drinking	790	11	< .01
Adaptation	239	3	---
Drink x Adap.	728	10	< .01

MS error = 74; df error = 39

Adapted Animals

HD	HND	MD	MND
19.2	36.1	23.5	32.9

S.V.	MS	F	p
Drinking	1729	15.7	< .001
Magazine	3	< 1	---
Drink x Mag.	135	1.2	---

MS error = 110; df error = 39

Adapted, 30 min.   Adapted, 60 min.

HD	HND	HD	HND
7.3	23.7	27.7	43.2

S.V.	MS	F	p
Drinking	2293	42	< .001
Time	3598	27	< .001[1]
Drink x Time	2	< 1	---

MS error = 85; df error = 35

[1] 60 min. animals were probably additionally stressed by disturbances occurring while removing 30 min. animals from adjacent cages.

tiveness of any hypothesis linking the previously
reported RNA changes to differential stress.

ACKNOWLEDGEMENTS

This research was supported in part by grant
numbers RR-0167 and 9-R01-NS09352 from the National
Institutes of Health. The authors thank Barbara
Beremen, Raul DeLuna, Louann Gonzalez and Barbara
Stark for their assistance in the technical aspects
of this research.

REFERENCES

ALTMAN, J., & CHOROVER, S. L. Autoradiographic
    investigation of the distribution and utiliza-
    tion of intraventricularly injected adenine-
    ^{3}H, Uracil-^{3}H and thymidine-^{3}H in brains of
    cats. *Journal of Physiology*, 1963, *169*,
    770-779.
APPEL, S. H., DAVIS, W., & SCOTT, S. Brain poly-
    somes: Response to environmental stimulation
    Science, 1967, *157*, 836-838.
BENNETT, T. L. Hippocampal EEG correlates of
    behavior. *Electroencephalography and clinical
    neurophysiology*, 1970, *28*, 17-23.
BOLLUM, F. J. Filter paper disk techniques for
    assaying radioactive molecules. In G. L.
    Cantoni & D. R. Davies (Eds.), *Procedures in
    Nucleic Acid Research*, New York: Harper &
    Row, 1966.
BOOTH, D. A. Vertebrate brain ribonucleic acids
    and memory retention. *Psychological Bulletin*,
    1967, *68*, 149-177.
BOWMAN, R. E., & DELUNA, R. F. Protein-binding
    assays for adrenocorticoids. *Behavioral Re-
    search Methods and Instrumention*, 1969, *1*,
    135-138.
BOWMAN, R. E., & STROBEL, D. A. Brain RNA metabo-
    lism in the rat during learning. *Journal of
    Comparative and Physiological Psychology*, 1969,
    67, 448-456.
BRYAN, R. N., BLISS, E. L., & BECK, E. C. Incor-
    poration of uridine-^{3}H into mouse brain RNA

during stress. *Federation Proceedings*, 1967, *26*, 709.

GLASSMAN, E. The biochemistry of learning: An elevation of the role of RNA and protein. *Annual Review of Biochemistry*, 1969, *38*, 605-645.

HYDÉN, H., & EGYHAZI, E. Nuclear RNA changes of nerve cells during a learning experiment in rats. *Proceedings of the National Academy of Sciences*, 1962, *48*, 1366-1373.

HYDÉN, H., & EGYHAZI, E. Glial RNA changes during a learning experiment in rats. *Proceedings of the National Academy of Sciences*, 1963, *49*, 618-624.

HYDÉN, H., & EGYHAZI, E. Changes in RNA content and base composition in cortical neurons of rats in a learning experiment involving transfer of handedness. *Proceedings of the National Academy of Sciences*, 1964, *52*, 1030-1035.

JOHN, E. R. *Mechanisms of Memory*. New York: Academic Press, 1967.

KANDEL, E. R., & SPENCER, W. A. Cellular neurophysiological approaches in the study of learning. *Physiological Reviews*, 1968, *48*, 65-134.

KARMOS, G., GRASTYAN, E., LOSONCZY, H., VERECZKEY, L., & GROSZ, J. The possible role of the hippocampus in the organization of the orientation reaction. *Acta Physiologica Academiae Scientiarum Hungaricae*, 1965, *26*, 131-141.

KOTTLER, P. D., & BOWMAN, R. E. A simple intracranial needle guide for presenting backflow of injectant. *Journal of the Experimental Analysis of Behavior*, 1968, *11*, 536.

RADULOVACKI, M., & ADEY, W. R. The hippocampus and the orienting reflex. *Experimental Neurology*, 1965, *12*, 68-83.

SHASHOUA, V. E. RNA changes in goldfish brain during learning. *Nature*, 1968, *217*, 111-113.

SHASHOUA, V. E. RNA metabolism in goldfish brain during acquisition of new behavioral patterns. *Proceedings of the National Academy of Sciences* 1970, *65*, 161-167.

CORRELATION OF THE S100 BRAIN PROTEIN WITH BEHAVIOR

Holger Hydén and Paul W. Lange

Institute of Neurobiology
University of Göteborg

Göteborg, Sweden

This paper summarizes investigations of the brain specific acidic protein S100 in the pyramidal nerve cells of the hippocampus as a possible correlate to learning during transfer of handedness in rats. The amount of S100 increased during training. Intraventricular injection of antiserum against the S100 protein during the course of training prevented the rats from further learning but did not affect motor function in the animals. Antibodies against the S100 protein could be localized after the injection to hippocampal structures by immunofluorescence, penetrating presumably through slight ependymal lesions caused by the injection. By contrast, control animals subjected to the same training and injected with S100 antiserum absorbed with S100 protein or with other antisera against γ-globulins showed no decrease in their ability to learn. The conclusion is that the brain specific protein S100 is linked to the learning process within the training used.

During the last few years we have investigated the acidic brain protein S100 in hippocampal nerve cells during a behavioral test in rats. We wish to report that the amount of nerve cell S100 protein increases in trained animals and that the

S100 protein is specifically correlated to learning. This linkage was demonstrated by the use of
antiserum against the S100 protein which was
injected intraventricularly during the course of
the training and localized in the hippocampus by
specific fluorescence. The presence of antiserum
against the S100 protein in the hippocampus prevents further learning during continued training.

The S100 protein is a defined and brain
specific protein and its correlation to learning
seems important since brain specific protein can
be supposed to mediate neural functions. This
protein described in 1965 by Moore and McGregor
(1965) has a molecular weight of 21,000, a high
content of glutamic and aspartic acid and, therefore, moves closest to the anodal front in electrophoresis at pH > 8. The S100 protein is mainly
a glial protein but occurs also in the nerve cells
(Hydén & McEwen, 1966) and constitutes about 0.2%
of the total brain proteins. The anodal band
containing S100 can be separated into at least
three components, two of which precipitate with
antiserum against S100 and have a high turnover
(McEwen & Hydén, 1966). The S100 protein seems to
be composed of three subunits of 7,000 molecular
weight (Dannies & Levine, 1969). Its appearance
in the human frontal cortex parallels the onset
of neurophysiological function (Zuckerman, Herschman & Levine, 1970).

Moore and Perez (1968, p. 343) have described
another acidic brain specific protein (14-3-2)
localized in nerve cells. Still another acidic
protein ("antigen α") unique to the brain has
been characterized by Bennett and Edelman (1968).
In addition, evidence for the existence of other
brain specific soluble proteins has been presented
by Bogoch (1968), MacPherson and Liakopolou (1965),
Kosinski and Grabar (1967) and Warecka and Bauer
(1967).

The training of animals involves a number of
variables, such as motor and sensory activity,
motivation, orientation reflexes, stress and the
learning processes, per se. Active controls are,

therefore, essential to the experimental animals
where these factors have become equated, except
learning.

In a well planned behavioral test surgical,
mechanical or electrical measures to the body
should be avoided and the stress factor should be
small. For these reasons, we have chosen reversal
of handedness in rats as a behavior experiment
(Hydén & Egyhazi, 1964). The active controls
perceive and act similarly to the experimental
animals.

Eighty-one Sprague-Dawley rats weighing 150
to 175 g were used. The experimental set-up has
been described previously in detail (Hydén &
Egyhazi, 1964). It may only be pointed out that
the rat retrieved one food pill at a time by reaching into the glass tube housing the pills. The
rats were induced to use the non-preferred paw
by arranging a wall parallel and close to the
glass tube on the opposite side of the preferred
paw. The controls used the preferred paw and
received the same amount of reward as the experimental animals. The rats were trained during two
sessions of twenty-five minutes per day. The
performance, defined as the number of reaches per
day, was linear up to the eighth day (Fig. 1).
The rats used in our experiments all showed performance curves similar to that in Fig. 1. Once
learned, this new behavior will remain for a long
time (Wentworth, 1942).

The three persons handling the training of
the rats and registering the performance, did not
know with what serum the rat was injected. Neither
did the three persons carrying out the injections
of sera and chemical analysis know about the performance of the rats.

In the present experiments, fresh pyramidal
nerve cells of the CA3 region of the hippocampus
were used. The method for dissection has been
described elsewhere (Hydén, 1959). The cell
sample weighing around 1 μg was homogenized in a
micro-homogenizer in the following solution: 20

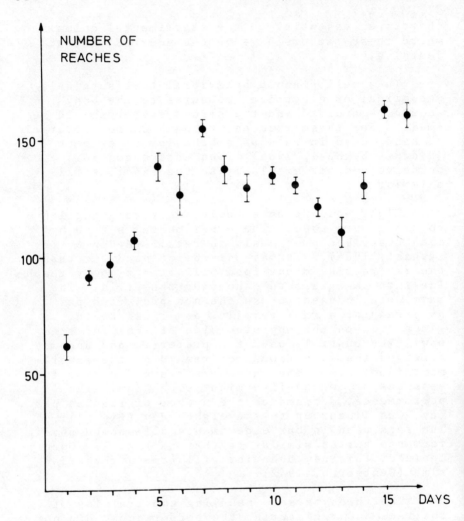

Fig. 1. Performance curve of a group of twelve
rats, given as the average of the number of
reaches as a function of the number of training
sessions (2 x 25 min. per day).

μmole sodium thioglycolate, 0.25 M sucrose with
0.1% Triton X-100 solution, buffered to pH 6.7 by
a solution containing 2.85 g Tris and 1 M H_3PO_4

and H_2O to 50 ml. After centrifugation, the
protein sample was separated electrophoretically
on a 400 μ diameter polyacrylamide gel in glass
capillaries according to a previously described
technique (Hydén & Lange, 1968).

INCREASE OF THE S100 PROTEIN

When the electrophoretic pattern of the
samples was studied, we observed the presence of
a double anodal protein band in trained rats. The
electrophoretic pattern from the samples of the
control rats, however, showed one single anodal
protein band. This observation was noted in a
recent paper on brain protein synthesis (Hydén &
Lange, 1970). Densitometric recordings were made
of 75 electrophoretic patterns from 23 rats
(Fig. 2).

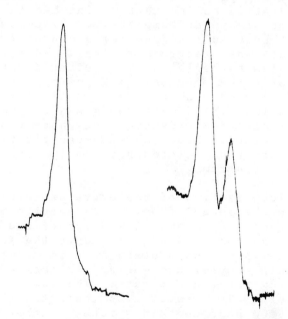

Fig. 2. Two recordings of the front anodal protein band from the electrophoretic pattern of the
soluble hippocampal protein from a control rat
(left) and a trained rat (five days). See text.

Table I shows the presence of two frontal protein bands in 30 recordings out of 55 (sixteen rats) from trained animals. One front band only was observed in all 20 recordings from controls (seven rats).

The following two tests were performed to see whether both or only one of these frontal protein bands contained S100 protein. Protein extracted from pyramidal nerve cells of the CA3 hippocampal region from five trained rats were separated. After the separation, the gel cylinders were placed for 15 minutes in saturated ammonium sulphate solution and briefly rinsed. The protein was fixed in sulfosalicylic acid and stained with brilliant blue. This treatment with ammonium sulphate caused the protein band closest to the anodal front to disappear, which is a characteristic solubility property of the S100 protein. The band immediately behind that diminished in size but did not disappear completely. Hippocampal nerve cell protein from another group of five trained rats was electrophoretically separated on 400 μ diameter gels and precipitated with 80% alcohol for three minutes. The gel cylinders were placed in fluorescein-conjugated antiserum against S100 (dilution 1:4) for 24 hours and then examined in a fluorescence microscope, and photographed. Both front protein bands showed specific fluorescence and had thus reacted positively with the anti-S100 antiserum.

The localization of the extra protein band closest to the anodal front, the reaction of both protein fractions to ammonium sulphate and antiserum against the S100 protein merit the following conclusion. A second protein band in front of the S100 protein complex had emerged in the nerve cell protein from the trained rats. This band contains S100 protein. The result also indicates that the original S100 band contains proteins other than the S100 component.

The question then arose if the amount of S100 protein had increased in the nerve cells of the trained animals. Measurements of the absorbance

TABLE I

Frequency of single and double front anodal protein fractions in the electrophoretic pattern of 75 polyacrylamide gels from 23 rats (7 controls, 4 resumed training on 14th day, 12 resumed training on 14th day and on 30th day).

Controls		Resumed Training on 14th Day		Resumed Training on 30th Day	
One Fraction	Two Fractions	One Fraction	Two Fractions	One Fraction	Two Fractions
20	0	5	10	20	20

of the single protein band from controls and the
two bands of the trained animals were performed
and compared with an integrating micro-photometer.
The same amount of protein from trained and control animals was used for the electrophoresis
and the procedure was identical in all experiments.
The protein was stained with brilliant blue. The
electrophoretic patterns were photographed together with a step wedge, and the areas under the
curves were calculated. It was found that the
amount of protein contained in the two anodal
bands of the trained rats was 10% greater than the
amount of protein contained in the one band of the
controls. Fig. 2 gives an example of the recordings of the S100 bands. The integrated value of
the largest peak of the bands from the trained
rats (right in Fig. 2) did not differ from that of
the single protein band of the controls (left in
Fig. 2). In addition, there is the new band
exclusively containing S100 protein in the samples
from the trained rats (right in Fig. 2).

THE EFFECT OF ANTISERUM AGAINST S100 PROTEIN

The next question was whether the increase of
the S100 protein during reversal of handedness
specifically relates the S100 protein to learning processes occurring in the hippocampal nerve
cells. As we pointed out above, training involves
several factors not related to learning *per se*.
In the reversal of handedness experiments, such
unspecific factors have been eliminated or reduced
to a minimum. The motor and sensory activity,
attention, motivation and reward are equated
between the experimental and control animals, and
the stress involved in reversal of handedness is
minimal. In the following experiments, designed
to test the specificity of the S100 protein
increase, even the stress factors have been equated
between controls and experimental rats. A group
of six rats were trained during 2 x 25 minutes
per day for three days. Between the first and
second training session on the fourth day, the rats
were injected intraventricularly on both sides
with 2 x 30 μg of antiserum against S100 in 2 x 30

µl. During further training for three days after
the injection, the rats did not improve in performance, i.e., the number of reaches per day
remained at the same values as those immediately
before the injection (Fig. 3). It is to be noted
that the rats were not affected by the S100 antiserum with respect to motor function and sensory
responses.

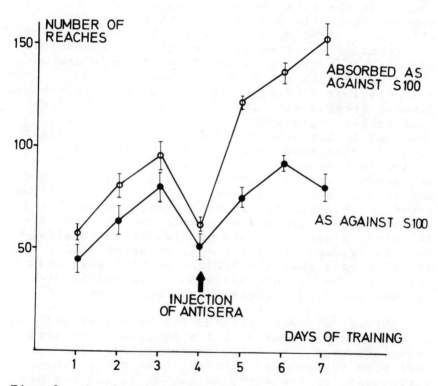

Fig. 3. Performance curves of six rats injected
intraventricularly on day four with 2 x 30 µg of
antiserum against S100 protein and eight rats
injected with 2 x 30 µg of antiserum against S100
protein absorbed with S100 protein.

To demonstrate the specific effect of the antiserum against the S100 protein, the following experiment was carried out. Antiserum against S100 was absorbed with S100 protein according to a procedure previously used (Mihailovic & Hydén, 1969).

The mixture of S100 antiserum and the S100 protein was left for six hours at room temperature and transferred to +4° C for further 65 hours. Three times a day the mixture was agitated for 30 minutes using a magnetic stirrer, and finally centrifuged. The supernatant was tested for effect of antibodies against the S100 protein by Coons' double layer method using sheep anti-rabbit γ-globulin conjugated with fluorescein (Flow Lab., Irvine, Scotland). The test material consisted of cryostat sections through the Deiters' nucleus taken from rats and fixed in cold acetone, after which both absorbed and unabsorbed anti-serum against S100 were applied to the sections and finally treated with the fluorescein conjugated anti-rabbit γ-globulin. When the sections were observed in the fluorescence microscope, a bright specific fluorescence was found in glial cell bodies in the sections treated with unabsorbed antiserum. On the other hand, using the absorbed antiserum, only a weak unspecific fluorescence was found in the glia cells, not stronger than that in the nerve cell cytoplasm. Since the S100 protein is mainly a glial protein and localized to glial cell bodies and to nuclei only of nerve cells, the result showed that the absorption with glia and nerve cell homogenate had removed the antibodies against the S100 protein in the antiserum.

Eight rats were trained for four days and injected on day four with 2 x 30 μg of S100 anti-serum absorbed with S100, as described. The rats were then trained for further three days. The performance of the rats, as number of reaches per training session (Fig. 3), increased in the same way as did the performance of the non-injected control rats shown in Fig. 1.

Since the active molecules of an antiserum have a large molecular weight it is important to know if the antibodies injected intraventricularly will reach and can be localized to the hippocampal structures. Therefore, rats were injected intraventricularly with 2 x 30 µg of antiserum against S100, and other rats were injected with 2 x 30 µg S100 antiserum absorbed with S100 protein. One hour (two rats) and eighteen hours (four rats) after the injection, the rats were decapitated and cryostat sections were made of the hippocampus. Coons' double layer method was applied on the two types of material to demonstrate the possible localization of antibodies to cell structures, using a rabbit-anti-rat-γ-globulin conjugated with fluorescein isothiocyanate (Behring Werke AG, Marburg-Lahn, Germany). Fig. 4 demonstrates specific fluorescence localized to nerve cells in the hippocampus of rats injected with antiserum against S100 (Fig. 4a). Evidently, the hippocampus differs from the brain stem, insofar as the astro- and oligodendroglia do not contain the S100 protein in amounts sufficient to give an immunofluorescent reaction. No such fluorescence can be observed in the material from rats injected with S100 antiserum absorbed with S100 (Fig. 4b).

A pertinent question is whether the effect of the S100 antiserum on behavior is due to a S100 antibody-antigen reaction in limbic structures since Klatzo, Miquel, Ferris, Prokop and Smith (1964) reported that fluorescein-labelled globulin does not penetrate through the ependyma into the brain tissue. When a small, local, cold lesion was produced on the surface of the brain cortex, Steinwall and Klatzo (1964) could show, on the other hand, that fluorescein-labelled globulin entered through the minute surface lesion and spread rapidly through the underlying subcortical area. In our present experiments, the antisera are injected into the narrow lateral ventricles. It can be suspected that the thin needle (gauge 20) may slightly damage the walls of the lateral ventricles when inserted and thus give free passage to globulins to enter. Sham-injections were, therefore, made with NaCl intraventricularly in

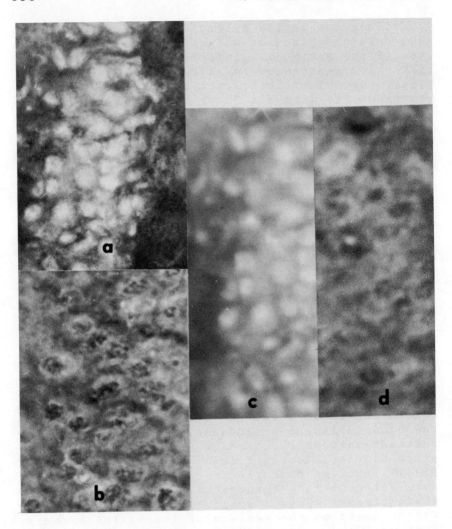

Fig. 4. Specific fluorescence showing the presence of antibodies against the S100 protein localized to the nerve cell nucleus and cytoplasm in the CA3 region of the hippocampus (a) and in granular cells of gyrus dentatus of rats injected with 60 μg of antiserum against S100 protein (c). There is no specific fluorescence to be seen in the corresponding structures of rats injected with antiserum against S100 protein absorbed with S100 protein (b and d).

rats in our standard way. The ventricles were
then carefully exposed, flooded for five seconds
with a 0.1% erythrocin solution in 0.9% NaCl and
after washing examined under low power magnifica-
tion in UV-light. From the remaining staining it
was seen that the walls of the lateral ventricles
were superficially damaged where the needle had
been touching the walls.

In conclusion it can be said that the S100
protein is specifically correlated with learning
processes within training. It does not mean, of
course, that injection of S100 protein should give
rise to a spontaneous change of handedness.

It was then of interest to study a possible
effect of injected antiserum containing antibodies
not directed against the S100 protein. Therefore,
six rats were injected with 2 x 25 μg of antiserum
against rat γ-globulin from goat, four rats with
the same amount of antiserum against rat γ-globulin
from rabbit and four rats with rabbit γ-globulin
from goat. As is seen from the curves in Fig. 5,
this has no impeding effect on their performance.
Before injection of antisera, all rats followed
an identical performance curve. After the injection of antisera, these rats followed a performance
curve which was an extrapolation of the performance curve before the injection. The same was
the case with a rat which was injected with the
same volume of physiological NaCl solution.

Another way to present the results is the
following. For each rat, the sum of reaches for
the first three training days is calculated, as is
also the sum of reaches for the last three training
days. The number of reaches during the day of
injection are thus not included in these sums.
The difference between the second and first sum is
calculated. The averages of this difference are
60 ± 14 for the rats injected with S100 antiserum
and 178 ± 14 for the control rats. The difference
between these numbers is highly significant (P <
0.001, 10 d.f.). It is clear that the experimental
rats show a decrease in learning capacity.

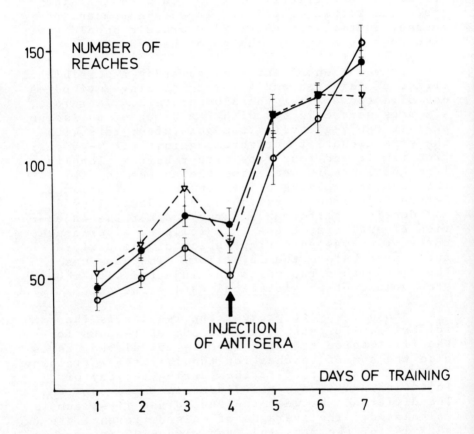

Fig. 5. Performance curves of rats injected intraventricularly on the fourth day with 2 x 30 μg of
antiserum against rat gamma-globulin from rabbit
(four rats), and from goat (four rats), and rabbit
gamma-globulin from goat (four rats).

DISCUSSION

There are so far no experiments reported which have aimed at correlating brain protein components to learning processes in mammals.

In the present experiments, we have used a uniform nerve cell population of the hippocampus in rats. This brain region was chosen because of its importance for learning (Hydén & Lange, 1970). In order to relate behavior to biochemical correlates, correct control experiments are essential. In an ideal learning experiment, all factors involved in the training should be identical for experimental and control animals with the exception of learning. The above experiments with four types of antisera fulfill these requirements. The increase of the S100 protein in hippocampal nerve cells, its alteration in physical properties and the blocking effect of the S100 antiserum on behavior point to the S100 protein as a true biochemical correlate to behavior. This conclusion is backed up by the localization of the antibodies against the S100 by specific immunofluorescence and by the lack of effect of antisera not specifically directed to the S100 protein.

Presumably the S100 protein is not the only protein of importance for behavior, and hence, the role of the rest of the brain proteins in this experiment may be discussed. A young adult rat's brain contains about 200 mg protein. The S100 protein constitutes around 0.4 mg thereof. Antisera were administered in amounts of 0.05 mg per rat, i.e., 0.025% of the total protein. The amount of antiserum against S100 constituted 12.5% of the total amount of the S100 protein of the whole brain. It is to be noted, though, that the antisera were injected intraventricularly and thus in the vicinity of the hippocampus.

Even so, it must be realized that the amount of anti γ-globulin serum is not only exceedingly small relative to the total amount of brain protein, but also relative to the total hippocampal protein. It is, therefore, questionable that the

antiserum would influence the total brain protein
synthesis in a measurable way. The antiserum
against the S100 protein is selective for the 0.2%
of the total brain proteins. The same conclusion
can, therefore, be made regarding the total protein synthesis. To confirm this assumption, the
incorporation of ^{3}H-leucine into the hippocampal
nerve cell protein was studied after the last
training session on the seventh day. No difference in incorporation of ^{3}H-leucine in the hippocampal protein was found between rats receiving
antiserum against S100 and rats receiving rat
γ-globulin antiserum intraventricularly. The
effect observed of the S100 protein antiserum on
behavior can thus not be explained by an influence
from a changed total protein synthesis in the
hippocampus.

In a recent paper (Hydén & Lange, 1970), we
studied the response during reversal of handedness of two protein fractions of hippocampal nerve
cell (CA3). These proteins move on the acidic
side during electrophoresis at pH 8.3. During
the course of one month of intermittent training (day 1 to 4, 14, 30 to 33), the values for the
incorporation of ^{3}H-leucine into the protein were
increased after the first and second training
period, but not after the last training. The rats
performed well at each training period. This
temporal link between behavior and protein synthesis indicated that the protein response was linked
to learning processes of the neurons and was not
an expression of increased neural function in
general. The two acidic protein fractions mentioned above are most probably not pure single
protein components. It is, therefore, of special
interest to observe that in the experiments presented in this paper we have been able to correlate a change in behavior to a single, defined
nerve cell protein which is, furthermore, brain
specific.

Jankovic, Rakic, Veskov and Horvat (1968)
reported the *in vivo* effect of anti-brain protein
antibodies on defensive conditioned reflexes in
the cat. Their results show that the intraventric-

ular injection of these antibodies produces significant changes in conditioned responses immediately after the administration and on subsequent
days. Injection of anti-liver antibody, normal
γ-globulin and saline produced no effect.

Mihailovic, Divac, Mitrovic, Milosevic and
Jankovic (1969) studied the effects of intraventricularly injected anti-brain antibodies on
visual discrimination tests performance in Rhesus
monkeys. The animals were injected with anti-
caudate nucleus, anti-hippocampal and normal γ-
globulin, respectively. The anti-caudate and anti-
hippocampal animals were significantly impaired
in the performance as compared to the normal γ-
globulin animals. The impairment was temporary.

It is also interesting to note that a high
level of environmental stimulation leads to a
thicker hippocampus with a higher density in both
oligo- and astroglia compared to those of control
rats living in isolation (Walsh, Budtz-Olsen,
Penny & Cummins, 1969).

ACKNOWLEDGEMENTS

We thank Dr. L. Levine, Brandeis University,
Waltham, Massachusetts, who kindly provided the
antiserum against the S100 protein, and Dr. Blake
Moore, Department of Psychiatry, Washington University, School of Medicine, St. Louis, Missouri,
who generously gave us S100 protein.

This study has been supported by the Swedish
Medical Research Council, Grant B69-11X-86-05B,
and a grant from Riksbankens Jubileumsfond.

REFERENCES

BENNETT, G. S., & EDELMAN, G. M. Isolation of an
    acidic protein from rat brain. *Journal of
    Biological Chemistry*, 1968, *243*, 6234-6241.
BOGOCH, S. *The Biochemistry of Memory*. London:
    Oxford University Press, 1968.

DANNIES, P. S., & LEVINE, L. Demonstration of sub-
    units in beef brain acidic protein. *Bio-
    chemical and Biophysical Research Communica-
    tions*, 1969, *37*, 587-592.
HYDÉN, H. Quantitative assay of compounds in
    isolated, fresh nerve cells and glial cells
    from control and stimulated animals. *Nature*,
    1959, *194*, 433-435.
HYDÉN, H., & EGYHAZI, E. Changes in RNA content
    and base composition in cortical neurons of
    rats in a learning experiment involving
    transfer of handedness. *Proceedings of the
    National Academy of Sciences*, 1964, *52*, 1030-
    1035.
HYDÉN, H., & LANGE, P. W. Micro-electrophoretic
    determination of protein and protein synthesis
    in the 10.9 to 10.7 gram range. *Journal of
    Chromatography*, 1968, *35*, 336-351.
HYDÉN, H., & LANGE, P. W. Brain-cell protein
    synthesis specifically related to learning.
    *Proceedings of the National Academy of
    Sciences*, 1970, *65*, 898-904.
HYDÉN, H., & MCEWEN, B. A glial protein specific
    for the nervous system. *Proceedings of the
    National Academy of Sciences*, 1966, *55*, 354-
    358.
JANKOVIC, B. D., RAKIC, L., VESKOV, R., & HORVAT,
    J. Effect of intraventricular injection of
    anti-brain antibody on defensive conditioned
    reflexes. *Nature*, 1968, *218*, 270-271.
KLATZO, I., MIQUEL, J., FERRIS, P. J., PROKOP,
    J. D., & SMITH, D. E. Observations on the
    passage of the fluorescein-labelled serum
    proteins (FLSP) from the cerebrospinal
    fluid. *Journal of Neuropathology and Experi-
    mental Neurology*, 1964, *23*, 18-35.
KOSINSKI, E., & GRABAR, P. Immunochemical studies
    of rat brain. *Journal of Neurochemistry*,
    1967, *14*, 273-281.
MACPHERSON, C. F. C., & LIAKOPOLOU, A. Water
    soluble antigens of brain. *Federation Pro-
    ceedings*, 1965, *24*, Part I, Abstract 272.
MCEWEN, B. S., & HYDÉN, H. A study of specific
    brain proteins on the semi-micro scale.
    Journal of Neurochemistry, 1966, *13*, 823-833.
MIHAILOVIC, L. j., DIVAC, I., MITROVIC, K., MILO-

SEVIC, D., & JANKOVIC, B. D. Effects of intraventricularly injected anti-brain anti-bodies on delayed alteration and visual dis-crimination tests performance in Rhesus monkeys. *Experimental Neurology*, 1969, *24*, 325-336.

MILHAILOVIC, L. j., & HYDÉN, H. On antigenic differences between nerve cells and glia. *Brain Research*, 1969, *16*, 243-256.

MOORE, B. W., & MCGREGOR, D. Chromatographic and electrophoretic fractionation of soluble proteins of brain and liver. *Journal of Bio-logical Chemistry*, 1965, *240*, 1647-1653.

MOORE, B. W., & PEREZ, V. J. Specific acidic pro-teins of the nervous system. In F. D. Carlson (Ed.), *Physiological and Biochemical Aspects of Nervous Integration*. Englewood Cliffs, N. J.: Prentice-Hall, 1968.

STEINWALL, O., & KLATZO, I. Double tracer methods in studies on blood-brain barrier dysfunction and brain edema. *Acta Neurologica Scandina-vica*, 1964, *41*, Supplement 13, 591-595.

WALSH, R. N., BUDTZ-OLSEN, O. E., PENNY, J. E., & CUMMINS, R. A. The effects of environmental complexity on the histology of the rat hippo-campus. *Journal of Comparative Neurology*, 1969, *137*, 361-365.

WARECKA, K., & BAUER, H. Studies on "brain-speci-fic" proteins in aqueous extracts of brain tissue. *Journal of Neurochemistry*, 1967, *14*, 783-787.

WENTWORTH, K. L. Some factors determining handed-ness in the white rat. *Genetic Psychology Monographs*, 1942, *26*, 55-117.

ZUCKERMAN, J., HERSCHMAN, H., & LEVINE, L. Appear-ance of a brain specific antigen (the S-100 protein) during human foetal development. *Journal of Neurochemistry*, 1970, *17*, 247-251.

CURRENT QUESTIONS IN BRAIN AND BEHAVIOR

Bernard W. Agranoff

Mental Health Research Institute
University of Michigan

Ann Arbor, Michigan

When scientists meet at a symposium such as this one they exchange findings and ideas in an attempt to answer one or more current questions. In the formative stages of a scientific discipline, they leave such a meeting with more questions than answers. The formulation and reformulation of questions is very often evidence of progress and may include clues to the answers. That is, being able to state a problem is a first step towards its solution. New areas of science also characteristically bridge gaps from more organized areas of science. Very often, new terminologies are needed to discuss interdisciplinary topics. In the study of brain and behavior, the term "memory" has a different meaning for everyone. Although the origin of the word is clearly behavioral, "genetic memory" and "immunological memory" are presently better understood than behavioral memory. It is natural to ask whether a common biological mechanism underlies behavioral, genetic and immunological memory or whether we are simply using the same word to describe very different phenomena. I would like briefly to consider this question and some other issues central to our understanding the brain. I shall include some studies from our laboratory regarding memory mechanisms in the goldfish.

347

HOW IS BEHAVIORAL INFORMATION STORED?
DOES MEMORY RESIDE IN A CHEMICAL FORM?

Much of what we infer about a chemical process
of memory formation comes from the consolidation
phenomenon. Various treatments can be shown to
affect memory when administered shortly following
training but not at some time later. Dr. Jarvik
has presented several examples. Our laboratory has
employed antimetabolites which are known to block
one or more macromolecular processes (Fig. 1;
Agranoff, Davis & Brink, 1966; Agranoff, Davis,
Lim & Casola, 1968, pp. 909-917). We have used
a shuttlebox in which a goldfish is trained to swim
over a barrier in order to avoid an electrical
shock (Fig. 2). With increasing trials, the animal
learns that if he swims over the hurdle when a light
goes on, he will avoid a punishing electrical shock
applied through the water. Because of the variability in responding between individual fishes we
use large numbers of animals. We administer twenty
sessions of one-minute duration each on the first
day of an experiment, return animals to "home"
storage tanks and then retrain them, usually three
days later, with ten additional trials. The result
of such an experiment is shown in Table I. When we
inject puromycin intracranially immediately following training, a memory deficit is seen three days
later. A similar amount of puromycin given one
hour later does not produce any memory deficit. The
animals are conscious throughout the experiment
including the period of time that memory block is
occurring. While one might argue that electroconvulsive shock simply disrupts electrical activity
and thus perhaps memory from being formed, in our
case there appears to be normal neurological activity during the block. We infer that an obligatory
process in memory formation fails to occur during
the time that the agent is acting. Since puromycin
is a protein inhibitor, the results suggest that
protein synthesis is required for memory formation.
In similar experiments, we have been able to demonstrate that a blocker of RNA synthesis (Agranoff,
Davis, Casola & Lim, 1967) but not of DNA synthesis
(Casola, Lim, Davis & Agranoff, 1968) prevents
memory formation and also that the fixation process

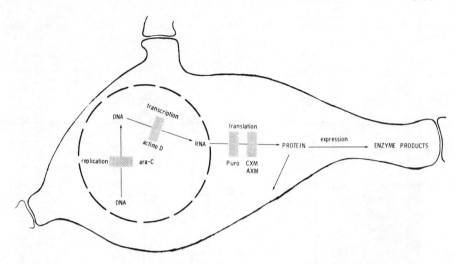

Fig. 1. Diagrammatic representation of the sequence of macromolecular synthesis showing sites of action of several blocking agents. Puro = puromycin; AXM = acetoxycycloheximide; CXM = cycloheximide; AraC = arabinosyl cytosine; Actino = actinomycin D. Nuclear DNA replication does not occur in mature neurons.

is temperature-dependent. The consolidation time derived from the use of blocking agents varies with the nature of the task used. In an apparatus somewhat different than the one shown in Fig. 2, we find that it takes over four hours for memory to become resistant to an agent which under other circumstances gives rise to a one hour consolidation period. A problem in quantitation of memory

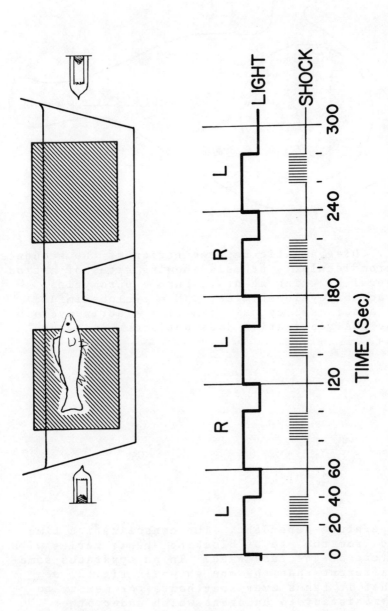

Fig. 2. The shuttlebox used for shock-avoidance training in the goldfish. The subjects learn to swim over the barrier during the first twenty seconds of a trial upon a light signal to avoid a punishing electrical shock.

TABLE I

Effect of Puromycin on Memory*

N	TRIALS Day 1		Treatment	TRIALS Day 4		
	1-10	11-20		21-30 A	21-30 P	Ret. Score (A-P)
72	2.3	3.4	Uninjected	5.3	5.3	0
36	2.5	3.8	Puromycin Dihydrochloride 170 μg, Immediate	2.7	5.4	-2.7
35	2.5	4.6	Puromycin Dihydrochloride 170 μg, 60 Min. Delay	5.5	5.6	-0.1

* Predicted scores are derived from a regression equation based on Day 1 scores for control fish. A-P, achieved – predicted responses (retention score) for Day 4, indicating degree of memory loss.

research is that we generally measure the performance of the animal. How the various brain mechanisms which ultimately lead to performance contrib-
ute is unknown but this observation, that consolidation time may vary with the agent and task used
within the same experimental animal, dictates
caution in interpretation of such results.

The concept of consolidation is derived from
the phenomenon of retrograde amnesia and has been
in the behavioral literature for over 100 years.
In man, a blow to the head will result in a retrograde amnesia, suggesting that memory is formed
following the actual experience. During the same
100 years, there have been many alternate explanations for retrograde amnesia which do not invoke a
consolidation phenomenon. It has been argued that
the disruptive agent, whether it be a blow to the
head or electroconvulsive shock, is unpleasant and
therefore acts as an unconditioned stimulus or
interferes in some other way with the learned
behavior in order to prevent its retrieval. Our
laboratory has devoted considerable amount of effort
in clarifying whether or not the antimetabolites
act specifically by preventing the formation of
memory or in some other way such as by interfering
with the retrieval of memory. It was at one time
argued that puromycin produced electrical abnormalities in the brain and this effect rather than the
inhibition of protein synthesis was responsible for
its amnestic effects in the mouse. Since that time,
the cycloheximides have been shown to block memory
formation in the mouse as had been originally
observed in the fish. These agents do not effect
electrical activity in the mouse or fish (Agranoff,
1970, pp. 35-39). At the present time the most
parsimonious interpretation of results in various
species would seem that RNA and protein synthesis
must be going on normally during the post-session
period in order for permanent memory to be formed
and further that some macromolecular process or
processes may mediate the formation of permanent
memory.

WHAT IS THE MECHANISM OF ELECTROCHEMICAL COUPLING? HOW DO NERVE IMPULSES RELATE TO STORED MEMORY?

As I indicated, the various antimetabolites used do not produce gross neurological change and in fact have remarkably little effect on initial acquisition. That is, animals who are making only a fraction of the normal amount of protein or RNA in their brain cells are able to learn a new behavior. Such animals do not, however, form permanent memory as tested some time following training. This remarkable dissociation of acquisition and storage has given rise to the concept of short- and long-term memory. The fact that acquisition is not affected by these agents suggests that the conventional tools of biochemistry, those dealing with the formation of covalent bonds such as incorporation of radioisotopes, macromolecular separation techniques, etc., will not be particularly useful in understanding the events leading to the development of a changed behavior but only to its storage. We must leave the former to the "electricians"!

From these observations, I am led to a brain model which much resembles the selective theory of immune body formation. The information stored in the brain is implicit in its complex neuronal networks. The brain is not a *tabula rasa*. We are born with a tremendously complicated pre-wired organ and more important for the understanding of plasticity in the nervous system, the brain also contains the potential for further differentiation. Experience evokes changes which may be likened to differentiation and growth. While there is a complex hierarchical structure in the brain making possible extremely large numbers of combinations of responses, the basic learning mechanism is the evocation of a potential connectivity that arose by natural selection and mutation (as well as fortuitously). This way of looking at the brain does not distinguish between what we ordinarily call instinct and learning. When an animal responds to the appearance of a predator that it has not previously seen in its life history, it is clear that his instinctive flight response has a completely genetic basis.

When we train an animal, we search such preprogrammed responses that will result in some desired
response from the animal's preprogrammed repertoire.

WHAT IS THE SIGNIFICANCE OF THE OBSERVED CHEMICAL CORRELATES OF BEHAVIOR? DO THEY REPRESENT CORRELATES OF FUNCTIONAL CHANGE?

Drs. Glassman and Bowman have presented results
indicating rather large changes in brain labeling
specifically related to learning and not to the
degree of excitation of the experimental animal or
to motor activity. Comparable changes in protein
labeling have not been observed. One would ordinarily expect messenger RNA to act catalytically so
that accompanying protein changes would be even
more dramatic than those seen in RNA. Such changes
have not been reported. We should keep in mind
that there is a considerable amount of RNA that is
metabolically active but never leaves the nucleus.
The function of such RNA is at present unknown but
it is interesting to speculate that it may be performing some special role in the brain. If a new
learned behavior results in the formation of a novel
nucleic acid or protein, the amount of "task-
specific" polynucleotide formed would probably not
be detected. The results reported here appear
rather to be correlated with some global brain
process that occurs concomitantly with learning as
Dr. Glassman has indicated. The relationship of
this RNA turnover to the minute changes seen in
protein in the hippocampus in Dr. Hydén's experiments in the rat are uncertain. If the new protein
is identical or very similar in composition to S-100
protein, some predictions could be made about RNA
labeling. If appearance of new S-100 protein is
dependent on the formation of new messenger RNA for
the protein, some predictions can be made about the
nature of the messenger because of the high content
of aspartic and glutamic acids in the S-100 protein
(Moore, 1965; Wender & Waligora, 1962). The calcu-
lations in Table II have also been made elsewhere
by Professor Hydén (personal communication) and by
Dr. V. E. Shashoua (personal communication). If we
assign bases according to the known codons (aver-

TABLE II

Expected Composition of mRNA for Brain Proteins

	U	C	A	G	$\dfrac{G + C}{A + U}$	$\dfrac{A + G}{C + U}$
	%	%	%	%		
S-100*	21.9	15.5	30.7	31.9	0.90	1.67
Total Gray Matter Protein†	25.2	17.5	24.4	33.3	1.02	1.34

* Calculated from analysis of rabbit S-100 protein[7].

† Calculated from analysis of guinea pig brain[8].

aging instances where more than one base appears in
the third position) and compare the base composition of the putative messenger for S-100 with that
for gray matter protein we can predict a high purine
content for S-100. This would lead to a low density
and should permit the flotation of messenger RNA
for S-100 and similar proteins by isopycnic centrifugation.

WHAT IS THE ROLE OF NEUROTRANSMITTERS IN HIGHER BRAIN FUNCTION? DOES THE NEURONAL NUCLEUS MEDIATE CHANGES IN FUNCTIONAL STATE OF THE PRESYNAPTIC TERMINALS?

If we postulate that macromolecular synthesis
under nuclear control regulates cell function and
further, that changes in neurotransmitter concentrations at the synapse regulate intracellular
communication, then the way in which the nucleus
communicates with its presynaptic terminal becomes
important. We have been studying the nature of
this communication in a model system in the goldfish
originally described by McEwen and Grafstein (1968).
If an isotope is injected into the right eye of a
goldfish, it is incorporated into protein in the
ganglion cells for several minutes, until the
remaining precursor is lost into the systemic circulation. The protein that is labeled in the
ganglion cell then begins to move down the optic
nerve to the contralateral optic tectum. The
radioactive amino acid which entered the circulation from the eye may also label the brain but will
result in equal amounts of radioactive protein in
the right and left tectum. Hence, the left-right
difference is an indication of axonally-transported
protein. While leucine has generally been used by
biochemists for protein labeling studies, Elam and
Agranoff (1970) have found that other amino acids
produce higher degrees of labeling of transported
protein and less systemic labeling than leucine,
particularly asparagine and proline (Fig. 3). We
have been able to demonstrate the temperature
dependency of rapidly transported protein, to
characterize the subcellular particles that are
transported and to study various other kinetic

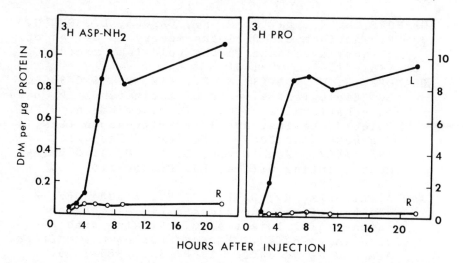

Fig. 3. The appearance of radioactive protein in the optic tectum of a goldfish following intra-ocular injection of labeled amino acid.

parameters. Even though we have measured a relatively rapid process, it is slow in terms of behavioral change. Radioactive protein formed in the ganglion cell does not reach the optic tectal presynaptic area for about six hours. Nevertheless, this interesting model may provide the insight we need to understand mechanisms of axonal flow in cells that may be more directly related to behavioral change such as the interneurons where the nucleus is closer to its terminals.

REFERENCES

AGRANOFF, B. W. Recent studies on the stages of memory formation in the goldfish. In W. L. Byrne (Ed.), *Molecular Approaches to Memory and Learning*, Academic Press, 1970.

AGRANOFF, B. W., DAVIS, R. E., & BRINK, J. J. Chemical studies on memory fixation in goldfish. *Brain Research*, 1966, *1*, 303-309.

AGRANOFF, B. W., DAVIS, R. E., CASOLA, L., & LIM,
    R.   Actinomycin D blocks memory formation of
    a shock avoidance in the goldfish. *Science*,
    1967, *158*, 1600-1601.
AGRANOFF, B. W., DAVIS, R. E., LIM, R., & CASOLA,
    L.   Biological effects of antimetabolites used
    in behavioral studies.   In D. E. Efron, J. O.
    Cole, J. Levine, and J. R. Wittenborn (Eds.),
    *Psychopharmacology, A Review of Progress,
    1957-1967*. Washington, D. C., U. S. Govern-
    ment Printing Office, PHS Publication No.
    1836, 1968.
CASOLA, L., LIM, R., DAVIS, R. E., & AGRANOFF, B.
    W.   Behavioral and biochemical effects of
    intracranial injection of cytosine arabino-
    side in goldfish. *Proceedings of the National
    Academy of Sciences*, 1968, *60*, 1389-1395.
ELAM, J., & AGRANOFF, B. W.   Rapid transport of
    protein in the goldfish optic system.   Sub-
    mitted for publication, 1970.
MCEWEN, B. S., & GRAFSTEIN, B.   Fast and slow
    components in axonal transport of protein.
    Journal of Cell Biology, 1968, *38*, 494-508.
MOORE, B. W.   A soluble protein characteristic of
    the nervous system.   *Biochemical and Bio-
    physical Research Communications*, 1965, *19*,
    739-744.
WENDER, M., & WALIGORA, Z.   Amino acids in the
    proteins of the developing nervous system of
    the guinea pig.   *Journal of Neurochemistry*,
    1962, 9, 116-118.

SUBJECT INDEX

Acetoxycycloheximide, 261, 263, 269
Acetylcholine, 97, 117, 118, 119
Acetylcholine esterase, 114, 116
ACTH, regulation of secretion, 153
ACTH, behavioral effects, 156, 259, 291
Actinomycin D, 104, 109, 138
Adenyl cyclase, 291
Adrenalectomy
    ACTH secretion, 154
    behavioral effects, 156, 291
    effects on incubation, 259
Adrenaline, 179
Adrenochrome, 179
Adrenolutin, 179
Alanine, 225
Albinism, 225, 230, 232
Aldosterone, 129, 130, 147, 150, 151
Alkaptonuria, 225, 230, 232
Amino acids, classification, 224-226
Amino acidurias, 223-240
Amphetamine, 100, 104, 107, 109, 117, 186
Amobarbital sodium, 186
Amygdala
    interaction with estradiol, 131-132
    role in hormonal regulation, 137-138, 155-156
    RNA during learning, 285
Antisera
    to brain, behavioral effects, 342-343
    to NGF, 25-34
    to S100, behavioral effects, 334-339

    to gamma globulins, behavioral effects, 339
Arginine, 225, 227, 229
Arginino succinic aciduria, 225, 228
Arousal, role in memory consolidation, 269, 281
Aspartic acid, 225, 227, 354
Asparagine, 225, 356
Axoplasmic flow, 111, 356
Behavioral trigger for brain RNA changes, 287-290
Biogenic amines, effects of steroid hormones, 135
Brain, proteins specific to brain, 328
Brom-lysergic acid diethylamide, 176
Bufotenin, 177-179, 183
Ceramide, 68
Cerebral cortex, role in ACTH regulation, 155
Cerebrosides, 65, 68, 71, 74, 80
Chemoencephalography, 301
Citrullinuria, 225, 230
Chlorpromazine, 185, 186, 190, 191
Cholesterol, 65
Choline, 107
Choline acetyltransferase, 101-119
    assays, 101
    distribution, 104
    drug effects, 109-116
    synaptic regulator, 107
Conditioning, effect on brain RNA
    classical, 290
    instrumental avoidance, 282-293
    instrumental appetitive, 305-313
Corticosterone
    brain uptake, 126, 127, 141-147, 157